CHAOS AND THE EVOLVING ECOLOGICAL UNIVERSE

THE WORLD FUTURES GENERAL EVOLUTION STUDIES

A series edited by Ervin Laszlo
The General Evolution Research Group
The Academy for Evolutionary Management
and Advanced Studies, Fulda, Germany

This book is part of a series. The publisher will accept continuation orders which may be cancelled at any time and which provide for automatic billing and shipping of each title in the series upon publication. Please write for details.

CHAOS AND THE EVOLVING ECOLOGICAL UNIVERSE

Sally J. Goerner

Triangle Center for the Study of Complex Systems
Chapel Hill, North Carolina

Gordon and Breach Publishers

Australia China France Germany India Japan Luxembourg
Malaysia The Netherlands Russia Singapore Switzerland
Thailand United Kingdom United States

First published 1994
Second printing 1995

3 Boulevard Royal
L-2449 Luxembourg

Library of Congress Cataloging-in-Publication Data

Goerner, Sally J.
  Chaos and the evolving ecological universe / Sally J. Goerner.
    p. cm. – (World futures general evolution studies, ISSN
  1043-9331 ; v. 7)
  Includes bibliographical references and index.
  ISBN 2-88124-635-4
  1. Chaotic behavior in systems. 2. Science–Philosophy.
  3. Evolution. 4. Human ecology.   I. Title.   II. Series.
  Q172.5.C45G64 1993   003.7–dc20   93-32484
                                                                        CIP

CONTENTS

INTRODUCTION TO THE SERIES

The World Futures General Evolution Studies series is associated with the journal *World Futures: The Journal of General Evolution*. The common focus is the emerging field of general evolutionary theory. Such works, either empirical or practical, deal with the evolutionary perspective innate in the change from the contemporary world to its foreseeable future.

The examination of contemporary world issues benefits from the systematic exploration of the evolutionary perspective. This especially happens when empirical and practical approaches are combined in the effort.

The World Futures General Evolution Studies series and journal are the only internationally published forums dedicated to the general evolution paradigms. The series is also the first to publish book-length treatments in this area.

The editor hopes that the readership will expand across disciplines where scholars from new fields will contribute books which propose general evolution theory in novel contexts.

PREFACE

This book describes a broad cultural shift and a parallel scientific shift. Scientifically and culturally, Western civilization is moving away from a Newtonian clockwork-machine universe toward a vision of a living, evolving, ecological universe. We are entering the "Ecological Transformation." In Stephen Pepper's (1946) terms, the shift represents a change in dominant world hypothesis — a shift in the dominant metaphor of how the world works.

This work builds a picture of this change in world view by showing the scientific discoveries that lead to it. Thus, the core of the book is a detailed exploration of the scientific shift. In the science section I show how a number of mini-revolutions in physics and biology connect and how together they create a literal (that is, a physical) picture of an evolving ecological universe. The goal is to build a very concrete path to the new understandings.

The core of the scientific revolution comes from a major conceptual shift in physics, the "nonlinear revolution." The nonlinear revolution includes three major elements: Chaos (modern nonlinear dynamics), Self-Organization Theory, and the thermodynamics of evolution. These elements combine to form a particularly important shift in understanding — a physical understanding of evolution as a single overall process from molecules to humankind. In place of a passive, directionless universe, we find an evolving, order-producing universe — that is, a universe that evolves toward higher and higher levels of ordered complexity through interactive ecological dynamics. This very different physical picture of how the world works produces a Copernican revolution, a shift in our understanding of how humankind fits in the universe.

The last part of the book describes shifts toward ecological thinking that are occurring outside the physical sciences (for example, in economics). It also examines how the radically changed physical understandings may affect human beliefs in general. For instance, the new physical view shows a remarkable ability to reconcile many traditionally oppositional schools of philosophical thought. It fits remarkably well with many understandings expressed in spiritual writings. Consequently — and perhaps most strangely of all — it is at once physical, pragmatic and spiritual. The result is a vision of the world that is at once radically different and deeply familiar.

This work shows how our assumptions about how the world works are changing — scientifically and secularly. It is about both, the secular and the scientific. It is my belief that the two are related though not in a one-causes-the-other way. Rather I believe both are part of a larger change in human doing and being. My goal is to paint a concrete, scientific picture of this big change in perspective.

The Human Side

This book talks a lot about scientific perspectives, yet its goal is fundamentally humanistic. One of my editors suggested that I give a sense of the human side by adding a section describing my personal reasons for choosing this topic and how it fits in my life. This is that section.

The simplest answer to why I chose the topic is that there *is* a new way of looking at the world emerging. It has worth scientifically, pragmatically and spiritually and I think it is important that the word get out. The more honest answer is that I think the new way of looking at things offers significant hope for making the world a better place. And, while I experience some embarrassment at the optimism and extravagance of this thought, I also say it with some degree of objectivity. I am a journalist reporting this new vision, not its inventor, and I am quite convinced that there is truth to it.

There is a third reason why I chose this topic. The new physics has provided a lot of answers for my own personal quests and I would like to share this vision with others. I, of course, reached this research topic by way of a complex set of personal reasons, including a 20-year quest to understand why psychology wasn't really a "science" — or rather, why psychology and the hard sciences seem so hard to reconcile. I've always felt like I had both of C.P. Snow's two cultures in one body; I'm a devotee of both psychology and the hard sciences and the two never really fit. Like many before me, I pursued this quest with fascination but without any real belief that something would get resolved — and yet, it did.

The new physical vision has put to rest a great deal of my searching. Frankly, I didn't believe such a thing could happen. And pleasingly, the resolution didn't come out of brilliant philosophical arguments, or esoteric subatomic science, or beautiful but sentimental New Age mysticism, though it speaks to all of these. No, there was simply a sudden reorganization of my understanding of how the physical world worked. This reorganization followed logically from a handful of simple discoveries. And in this reorganization the various dissonant parts of me came together in peace. A few small conceptual changes, a very big change in perspective. It is quite an amazing transformation.

How the Book Is Organized

Assuming a change of perspective is at hand, the three big questions are: 1) what is it? 2) how did it come about? and 3) how will it affect us? The book's three parts parallel these three questions. They examine: 1) the change of perspective (called the Ecological Transformation); 2) the new physics (called the Nonlinear Revolution); and 3) the human implications.

Part I: The Ecological Transformation — The first part provides an overview of the change in vision. Chapter 1 describes the Ecological Transformation — what is it and how it fits Pepper's theory of world hypotheses.

Part II: The Nonlinear Revolution — Any explanation of a change of vision must include a convincing argument for why one should believe a big change could happen at all. This is the story of the science. Thus, the second part walks through the basic scientific concepts, facts, discoveries and insights that lead to the new perspective. I center my discussion on the new physics (called the Nonlinear Revolution) but I also include elements of the New Biology.

Chapter 1 introduces the nonlinear revolution and chapters 2–5 review how its various elements build from a general understanding of spontaneous physical structuring to an overall vision of evolution. These discussions also describe how the new physics fits the Ecological vision. I include references for those who would like more detailed discussion.

Part III: The Human Dimensions of the Ecological Universe — The last section looks at the human implications along four dimensions: power, re-enchantment, reconciliation and empowerment. Power has to do with how useful a model is, whether it improves our ability to navigate the world. Thus, for example, the power section looks at how ecological perspectives are improving our understanding of economies and how they work. The chapter on reenchantment explores the new science's consonance with long-standing spiritual traditions. The chapter on reconciliation discusses how the new physical view helps reconcile previously antagonistic philosophical traditions. And finally, the chapter on empowerment looks at how the new view changes our sense of how individuals fit in and affect the world.

Note. Because the change of perspective is so ubiquitous, I can only provide a small sampling of both the science and the human implications. I regret not being able to include more of the biological work, particularly that coming out of the cybernetics community, and more of the philosophical work, including individuals such as Gregory Bateson and Arne Naess whose views are exceedingly in line with this work.

ACKNOWLEDGMENTS

"It all seems extremely interesting, but for the life of me it sounds as if you pulled it out of the air," my good friend Ray Lassiter exclaimed to me after enduring about 20 minutes of my enthusiasm for the newly formulated concept...

"It wasn't," I replied, "but it would take a book to show you where it came from."

Robert Ulanowicz (1986)

I strongly identify with friend Ulanowicz's experience. This is my book. And it is a great pleasure to have finally been able to write it. It is also a great pleasure to thank some of the people who helped make it possible.

First, thanks to Michel Baranger, my very beloved scientific mentor and coach, who always insisted that I was trying to know too much while simultaneously insisting that I make some point clear. He was always right. He is not only brilliant but a wonderful human being.

Thanks also to Ralph and Fred Abraham who helped get me started in Chaos; to Bela Banathy and Cliff Josyln who connected me with the Systems movement; to Marty Groder who introduced me to the tie between Chaos and ecology; and to Rod Swenson, whose work provided the basis of the vision of evolution and life that I report here. Finally, my deepest thanks to Debra Weiner and to my husband Jack Petty who provided unstinting moral and editorial support.

My acknowledgment also to Ralph Abraham, Christopher Shaw and Aerial Press for their permission to reprint figures from *The Geometry of Behavior* in this book.

This book is a contribution of The General Evolution Research Group.

Part I:

The Ecological Transformation

CHAPTER 1

The Ecological Universe

There are no separate problems anymore.

John Lovejoy, CBS Sunday Morning, 4/21/91

A remarkable cultural phenomenon occurred in Western civilization between the 16th and 19th centuries: people began to see their world as a giant clockwork universe. Mechanistic themes — material reality, logic, lawfulness, and precision — emerged in all areas of human endeavor, from a growing economic focus on technology to the scientific revolution and the Enlightenment belief in a lawful, controllable universe. All of these elements fed each other.

A similar and equally remarkable cultural phenomenon is happening in our own time. Western civilization is beginning to see its world in terms of ecologies and change. One finds ecological images — the sense of things being made of intricately interconnected, interdependent elements — everywhere. Global economy, global community — in the modern view the world appears to be a tightly coupled system in which everything affects everything else. And not only interconnected but changing. The rapid rush of change — accelerating, unpredictable, unstoppable — has become a foundational part of the Western understanding of the world. The clockwork model is falling away. The modern Western sense is of a rapidly unfolding, complexly interconnected world, an evolving ecological universe.

This new sense of things is more than just a surface phenomenon. It represents a fundamental shift in Western understanding of how order — both in the universe and in individual lives — works.

This book builds a picture of this change in world view by showing the scientific discoveries that lead to it. We are in the midst of an intellectual, scientific, and cultural revolution that holds the promise of being every bit as dramatic and drastic to Western thought as the Mechanistic Revolution of the 16th through 19th Centuries.

MODELS OF HOW THE WORLD WORKS

> You don't see something until you have the right metaphor to let
> you perceive it.
>
> *Thomas Kuhn*

The usual approach to a topic like mine is to proclaim a paradigm shift and point to Thomas Kuhn's (1972) work as a theory. However, Kuhn's work is not an appropriate model for the type of large scale change that I am addressing. Kuhn's notion of paradigm is a conceptual framework shared by a community of scientists that provides them with model problems and solutions. It is too narrow and nonspecific to guide our understanding of a conceptual framework shared by a community of human beings engaged in all forms of endeavor.

There is, however, a body of work that describes conceptual frameworks that exist over long periods of time and that are used by people in all walks of life. The work is Stephen Pepper's (1946) theory of world hypotheses. A world hypothesis is like a paradigm, only broader. It is a tacitly held model of "how the world works." Pepper's theory describes how these tacit conceptual models arise from and become grounded in commonsense metaphors originally used to describe a new view of the world. Pepper explains the process as follows:

> A man desiring to understand the world looks about for a clue to its comprehension. He pitches upon some area of commonsense fact and tries to understand other areas in terms of this one. This original area becomes his basic analogy or root metaphor. (pp. 91–92)

For example, one might tacitly hold a model of the world as a machine, very lawful, logical and knowable. Or one might see the world as an unfolding organism, developing through various stages of history and having an overall coherence to it. Pepper's work shows us that there have been — or rather, that there *are* — a number of such tacit models in existence. Mechanism and Organicism are two of them. (I discuss others and the theory in more detail in Chapter 8.) This book's thesis is that our time marks the emergence of a new world hypothesis based on the root metaphor of an evolving ecology.

Note: For brevity, I will talk about "the ecological world hypothesis" or "ecological thinking," rather than the more bulky "evolving ecological world hypothesis." I do this only for simplicity, not because evolution is a secondary aspect of the model. I refer to the emergence of the new world hypothesis as the ecological transformation.

Mechanism is well known enough to provide a strawman sense of what a world hypothesis is like.[1] Mechanism tends to portray things in terms of separate elements connected by lawful relationships into a working system that produces well-defined, controllable outcomes. For example, Wolmuth (1991) notes that the Western model of contract law describes two independent parties that come together and sign an agreement which is satisfied on performance of the particulars. This model is used despite the fact that in actuality most contracts are created between two parties with long-standing interconnections that strongly mitigate both the stated agreement and how much performance will actually be required for satisfaction. Mechanistic beliefs can easily be seen in business, marriage, government, and of course a vast number of intellectual and scientific theories. For example, Goldstein (1990) notes that the Freudian model of the human psyche also uses a mechanistic understanding.

These are formal intellectual examples of mechanism. But mechanistic thinking is just as common in the informal aspects of daily life. For example, mechanism is intrinsically a materialist hypothesis. It emphasizes physical law and the real world. Anything that does not fit its sense of physical law is dubious. Spirituality, the caring-connection ethic, meaning, purpose and many other "nonphysical" phenomena are not important operators in the mechanistic belief system. Extreme mechanists do not believe such phenomena exist; they are epiphenomena or "illusions."

Such phenomena, however, are powerful and real in other world hypotheses. For example, organicism emphasizes coherence, hidden order, and direction. From its perspective meaning and purpose are quite reasonable outgrowths of the organic process. Organicism is not anti-physical per se; rather, coherence, order, and direction are central and how such things work physically is secondary. If physical understanding cannot yet explain these things, then it is physical law that is in doubt not the phenomena.

This brings me to a major point. Until now, the various world hypotheses have seemed fundamentally irreconcilable. This in turn means that people with different world hypotheses are very likely to find each other's positions intolerable. It may seem as if they are fighting about facts or logic but often the problem is one of deep-seated, often tacit assumptions about what is possible, what is reasonable, what is important, what is most real. Efforts to establish the "Gaia hypothesis" in mainstream science is an example of this kind of conflict of visions. The Gaia hypothesis suggests that the dynamics of the biosphere (oceans, atmosphere, and biota) function like a single coherent self-organizing, self-regulating system. In short, the biosphere works a lot like a living organism. And Gaia researchers, though they are very much empirical scientists, find themselves deeply at odds with their mechanistic scientific brethren. Debates are couched in terms of science but at heart the problem is one of root metaphors. Machines do not self-organize. A nonliving physical system does not spontaneously organize and regulate itself — at least not according to traditional mechanistic beliefs.

Thus, debates that cross world hypotheses have an element of arguing over whether the cup is half-full or half-empty. As long as underlying assumptions seem irreconcilable, such debates are not just about different visions, they are about *conflicting* visions. It is as if one denies the other. The first important and unusual aspect of the ecological transformation then is that it offers the potential of reconciling previous world hypotheses by showing how their basic observations fit together. Thus, ecologism does not merely depart, it connects the previous visions and subsumes them. Ecologism allows us to see that the cup is *both* half-full and half-empty. This does not mean that different visions see the world exactly the same or that all points of contention immediately disappear. It simply means that the main premises of each are now seen as compatible. For example, mechanism begins to comprehend spontaneous self-organization, self-regulation and ordered developmental unfoldings as part of materialism and physical law. Conversely, organicism finds its sense of a *living* process connected to and potentially informed by an expanded physical/mechanical understanding.

To sum up, world hypotheses are deep-seated, tacitly held models of how the world works that powerfully shape how their owners see and consequently how they act in the world. Often seeming to be only what's "obvious" or "reasonable," world hypotheses have also been a major source of division in human knowledge systems. And yet, they are very powerful vehicles for navigating the world, for organizing experience, for communicating with fellows, for coordinating efforts. World hypotheses are tacit mental models, no more no less. They aid vision and they create conflicts.

THE ECOLOGICAL TRANSFORMATION

The germ of the idea grows very slowly into something recognizable. It may all start with the mere desire to have an idea in the first place.

Walt Kelly

The first thing to know about the ecological transformation is that it has a dual nature: it is both evolutionary and revolutionary. On the one hand, the move to ecologism is part of a slow gradual change of vision that is accruing as we develop new tools, new abilities and more subtle understandings of how things work. This evolutionary aspect makes the transformation seem obvious, a maturing of commonsense.

Yet, the ecological transformation also contains a revolutionary shift. It is quite literally a turning point. The key has to do with the development of a physical understanding of how order arises. It is this physical understanding of how order arises that allows mechanistic science to comprehend phenomena and concepts that have previously seemed "nonphysical." This means the tension between a whole array of pairings — holism/reductionism, mind/body, and physical/spiritual — begins to melt away in a way that leaves one wondering why they ever seemed oppositional at all.

The story of the ecological transformation is the story of its two faces. I call the evolutionary part of the transformation "basic ecological thinking." I call the revolutionary part "the deep ecological vision." The next two sections introduce each of these.

Basic Ecological Thinking

The metaphor of an ecology provides the basic image of what the new world hypothesis is about. Biologists and social activists made "ecology" a household word in the 1960s. The model they created was of a whole arising out of many interdependent elements. An ecology shows us how connection can be hidden in complex systems. An ecology's components are bound together in a network of mutual effect; if you change one thing, another is affected. No component can be separated from the others and the welfare of each is bound to the welfare of the whole. For example, concern has recently been raised over the mass annihilation of South American rain forests because these forests house huge numbers of insects that emit nitrogen needed for proper balance of the atmosphere. Our common health and welfare is affected by (connected to) insects in South America. In general, ecological thinking emphasizes 1) a whole built of diverse elements; 2) interdependence/interconnectivity; 3) hidden patterns; 4) complex causation (i.e., chains of effects, mutual effects, circular effects) and 5) ongoing change.[2]

Examples of ecological themes in the current thinking abound. For example, economic interconnectedness becomes a greater and greater factor in changing international relationships. Businesses begin to add exercise facilities and alcohol counseling to their venue because productivity is connected to employee health. Psychology increasingly treats clients as part of a system and places a growing emphasis on mutual causality in dysfunctional relationships (e.g., co-dependents). Dieting becomes less a function of calories and more a function of an entire metabolic system in which exercise, types of food, timing and size of meals all play important roles.

Contrast this ecological sense of things with mechanism. Mechanism emphasizes: 1) lawfulness; 2) precision; 3) physicality; 4) separability/separateness; and 5) simple (i.e., isolable) causation. For the most part the two visions are different but not glaringly oppositional. The two notable shifts are ecologism's emphasis on interdependence and complex causation (versus mechanism's emphasis on separability and simple causation). In retrospect, mechanism contributed to a type of commonsense that is rapidly becoming outdated. Thus, previously businesses seemed willing to believe that exercise and personal well-being were separate issues from the work place and productivity. Psychology was apt to treat client difficulties *as if* they had a single basic isolable cause, say childhood trauma or a chemical imbalance. And dieting seemed to be a matter of calories, like heart disease seemed to be a matter of cholesterol. None of these is completely wrong. Ecologism just adds a degree of sophistication to the basic mechanistic approach. It sees a more complete system. It is as if each theory evolved a little such that the earlier version can be seen as somewhat simplistic — just a starting place. And so it is with basic ecological thinking, it consists largely of more sophisticated understandings arising out of earlier attempts. It stands on the shoulders of the previous as it were.

So, this is what the ecological thinking looks like in general — a different, slightly more complete picture of things. What is the revolution?

THE DEEP ECOLOGICAL VISION

> Every thoughtful person who hopes for the creation of a contemporary culture knows that this hinges on one central problem: to find a coherent relation between science and the humanities.
>
> *Jacob Bronowski (cited in Bartlett, 1980, p. 871)*

Philosophers from Kierkegaard to Marcuse have argued that mechanism does not address the *human* aspects of humanity, from meaning and morality to spirituality and wisdom. Unfortunately, mechanism's close ties to science has made its shortcomings seem to be part of the real/physical world, just the facts of life. One might bemoan meaning, caring, wisdom, spirituality, etc. not being part of the real world, but it is hard to argue with science's well-worked out understanding of physical reality.

A truly revolutionary transformation would resolve the dilemma stated in the opening quotation — expanding Bronowski's term "humanities" to include life-centered discourses of all kinds. And the upshot of this resolution would also provide a fundamentally more sane way of seeing the world. This is precisely what the deep ecological vision is about.

It is clear that this requires a scientific revolution which includes mechanism and yet comprehends the missing pieces as well. The old must be retained as a limited subset of a broader case and, in the process, it must also be "reframed" and "renewed." This, of course, is a tall order. Thus, the ecological transformation's most remarkable facet is its quiet and already occurring scientific revolution. This revolution does, in fact, recast science's understanding of itself while nevertheless preserving the facts and fundamentals that went before. Mechanistic science's claims are reduced, but science is reframed and renewed in a larger context.

The summary of revolution is as follows: A general scientific revolution is emerging out of a variety of small evolutions and mini-revolutions in various fields from physics to biology. It has been hard to see this revolution as a single piece because it has been spread over a number of fields and mired in the jargon and concerns of various specialty areas.

This scientific revolution produces two major events:

1. A general shift in scientific frame of reference — In physics terms, the shift is from linear to nonlinear and independence to interdependence.

2. An understanding of spontaneous ordering in the physical world — The new physical understanding of how order emerges has particularly profound implications. This physical understanding started quietly enough with new understandings of how order works in such everyday phenomena as dripping faucets and the human brain, but it ends radically, in a transformed understanding of evolution. No longer just a matter of genes and species, evolution becomes visible as a general all-encompassing physical process, an order-producing process that created and is still giving rise to this intricately ordered world of ours. Life is not an accident but one of many natural products of an order-producing universe.

The idea that the physical universe is ordering itself is indeed a radical shift in perspective. We are not masters of the universe nor accidents of the universe. We are part of an ongoing unfolding process that is *the* quintessential creative process. We co-create this unfolding along with all other elements of the world. Being able to describe this process scientifically makes it more palpable, more real.

The new physical scientific understanding connects much more simply and elegantly to life-focused discourses such as biology and human/social sciences than did its predecessor. It fits remarkably well with many spiritual descriptions. The new physical model is compelling because it allows us to unify an enormous number of facts and ideas in a way that is so reasonable as to seem common sense.

It also allows us to derive pragmatic implications for living in what now appears as an active, on-goingly creative world. For example, it provides a very different perspective on the pressures driving transformation and the patterns by which transformation proceeds. This helps inform and reframe our understanding of the historical juncture in which humankind is now poised. The net result is a very different perspective on what it means to be human in a physical world.

Yet, this revolution is *significant* because it opens the door to reconciling our conceptualizations of the physical world with many of our loftier philosophical observations. Consequently, it offers a greater potential for sanity. Mechanistic science found no basis for caring, meaning, intentionality, consciousness, morality, ethics, and connection to a higher whole. A civilization whose physical conceptualizations are irreconcilable with so many fundamentally important life concepts is of necessity split within itself and split off from the world. Consonance between science and life-centered discourses creates the possibility of a vastly less *schizophrenic* understanding of what it means to be human in a physically real world. This is a fundamental change.

This then is the revolution: a transformed vision of the physical world, resulting in a transformed vision of ourselves with implications for how we live and act in the world, and a very different interpretation of our times. Basic ecologism creates a root metaphor for an evolving ecological universe. The deep ecological vision creates a literal one, i.e., a physically based understanding of an evolving, order-producing universe that consists of and is governed by ecological dynamics.

BEGINNING THE STORY

> Alas, all is Newtonian. The rationalists have taken over the world and there is no longer room for magic.
>
> *Character in television series Northern Exposure*

The mechanistic transformation gave us the Scientific Revolution and the Scientific Revolution's foundational discipline was Newtonian physics, or more precisely, Newtonian mechanics. Since that time, Newtonian mechanics has served as the model of how science can and should be. The first revolutionary news is that Newtonian successes created an impression of how the world works and this impression is not valid. For example, Newtonian successes created the impression that the world was not just "lawful" but that it had the potential to be completely predicted and controlled. This is not true. The nonlinear revolution *proves* that there are very real limits on prediction and control and that these limits are due to the nature of things, not just practical problems.

As inheritor of the mechanistic dream, Western understandings are now thoroughly and invisibly riddled with Newtonian assumptions. Thus, a modern Newtonian thinker believes that the weather may some day be precisely predictable given enough data and powerful enough computers. A Newtonian businessman tries to figure out how to perfect control of his business' process. The nonlinear revolution shows exactly why these attempts are wrong and, in the process, suggests vastly transformed approaches to the same problems.

The story of the nonlinear revolution or physics' "revolution of the broader case" is the story of physics' discovery that the world does not work the way Newtonian impressions suggested it did. It is also the story of a new impression of how the world works that arises, as it were, from the ashes of the old. Not surprisingly, the central themes are evolution and ecological dynamics — that is, how order is produced by the dynamics of interdependent elements. And though the nonlinear revolution comes out of physics, it has implications for science in general precisely because Newtonian images have dominated so much of science and our beliefs about the world.

The next section provides a brief introduction to the who, what, where, when, and why's of this nonlinear revolution.

The Nonlinear Revolution or The World Hidden in the Broader Case

Think how many absolutely new scientific conceptions have arisen in our own generation, how many new problems have been formulated that were never thought of before, and then cast an eye upon the brevity of science's career... Is it credible that such a mushroom knowledge, such a growth overnight as this *can* represent more than the minutest glimpse of what the universe will really prove to be when adequately understood? No! our science is a drop, our ignorance a sea.

William James

I call this the nonlinear revolution because physics found this new vision while following nonlinear phenomena. I call it the "revolution of the broader case" because the old vision was based on physics' first solvable problems which turn out to be limited cases of the new.

The idea of the "broader case" sets the tone for this revolution. A truly more powerful model subsumes the previous model, it adds new dimensions while keeping all of the abilities of the previous. Relativity's revision of mechanics is an example of this type of revolution — by changing a single assumption, relativity showed how Newtonian mechanics was a limited subset of a broader case. The old is reduced, but also reframed and reborn in a larger context. The nonlinear revolution is exactly such a case of expansion, reframing, and rebirth.

What discoveries/theories make up this revolution? This revolution is about changing our understandings of nonlinear interdependent systems (nonlinear and interdependence are described below). Since nonlinear phenomena are found in every specialty, — quantum mechanics, atmospheric physics, thermodynamics, etc. — the nonlinear revolution really applies to physics as a whole. Thus, where most scientific revolutions of this century were localized in a particular specialty area or around a particular theory (for example, relativity and quantum mechanics), the nonlinear revolution is much more widespread.

This broad nature makes the revolution's implications more widely relevant, but it is something of a problem when it comes to listing the particular discoveries/theories that make up the revolution. There are a large number of such discoveries/theories (see Appendix A) and more coming in every day. These findings have been published by people who operate in many different fields in and outside of physics. What unites them is the exploration of the newly opening field of nonlinear interdependent dynamics.

Because it is more than a single theory, various cohorts of the revolution rally around a variety of broad and sometimes rather loose labels. The most well-known labels are: Chaos, the sciences of complexity, dynamical systems, dissipative systems, far-from-equilibrium systems, fractals, modern nonlinear dynamics, and self-organization theory. Some of these labels refer to specific identifiable theories but most are umbrella labels which might include any number of particular theories. To these already popularized components, I add the notion of the thermodynamics of evolution. Chapters 2 through 6 describe these pieces of the revolution and how they relate.

In order to give some insight as to what unifies this broad group, I should explain how there came to be a nonlinear revolution. James Burke (1978) has done a remarkable job tracing the transformation of ways of looking at the world as a function of technological innovation. The nonlinear transformation is no exception. It has been made possible largely as a result of a single technological advance, the computer. Before the computer, computational difficulty tacitly limited the types of problems science could handle and the types of approaches that could be applied. The computer's speed and power created an incredible leap in human ability to do science. A whole assortment of tools, approaches, and ideas that had previously been oddities of mathematical imagination suddenly became practical.[3] It even became possible simply to experiment mathematically with models. People could see what happened as parameters and input varied over wide ranges.

The new approaches opened realms that used to be inaccessible. This is where the "broader case" concept comes in. We're not talking about a breakthrough concerning a particular question — say, how the human gene works. We're talking about a breakout of new tools, concepts and approaches that can be applied to all sorts of questions. In fact, since most of the new tools and insights come out of the mathematics, they apply to things in general, not to any particular discipline or topic area. It is a bit like finding that the bell-shaped curve applies to all sorts of phenomena from grades in school to genetic characteristics. The concept and the fact that it applies makes us see the world differently. One learns as much about the nature of things as one does about grades or genetics per se.

The interesting thing about the nonlinear revolution is that, retrospectively, one sees just how small a piece of the world physics had been dealing with because that is as far as the earlier tools could go. Classical physics has seemed so well worked out that one expected radical insights only in nature's most esoteric regions — subatomic particles, near-light speeds, or perhaps the origins of the universe. The nonlinear revolution is startling precisely because it applies to the *everyday* world not just near-light speeds or subatomic levels.

How does all of this apply to Newton, mechanism, and our current sense of things? Retrospectively, physics had a tool (actually a set of tools) that particularly shaped its vision of the world. The tool is calculus, the quintessential tool of the Newtonian revolution. Like the computer today, calculus made the first scientific revolution possible by allowing a quantum leap in human ability to do science. It was so successful in helping physics unravel the world, that it set expectations about the way the world was.

The catch is that calculus makes certain assumptions and hence only works on certain problems. For example, calculus presumes smooth continuous change. It also presumes that a problem can be broken down — approximated to precision — by lines or simple curves. This technique of breaking down to approximate by simple curves is used in a wide variety of tools besides calculus so these tools too have supported calculus' sense of things.

Unfortunately, while calculus and analytic techniques worked wonderfully for the simple systems physics cut it teeth on, they are inadequate for the vast majority of real world problems. It has been known for nearly 100 years that the number of problems that can be integrated (i.e., solved with calculus) is minuscule compared to the ones that cannot be integrated. Most systems do not exhibit only smooth continuous change. Less obviously, most problems cannot be adequately approximated with lines or simpler curves. One of the nonlinear revolution's more interesting discoveries is that a large number of common phenomena have a *fractal* nature; there is strong evidence that much of nature's geometry is fractal (Mandelbrot, 1983). And fractals cannot be approximated by simpler curves (I discuss this more in Chapter 2.)

Of course, systems that can be solved via calculus exhibit certain characteristics — otherwise they would not be solvable via calculus. For example, any system that can be integrated can be represented as a set of independent elements, all changing in isolation from each other. All integrable systems exhibit smooth continuous change. They can all be broken down and approximated by simpler curves. And once their equations of motion are known, precise prediction and control are possible in principle, if sometimes difficult in practice.

In short, calculus-solvable systems create a Newtonian mechanistic image of how things work. They lead us to believe we can isolate causes, predict precisely, reduce to independent elements, and control change. These images move insidiously into our everyday beliefs about how things work. Take for example, the image of change. In a Newtonian world, if we make a small change to the system we believe this change will affect the system in predictable and traceable ways. Soviet five-year plans epitomize such thinking about change: if I add 40 workers and 5 machines, in 5 years I will have **X** level of production.

Such Newtonian beliefs are not only inaccurate, they are also dangerous. Newtonian images support belief in "technique" — precise interventions that produce precise, predictable, *controllable* results. We get the kind of thinking that says: if I apply this technique to my children they will grow up happy or, if I present this propaganda to my employees, or the voters or … fill in the blank, it will raise their morale, make them more efficient, i.e., make them do what I want. Thus, the profound and problematic part of the Newtonian mechanistic image is that it provides an excuse for an ethics of power. It leads directly to the idea that we can make the world do what we want. Eisler (1988) calls this the "dominator" mentality, and though she associates it with much earlier roots, it is also a logical consequence of the Newtonian world view.

Soviet five-year plans seem ludicrous in the face of current events, but other kinds of mechanism-shaped thinking — like the potential for complete control — remain quite unchallenged. They remain unchallenged because they have a partial validity, i.e., techniques have a valid place in the world, we *can* control some things. Yet, they also remain unchallenged because there has been no scientifically substantiated broader case context that shows how, when and why such thinking is wrong. Consequently, there has been no reason to change (at least not for a good pragmatic mechanist) and no alternative. One of the nonlinear revolution's benefits is that its science-supported broader-case context helps show what parts of technique-ism are baby and what are bathwater. This gives the pragmatists reason to change and some budding alternatives.

The nonlinear revolution destroys the science-supported vision of domination and control by showing that many if not most systems cannot be fully predicted even with equations of motion and precise initial conditions. This means the dysfunction that comes from a controlling master-of-the-universe mentality can now be challenged on a pragmatic/scientific basis as well as a social/humanistic one.

The sense of isolable causes, of precise prediction, of reducing to independent elements, of controllable change — all these images fit the mechanistic calculus-approachable part of the world. They are a very limited case of the broader context.

How does all of this apply to nonlinearity? The nonlinear realm is where one finds the types of systems that do not succumb to calculus. Though some nonlinear systems can be solved by calculus, most cannot. So, the nonlinear realm presents important classes of problems that couldn't be solved in traditional ways and these succumbed to the new ways. And lo, these systems didn't fit the Newtonian image of the world. For example, among the nonlinear revolution's many paradoxical findings are: systems can be both completely determined and completely unpredictable/uncontrollable; what looks random often has hidden structure; the structure of things often does not get simpler as you break it down; infinitesimal causes can have a massive effect; complex systems often have simple solutions; and simple equations often produce very complex results. Such findings and others don't fit Newtonian expectations. Thus, nonlinear systems opened the door to understanding that the Newtonian world view was a limited case of a broader world.

What is special about nonlinear systems? First a definition of "nonlinear" is in order. A nonlinear system is any system in which input is not proportional to output; that is, an increase in x does not mean a proportional increase or decrease in y. For example, 140 Fahrenheit is not twice as pleasant as 70; 8 aspirin do not reduce a headache 8 times as much as one aspirin. In other words, if you graphed temperature or aspirin versus comfort, the graph would not be a straight line. Nonlinearity is as simple as that. It is everything whose graph is not a straight line — and this is just about everything.[4]

As this definition suggests, there is nothing "special" about nonlinearity. It's as common as sliced bread. Nor is nonlinearity necessarily out of the realm of calculus or linear approximation methods. Calculus can solve many nonlinear problems. Much of the popular Chaos literature tends to hype "nonlinearity" as something important and this is simply not the case.

So, it's not nonlinearity per se that is "special." Then what is so special? Let me introduce the concept of interdependence, also called interaction effects. Interaction effects — the notion of elements of a system mutually affecting and being affected by each other (either instantaneously or in a loop fashion) — is at the nexus of a whole string of concepts, for example, feedback, recursion, and self-referentiality (see also Chapter 2). Chaotic phenomena are thought to be the result of interaction effects, particularly self-referentiality and recursion. In fact, calculus' deep limitations were first discovered as a result of an interaction-effect problem, the three-body problem. Newton had modeled the solar system using the interactions of only two bodies, i.e., sun and planet. When people attempted to expand the model to include the interactions of at least *three* bodies (for example, sun-planet-moon), they discovered that the problem was provably unsolvable with approximation methods like calculus (see discussion in Chapter 2).

So, it is interdependence that is "special" right? Unfortunately, interdependence isn't the single crucial factor either. Calculus can handle some interdependence, specifically, linear interdependence. It is the *combination* of nonlinearity and interdependence that is crucial. Chaotic phenomena are found in *nonlinear interdependent* (interdependent) systems.

Yet, the final twist is that nonlinear interdependent systems are anything but "special" in the sense of odd, unusual, different or somehow anointed with special powers. All real world systems have some element of non-linearity and interdependence. "Linear" and "independent" are idealizations. The systems we call "linear" are so line-like that linear models are effective. Similarly, the variables or systems we call "independent" are so relatively independent that independent models are effective.

This brings us to the main point of this discussion. Probably *the* most revolutionary point about the science of Chaos is that the systems it deals with are anything but special, odd or unusual. And if they are "different," they are only "different" from the systems that physics has been able to deal with heretofore. The very startling upshot of this is that physics has not previously been able to deal with the most common types of system in the world at large. And this is quite shocking because we tend to think of science as somehow pretty comprehensive. This idea is startling enough to warrant its own section.

How does Chaos reorganize our perception of what physics has been able to do up until now? Until Chaos there have been not one but two types of mathematics/physics. One is linear. There are all kinds of topics taught in a wide range of disciplines — from physics to business and economics — that have the word "linear" in their title: linear programming, linear algebra, and linear regression. The linear branch is huge and well developed. The second type of mathematics/physics deals with nonlinear *in*dependent systems. This branch develops solutions to equations that are nonlinear but have only one variable (i.e., nonlinear non-interdependent). In this field one learns special functions (the Bessel functions, the Elliptic functions, etc.) that are solutions to simple nonlinear equations with only one function. The nonlinear branch is also highly developed and very useful in dealing with many problems, for example, in electrical circuits and radio propagation. Though both of these branches are highly developed and important, neither has much to do with the other, and more importantly, neither encompasses the bulk of the real world because both linear and nonlinear independent systems are exceptional cases.

Up until Chaos, physics could deal with linear problems (with or without interdependence) and nonlinear problems with independent variables. These formed the two directions in which one could go and do reasonable mathematical work and in neither of these two directions did one find

chaos. It is only if one couldn't go in either of these two special directions
— when people *had* to go in the middle — that they ran into the non-Newtonian world ... the phenomenon of chaos. Before Chaos people didn't
want to enter this middle ground if they could avoid it because there were
no adequate tools. But, of course, the middle is where the real world is.

Chaos provides tools that open up the mid-ground, the world of nonlinear interdependent systems. And, in the process it allows us to see just
how much of the world has been inaccessible before — and how much is
still inaccessible. It helps human humility to realize that these two huge,
important and well-developed directions were nevertheless drops in the
ocean.

There is also a relatively easy way to understand the nature of the new
perspective and this has to do, not with nonlinearity, but with causality.

What is the nonlinear revolution's key change in perspective? The key to
why Chaos represents a big change has to do with complex causality, that
is, everything that isn't simple, sequential, or independent causality. Traditionally we look for independent variables and "the" cause (i.e., the singular, antecedent cause). Nonlinear interdependent systems force physics
to acknowledge that the vast majority of causality is irreducibly complex
and that complex causality creates a distinctly non-Newtonian world. The
classical vision is wrong because causality is virtually never simple. The
world can rarely be broken down into independent elements or essentially
linear systems. And all this is now provably so.

The change in our understanding of causality can be seen in two simple
examples. The classic Newtonian image of causation is that of a billiard ball
shooting across a table and colliding with another ball. In this image, the
balls collide and career off in their separate ways. Though the two balls are
mutually affected, the traditional approach is to focus on the effect one ball
has on the other. This approach produces a unidirectional, one-shot, and no
return image of causality and of the system's behavior. It pushes interaction
effects aside, treating them either as negligible, transitory, too complex, or
irrelevant. This approach's helpful simplification has served science well
over time, but it is limited.

An image of interdependent causality is seen in a whirlpool. In a
whirlpool, each water molecule affects and is affected by the ones around
it. It is pulled in after the one in front of it and in turn sucks ones behind it
into the same line. The whirlpool's shape is maintained by this circle of
acting and being acted on — a dog-chasing-its-tail effect. The whirlpool is
nothing but a bunch of molecules chasing each other. But it is also a system,

it has a coherent wholeness to it. The whirlpool shows us that interdependent causality generates form and structure.

The phenomenon of entrainment of clocks on a wall provides another important image of interdependence effects. If you place a number of cuckoo clocks on a wall and set their pendulums in motion in different directions, they will nevertheless end up with their pendulums all perfectly synchronized. As the pendulums swing they send small perturbations through the wall such that each affects and is affected by the others. The net result of this mutual affecting is that together the pendulums arrive at a common mutually enhancing rhythm. This collection of interacting elements start looking and acting as if they were a whole. Interdependent causality produces coherence and synergy.

These examples are both very physical, simple, and well known. Yet, they give some sense of why a science centered on interdependent causality produces a very different image of the world than one centered on independent causality. Affecting and being affected is a kind of linking causality. It is not one-shot, one-sided, and independent, but looping, two-sided, and reflects interconnection and interdependence between variables/components. And, as the whirlpool and cuckoo clocks show, it often produces coherence, synergy, structure, and form.

This discussion of interdependent causality also suggests how the non-linear revolution connects to ecological thinking and why ecologism subsumes mechanistic thinking. For example, classical mechanistic thinking emphasizes how parents affect the child, how interest rates affect the economy, and how germs affect the body — all unidirectional effects. Nonlinear ecological thinking restores the other side of each of these equations. And, in the process, it creates an image of the two sides being part of one system. The parent and child are part of a mutually affecting family system; interest rates affect and are affected by the economy; and a germ's effect on the body is strongly determined by the body's overall condition.

Why does the nonlinear revolution make such a big difference? I believe it is because it houses a change in science's focal type of causality — from independent, isolable and sequential causality to interdependent causality. Thus, "nonlinear interdependent systems" labels a type of mathematical model but the key difference is that such models highlight a type of causality that was short-changed in classical science because it was too hard to follow. The nonlinear revolution is physics' emerging understanding that structure arises from complex interdependence.

So, this is how we change from a Newtonian to an ecological world — by being forced to give up the idea that we could (or should) always break things down into simple independent causal systems. The new physics focuses our awareness on the web of mutual causation rather than a sequence of non-interacting causes. It makes ecology part of the whole physical spectrum not just biology and life. (It expands and adds new twists to ecological understanding as well, but that is for later chapters.)

Still, as profound as this shift in vision may be, it is not the only or even the most fundamental shift in world view that the new physics provides. There is a more fundamental shift in vision. Hence, the next question is:

Where else is the revolution? In a nutshell, in paying attention primarily to independent causality, classical physics missed how the universe goes about ordering itself. Interdependent causality plays a much more important role in the nature of things than classical science imagined. Specifically, interdependent causality is the key to the natural, spontaneous, physical, emergence of structure and order.

The nonlinear revolution's appreciation of this started small. It started with the discovery of patterns hidden in what had previously looked like random behavior. It discovered a number of interesting effects that relate to cohering, i.e., coming or staying together, forming patterns and shapes. It discovered that this taking form is a very ubiquitous process. People hadn't seen how common this "taking form" was before because it frequently looks like chaos. The popular name for the branch of the revolution that made these discoveries is, in fact, "Chaos" (less popularly, "modern nonlinear dynamics"). The science of "Chaos" is known for revealing the order in chaos. Its mathematical nature means its insights can be applied to virtually all scientific disciplines.

Chaos' tools and insights are particularly useful in another branch of the revolution, self-organization theory. When tied to rules of energy flow, Chaos' discoveries help explain how things organize themselves into coherent structures, for example, how systems like the whirlpool arise and maintain their form through energy exchange operations. Jantsch (1980), Prigogine (1984), Laszlo (1987) and many others describe how far-from-equilibrium nonlinear dynamics lead to self-organization.

The thermodynamics of evolution then adds a final piece to the puzzle. It provides an understanding of why higher and higher levels of organization are driven into being and finds basic patterns and mechanisms by which such driven evolution proceeds. In short, it produces the beginnings of a general theory of evolution that covers everything from molecules to humankind. And perhaps most surprisingly, it suggests that this evolution is both inexorable and ongoing. This "physics of evolution" crystallizes the work that has gone before into a vision of a directed order-producing universe. In this universe life, civilizations and consciousness are not accidents but logical products of an unfolding order-building process.

This is the crux of the nonlinear revolution's truly revolutionary nature. Through it the concept of ordering is added to physics. Mechanistic science could not comprehend and actually rejected the spontaneous emergence of order. Without a physical understanding of order production, life and consciousness appear to be an anomaly in an otherwise inanimate physical world. Direction, order, intent, and many other characteristics of the living need somehow to be discounted. Small wonder the relationship with life-centered discourses was strained.

A physics of order-building and evolution has dramatic implications for human beings because, like the Copernican revolution, it creates a radical change of perspective. Nonlinear science produces an image of an active, creative, order-producing universe. It denies classical science's image of a sterile mechanical universe of directionless colliding particles and accidental life. The Copernican revolution showed that we were not the center of the universe. The nonlinear revolution shows that we are embedded in a deep, creative, and directed process that *is* the physical universe. We are part of something much larger, more coherent and more miraculous than just ourselves. Retrospectively, nonlinearity opened the door to a physical understanding of order-building. And, retrospectively, hidden in the physical understanding of order-building is a complete reversal of classical physics' vision of itself and the world.

Summary

The nonlinear revolution is a classic case of reframing and renewal (see Diner's, 1986, *Renewal of Mechanism*). Science is still science and none of its old tools go away. Yet, many classical scientific connotations do go away. Science is reborn with a very different nature. Nonlinear discoveries show just how much science's view of the world has been shaped by the models it used. Classical science believed the world could be broken down into isolable elements. The result was extremist beliefs about prediction, control, quantification, and reductionism. The nonlinear revolution provides concrete reasons why extreme claims of prediction, control, quantification, and reduction are false. Science can still do all of these — to an extent — but there are very strong restrictions on scientific ability to know, control, predict and reduce.

There are also alternative ways of doing scientific business so that these restrictions do not amount to the end of science. Rather they are the basis of a new beginning. The only thing that is limited is the old way of doing things, the only things lost are absolutist ideas. "Physical" and "scientific" no longer mean reductionistic, control-oriented and completely determinable. Science's self-image becomes less "mechanical" because machines are very simple non-interacting over-constrained mechanisms. Science's external image becomes less megalomaniacal because it can suddenly imagine things mechanistic science arrogantly discounted. All this reduces the rift with life-centered discourses. Suddenly a physics of the commonplace explains exactly why we cannot control the universe. Philosophically and ethically this alone is a gigantic idea.

The net result is a very different situation. Usually physics' world view threatens to *dominate* life-centered discourses and this seems to include stamping out certain observations, models, and types of thinking. This time physics threatens to *join* life-centered discourses. It begins to *fathom* things life-centered discourses have been talking about for a long time. A closer collaboration between the two becomes possible in many surprising ways. For example, cooperation is found to be as much a part of the physical/biological world as competition — and perhaps a more important one (see Chapters 4 and 5). Even art is affected. For a long time art has had an ambivalent relationship with the simple idealized shapes of classical Greek geometry — circles, triangles, and regular figures of all types. The new physics also discovered a new geometry, fractal geometry (see Appendix A). Fractal geometry ties physical dynamics to the creation of form. It is found to be the most common geometry of natural forms — and it is not at all of the Greek form. Fractals show how rich, beautiful, natural complexity grows out of simple dynamics. Various art shows have been produced out of this new geometry and the common reaction has been of awe, beauty, *and* recognition. Dynamics, beauty, simplicity, complexity, and nature blend into one image.

Discoveries like these and many more move us toward a rejoining of C.P. Snow's "two cultures." They move us one giant step toward reconciliation between humankind's many fragmented ways of knowing. The net result of the nonlinear revolution is something most of us find quite unbelievable — a radical change of perspective grounded in physics and yet profoundly humanistic and spiritual.

MODELS AND METAPHYSICS

> Metaphysics is a set of basic assumptions about the general struc-
> ture of existence... Thus, various Greek philosophers enunciated
> views, such as "All is fire ... water ... atoms," etc. Scientists later
> assumed that all is a universal mechanism, following Newtonian
> laws. Metaphysics is something that pervades every field ... in
> varied and subtle ways, of which we are often not conscious. The
> proper role of metaphysics is as a metaphor which provides a
> perceptual grasp of the overall structure of one's thoughts. It is
> therefore a kind of poetry. Some "hard-headed" individuals may
> object to bringing such "poetry" into science. But, just as Moliere
> spoke of the man "who talked prose all his life and never knew it,"
> so even the practical man is speaking poetry all his life without
> knowing it ... all of us will think more clearly when we openly
> admit that a lot of "factual science" is actually a kind of poetry,
> which is indispensable to our mental functioning.
>
> *David Bohm (1972, p. 41)*

The topic of this book is extremely broad. It touches on everything from
physics and philosophy to economics and spirituality. It seeks to portray the
underlying simplicity and commonsense in a major change that embraces
all of these areas. Its topic is the ecological transformation. Its primary
theme is the inseparable circular relationship between tools and tacit assumptions about how things work — or, using David Bohm's words,
models and metaphysics.

The rest of the book examines three things: (Part 1) the ecological
transformation; (Part 2) the nonlinear revolution; and (Part 3) the
transformation's implications for humankind. These topics fit the model-
metaphysics theme as follows:

The nonlinear revolution amounts to a major shift in physics' tacit model.
Bartley (1987) notes that "the scientific view of how the world works has
not only been dominated by physics but by a particular *interpretation* of
physics" (p. 7). Chapter 2 discusses how physics' dominant "Newtonian"[5]
interpretation is something of a byproduct of classical tools. Here "interpretation" refers to a type of metaphysics. It does not refer to a set of facts,
or formal assumptions, but rather a set of tacit assumptions that set the
framework in which facts were interpreted. Thus, the nonlinear revolution
is not a disputation of facts, it is a radical transformation of the framework
in which physicists interpret facts.

Retrospectively, the Newtonian interpretation has dominated the Western world view and has been the cause of much of the fragmentation in modern thought. This interpretation, this model, is being outgrown. Physics is producing a new metaphysics (Chapters 2–5).

The ecological transformation represents the emergence of a more powerful model of how the world works. Previous world hypotheses also represented models of the world. Each was stronger than its predecessor in some ways and weaker in others. The ecological world hypothesis is particularly powerful because it reconciles the major elements of all previous world hypotheses. From its perspective we can begin to see how many feuds are model-based not observation-based. The ecological transformation implies a new metaphysics, a new sense of how the world works (Chapters 6–10).

Broader implications for humankind. I organize the ecological transformation's implications for humankind along four dimensions: power, empowerment, reconciliation, and reenchantment. I also add a special chapter on how ecologism can be applied to current times.

Power accrues because models help us navigate the world; the more complete and accurate the model, the better it helps us navigate, the more power it provides. Ecological thinking (both the basic and nonlinear versions) help us see more than we did before. I examine some economic, psychological and philosophical examples of how ecologism helps us better see and navigate the world (Chapter 6).

Reenchantment comes from the ecological transformation's effect on perception. The modern Western context is a composite of the fruition and exhaustion of the Newtonian mechanistic dream — vast physical power and anomie born of little sense of connection to anything beyond ourselves. General ecological thinking is already changing that. It already shows us that we are part of a larger whole. The deep ecological vision takes this movement a leap beyond. It provides physical conceptualizations that substantiate and transform our sense of belonging. A meeting of heart and mind becomes possible in a way not imagined in the current milieu. If the 21st century finds our context unfathomable it will be because they cannot imagine how we could have seen ourselves as so divided from the world and each other (see Chapter 7).

Reconciliation comes from the new science's ability to support and connect the major observations of existing world hypotheses. Where new world hypotheses traditionally cause a break and thus increase fragmentation in human knowing, the ecological view builds bridges across existing breaks and offers the possibility of reconciliation of traditionally irreconcilable views of the world (see Chapter 8).

Empowerment is another implication of the shifted physical view. One's perception of how the world works shapes how one acts in the world. For example, if you believe that things always stay the same (it's genetic, it's human nature, it has always been like that...), this affects your actions. If you believe that big things can only be changed by big forces, this affects your actions. If you believe that the universe is a bunch of colliding particles going nowhere and the only thing that determines survival is competitive self-interest, why should one act for any reason other than competitive self-interest? The mechanistic model supports all of these impressions. The evolving ecological model supports none of them.

Ecologism empowers the individual in ways that mechanism did not. From the potency of small actions and the inexorability of change to the importance of inhomogeneity and membership in community of Being, the ecological perspective suggests individual human beings count, have power, and belong (Chapter 9).

Thoughts on Our Times. Chapter 10 looks at how nonlinear ecological insights may relate to the changes going on today in the world at large.

Very much out of awareness, often appearing as fact, one's model of the world tacitly sets the context for all action — how we act on the world and how it affects us. Can the world be both demystified and re-enchanted, better understood and more humane? That is precisely the implication at hand.

NOTES

1. The goal here is only to provide a sense of mechanism's essence. It is a strawman because space permits only caricature of mechanism's complexity.

2. Ecological thinking follows the common impression of ecology and not necessarily its technical definition; ecology is only a metaphor. The same is true for "evolution."

3. Time and again, approaches that make dramatic changes to established disciplines can be found in the writings of much earlier workers. They appear to have been the method of choice but were not pursued because of computational difficulty.

4. The basic definition of nonlinear as input not proportional to output results in several other equivalent "definitions" of nonlinearity, for example: any model whose graph is not a straight line; any function with an order higher than one (for example, $y = x_2$); and, in engineering, any system that does not hold to superposition, i.e., you cannot break the system down into separate summable component cycles. The basic definition describes the fundamental property of nonlinearity; the other definitions just reframe this property for particular situations.

5. It is notable that Newton himself did not make the claims for absolute prediction and control that are made in the name of "Newtonian" mechanics. However, Pierre Simon de Laplace (1749–1827) did. His famous quote is: "Given for one instant an intelligence which could comprehend all the forces by which nature is animated, and the respective positions of the beings which compose it, if, moreover, this intelligence were vast enough to submit these data to analysis, it would embrace in the same formula both the movements of the largest bodies in the universe and those of the lightest atom; to it nothing would be uncertain, and the future as the past would be present to its eyes" (from *Bartlett's Familiar Quotations*, 1980, p. 397) Thus, the current world view should really be called Laplacian mechanics.

Part II

The Nonlinear Revolution

The next several chapters outline the changing physical model of how things work. Note that this is not a traditional scientific effort. In a traditional science section, the author tries to establish the detailed correctness of his/her theory of physical reality. Although, I present quite a number of theories and supporting data, I do not claim that everything is worked out. Rather, my primary goal is to show the emerging picture of which these theories and observations all seem a piece. This picture is of a physics with very different metaphysics and of a decidedly more-than-mechanistic world. In this world interdependence is both fundamental and inescapable.

Note. I would not be at all surprised if there are some errors in some of the theories I will present. To maximize reliability I stay primarily with well-established work and identify very new and as yet speculative work before presenting it.

CHAPTER 2

Chaos: The Revolution in Mechanics

> Chaos is the anti-calculus revolution. Calculus is the science of replacing smooth curves with little bits of straight line. Chaos is the science of dealing with things that cannot be described by smooth curves and therefore cannot be replaced by little bits of straight line.
>
> *Michel Baranger*

This chapter looks at Chaos: what it is, what it has found, and how it changes the classical sense of how things work. I provide a more technical review of Chaos' major tools and discoveries in Appendix A.

FROM NEWTON TO CHAOS: THE BEGINNINGS OF NONLINEAR THINKING

> In 1953 I realized that the straight line leads to the downfall of mankind... The straight line is something cowardly drawn with a rule, without thought or feeling; it is the line which does not exist in nature. And that line is the rotten foundation of our doomed civilization.
>
> *Friedensreich Hundertwasser*

Let us begin with a brief history of how Chaos came about.

Physics established its reputation for success in the first scientific revolution by applying calculus to certain basic systems, for example, rolling balls, pendulums and the solar system. In using calculus to unravel planetary motion, Newton actually created the foundational model of science — he created the idea that systems can be precisely predicted through equations of motion. At the heart of this common model of science

Figure 2.1. Trajectory of the three-body problem (Peitgen and Richter 1986, p. 2).

is a particular winning combination — calculus and calculus-approachable systems. But as I've said, calculus cannot unravel the world, a fact first proven by Poincaré in 1892. Thus, Poincaré's work is a logical starting place for a history of Chaos. The question is: why can't calculus unravel the world?

Newton had set science's agenda (precise prediction) by solving "the" equations for planetary motion. But the equations he used were a two-body model of motion; they used only the sun's effect on a planet. To get a more precise model, the effects of other bodies had to be included. The next simplest model would be a three-body problem (say, sun-planet-moon). As Figure 2.1 shows, the three-body interaction problem is very messy.

For over 100 years the best mathematical minds tried to solve the infamous "three-body problem" to no avail. They tried more and more sophisticated ways of breaking the motion down so that it could be approximated by simpler curves. This approximation approach was how calculus had conquered the curve. It was (and is) a fundamental part of the classical scientific approach. Poincaré made the first dent in the three-body problem by coming from the opposite direction. He proved that the three-body problem could *not* be solved by such approximation methods. The nasty upshot of this is that the class of integrable problems is very small. Calculus won't work on the world at large, classical physics' fundamental approach cannot even handle the interactions of three or more bodies.[1]

Poincaré's proof set very clear boundaries on how far the classical approach could go. It suggested that the ability to dissect and delineate direct cause and effect was an exception, the nature of more-than-two-bodied interactions makes this impossible. But, since no other viable approaches really existed, this was just a depressing fact of life. Rather than dealing with Poincaré's insight, most physicists continued to focus on problems that could be integrated. Other problems were pushed aside as uninteresting, though more likely the reason was that they were just too hard.

The belief that the world can be predicted, controlled and understood by breaking things down comes from assumptions hidden in Newtonian approaches. Changing such a well-established view requires both reasons to change and alternatives. The 20th century produced both of these in the form of new sets of problems and a pivotal new tool — the computer.

In the early 1900s Poincaré and others began to develop alternative mathematical approaches, notably the qualitative geometric approaches of topology and mathematical systems theory. And while physicists often regarded these as bizarre figments of mathematical imagination, by mid-century these approaches were pretty well developed.

The expansion of electronics in the 20th century created important sets of problems that could not be adequately addressed through definite integrals. Such problems created pressure to develop new approaches. Van der Pohl, for example, in studying electronic oscillation began to develop new ways to solve nonlinear differential equations and, in the process, he began to draw interesting conclusions about the behavior of such systems.

But it was the development of the computer that allowed science to move beyond Newtonian assumptions. Like the development of the microscope in the last century, the computer opened up realms of research and understanding that simply were not possible before. In particular, those alternative approaches that mathematicians had been developing required huge numbers of calculations to be useful for real-life problems. In a very real way science couldn't move beyond Newtonian conceptions until the computer came of age. Poincaré glimpsed some of the order in three-body interactions but found it impossible to follow. Today computer graphics show us what he could not see. As Figure 2.2 shows, these graphs reveal order and simplicity in what looks like chaos when viewed the old fashioned way.

Through the middle part of the century numerous workers made inroads into a new understanding. But in the beginning they worked in isolation, with no awareness of the commonality of the issues they were dealing with or the conclusions they were reaching. Gleick's popular book, *Chaos: Making a New Science*, outlines how these various workers found each

Sally J. Goerner

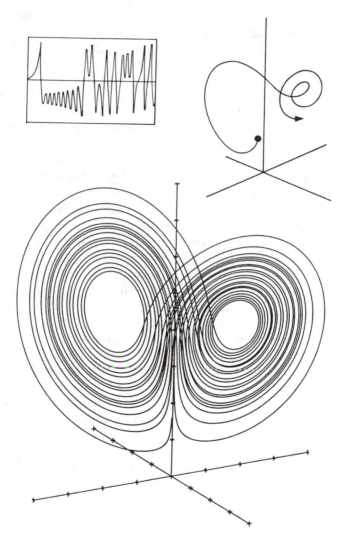

Figure 2.2. Lorenz attractor with time series insert (reprinted with permission from James P. Crutchfield).

other in the early 1970s, began to collaborate, and, finally, how their disparate activities began to take shape as a new understanding of "Chaos" or, alternatively, "complexity" (see Rosen 1985 and Pagels 1988).

But what are "Chaos" and "complexity"? We now run into the first of many terminology problems. Let me take the term "complexity." The term "complexity" is used because the new approaches and understandings are particularly helpful in dealing with complex interdependence (like that found in weather, the brain, economics, etc.). However, "complexity" is a very misleading term for a number of reasons. First, one of the new insights is that much of what *looks* complex is actually very simple. Even very complex "infinite-dimensional" systems can be described by very simple equations with only a few dimensions (see Thompson and Stewart 1986). Thus, complex systems theory shows simplicity hidden in complexity. The same point can be made about "Chaos": a major insight is that what looks chaotic actually has a lot of structure, we just couldn't see it before.

The biggest problem with the terms "Chaos" and "complexity," however, is that they make it sound as if the new understandings apply to some limited type of system (chaotic or complex ones). This is very misleading. In fact, it is fundamentally wrong. In the classical view, linearity is the baseline; everything else is a deviation ("non"-linear). What Chaos brings out in big bold letters is that the reverse is actually the case. Everything is nonlinear. Thus, as Stanislaw Ulam quipped, "to call the study of chaos, nonlinear science is like calling zoology the study of non-elephant animals" (Gleick 1987, p. 68).

Ulam's comment brings out the fundamental reason that Chaos is important. Chaos reverses the context. It flips the classical order of things on its head. Classically, linearity and isolable elements are used as the standard case (from which deviations were measured). In opening the door to the exploration of nonlinear interdependence, Chaos allows us to admit that nonlinear interdependence is the norm. In the process, it shows that interdependence plays a much deeper more productive role in the nature of things than Newtonian physics imagined. Thus, Chaos is important because it completely reverses our frame of reference — it changes our assumptions from ones based on a limited case to the ones based on a broader case.

"Chaos" and "complexity" are mainly pop labels for modern nonlinear dynamics. They highlight a new perspective on what physics has always studied, dynamical systems — literally, systems that move. This new vision reflects an expanded appreciation of interdependence and how it makes things work. Armed with new tools, modern nonlinear dynamics (hereafter called "Chaos") shows precisely how prescient Poincaré's insight about the nature of three-(or more-)body interactions was. The nature of interaction, the nature of change — the nature of systems in the general case — does not fit calculus' image of isolable causation or smooth, continuous and predictable change.

Note. In these discussions I use the word "Newtonian" to refer to the calculus-shaped sense of things. This implies no disrespect to Newton himself, who (using these terms) was probably not a "Newtonian." Newton used certain assumptions to attack problems; it was generations of followers that changed his problem-solving approach into beliefs about the world.

WHAT DOES CHAOS DO DIFFERENTLY?

Chaos theory is discussed more thoroughly in Appendix A. However, to provide some feel for how Chaos differs from Newtonian approaches, this section looks at two foundational Chaos approaches, attractors in phase space and bifurcation diagrams.

Physics' traditional methods focus on solving equations and predicting where something is at a specific time. The idea is that with an equation and a starting point (initial conditions), one can predict what the system will do at any time in the future (and presumably what it did do at any time in the past). But, calculus can only construct solutions for a certain limited set of systems. Even if this weren't a problem, for most systems initial conditions are completely unknown (e.g., the weather, the economy, human beings). If this approach doesn't work, what else can one do (besides statistics)?

The answer that has come to fruition in Chaos is: 1) one develops models, 2) that bring out the relationships between variables (show how they affect each other); and 3) that show the system's overall pattern of flow. Then you graph these models so you can *see* patterns of flow. The result is a graphic "overview of how the whole system evolves and how this is influenced by the starting conditions" (Thompson and Stewart 1987, p. xi).

Phase space maps are a good example of Chaos' approach. Each axis of a phase space map represents a variable. For example, if you graphed the behavior of a pendulum in phase space, one axis would be the velocity and the other axis would be the position of the bob in the horizontal direction. A plot of the pendulum in phase space shows how velocity and position change together and it shows all the velocity/position pairs that the system generates. Figure 2.3 shows the phase space diagram for a imaginary frictionless pendulum starting from some particular set of initial condition.

This map is simple and relatively uninteresting but it does bring out the slightly different way that Chaos treats things. Phase space maps highlight

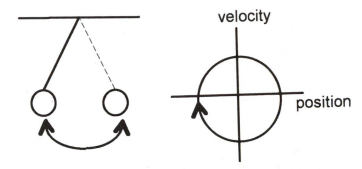

Figure 2.3. Frictionless pendulum in phase space (after Crutchfield et al. 1986, p. 49).

the relationships between variables and the flow of change. It also emphasizes the system's whole range of behavior. The map shows the whole picture of how pendulum speed and direction *vary together* as the system evolves over time. It gives a better picture of the flow of mutual effects.

Seeing the flow of mutual effect is crucial to seeing the order in complex systems. The first researchers literally *saw* very clear order demonstrated in the graphs of what had previously been considered essentially random behavior of a complex system. For example, Figure 2.4 compares a system's behavior as seen in a traditional time-series graph to a relational map.

The forms shown in the relational maps in Figure 2.4 are called *attractors*. Many attractors are striking because of their beauty and disarming because they reveal a deep structure hidden in what looks like jumbled, erratic behavior. They are pictures of the order in interactive chaos.

Bifurcation diagrams provide another example of what Chaos does differently and how it results in a different impression of how things work. An attractor only shows the system's behavior for a particular value of a parameter. For example, you might have a model for how water moves and at 95° this movement would follow a particular attractor. At 100° the movement might be very similar. The 100° attractor will look essentially like the 95° attractor (technically, they are topologically conjugate). However, at 100.1°, suddenly the system's behavior changes. A new, very different attractor now describes the system's behavior. It turns out that different forms of behavior are hidden in the same equation. Figure 2.5 shows a system moving through various attractors (i.e., through various *forms* of behavior).

Sally J. Goerner

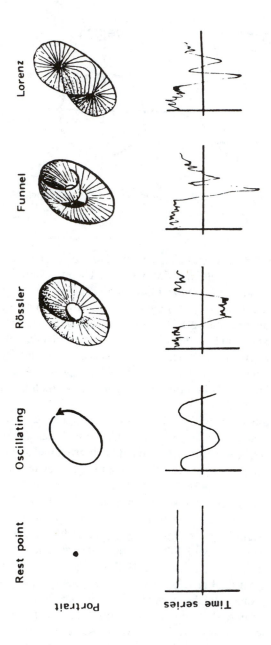

Figure 2.4. Strange attractors versus time series (Abraham and Shaw 1987, p. 556).

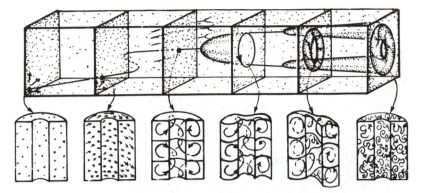

Figure 2.5. Bifurcation diagram (Abraham and Shaw 1988, p. 46).

You can condense the information in Figure 2.5 into a two-dimensional graph, called a *bifurcation diagram* (shown in Figure 2.6). Bifurcation diagrams provide an overview of how the system's behavior varies for different values of a parameter (called a control parameter). The parameter's values are given on the horizontal axis and number of cycles before the attractor repeats itself is shown on the vertical axis. In Figure 2.6 the single line part of the graph represents attractors that repeat themselves after one cycle, the first parabola represents two-cycle attractors, the double parabola four-cycle attractors, and so. The bifurcation diagram allows us to see at a glance where the system's behavior is essentially the same and where it undergoes qualitative transformations of behavior, called *bifurcations*.

The bifurcation diagram also produces a very different image of how change takes place. The classical calculus-shaped image was of smooth, continuous and traceable change. The bifurcation diagram shows a type of change called *punctuated equilibrium*. As the control parameter increases, the system goes through periods of stable sameness, punctuated by abrupt transitions to qualitatively different forms of behavior. Change is sometimes smooth and sometimes discontinuous. And notably, the effects of a particular perturbation cannot be tracked across a bifurcation.

The mathematics of attractors and bifurcation provide a good model for a lot of real-world behavior. Psychology has long struggled with the observation that a person's behavior can appear incredibly resistant to change, like a fixed "trait," and yet become completely different in a slightly different context. Is behavior trait-like or context dependent? Attractors and bifurcations provide a concrete model for how they can be both. Behavior

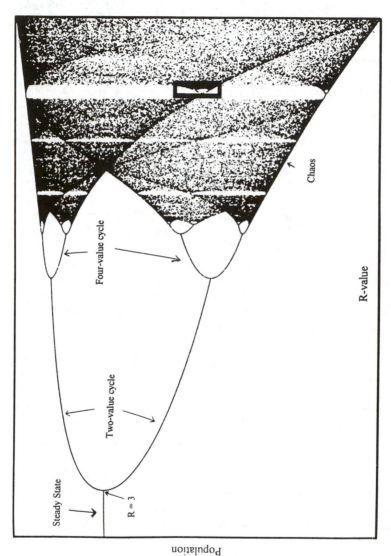

Figure 2.6. Bifurcation diagram (after figure from James P. Crutchfield).

is stable and resistance to change within the domain of an attractor. Behavior is context sensitive in that a small change in a parameter results in a transformation of attractor.

The mathematics of attractors and bifurcation twist the usual sense of things in a lot of ways. For example, May (1974) used bifurcation diagrams to investigate how population levels vary as a function of fertility rates. On the one hand, the bifurcation diagram suggests that many ups and downs of population are just part of an overall pattern (attractor). On the other hand, very different patterns are just a decimal point away. Such insights apply to economic patterns as well. It may well be the case that interest rates going up one month and down the next is less a reaction to a particular event than part of a general pattern. Conversely, longstanding economic patterns may be a hair's breadth from demise.

These examples provide some sense of the difference between Chaos and classical science. Instead of focusing on following a particular causal chain, Chaos tends to look at overall maps of the system's behavior. The result is fewer questions of the form "did this cause that?" and more of the form "when and why does this happen?" Instead of trying to nail down particular trajectories, there is a greater belief in and search for hidden patterns. These patterns give very precise quantitative information but not necessarily of the form "where is this piece of matter at this particular time." Thus, Chaos' patterns suggest when a heart is about to fibrillate and what parameters control fibrillation but it cannot predict on which specific heart beat the fibrillation will begin.

WHAT DID CHAOS FIND? A BRIEF SUMMARY

Some key findings and concepts of Chaos are:

Attractors Roughly speaking, an attractor is a picture of the stable behavior a system settles into over time. Attractors can be simple, for example, a point attractor means the system stabilizes at a single stable point (for example, no motion). And they can be amazing, for example, strange attractors are complex and often beautiful forms that describe behavior that never repeats exactly the same way yet conforms to a bounded pattern.

The concept of attractors adds two important elements to science's conceptual scheme: the idea of attraction itself and the idea of form. A system's behavior can be thought of as being drawn toward the attractor's form. Here form implies both the attractor's actual shape and the "form of behavior." The section on "Characteristics of An Interdependent World" discusses the sense in which attractors "attract" behavior.

Bifurcations. A bifurcation is a transformation from one type of behavior to a *qualitatively* different type of behavior. A corollary to the concept of bifurcation is that a system may have multiple attractors. i.e., a single system may have multiple forms of behavior.

Chaos. Technically, the term "chaos" (with a small "c") refers to a particular state of the system characterized by a particular type of behavior. Specifically, "chaotic" behavior: 1) never repeats itself and appears erratic; 2) has sensitive dependence (described below); 3) yet, is nevertheless orderly and follows deterministic rules. Technical chaos adds two more important caveats to classical thinking as follows:

> *Sensitive dependence on initial condition*. Minute differences in initial conditions may lead to widely divergent outcomes. This phenomenon is also known as the Butterfly effect because the smallest action at any level can produce a critical effect (e.g., the flapping of a butterfly leads to monsoons in India). When a system is in the technical state of "chaos," small differences are determinative.

> *Unpredictable Determinism*. Sensitive dependence creates an "uncertainty principle" for the macroscopic scale. During chaos, the system's actual path cannot be predicted even with a perfect model, i.e., the exact equations of motion and very precise initial conditions. Because of limitations in precision and differences in how roundoff errors are handled, the same equation with the same initial conditions won't even produce the same result when run on two different computers (see Stewart 1989). Systems in chaos are lawful, orderly, deterministic *and* unpredictable. The concept of chaos contradicts the classical idea that "deterministic" means "predictable in principle."

Strange attractors and homoclinic tangles (described in Appendix A) are both maps of chaotic behavior; both are fractals (described below).

Fractals. Fractals refer to a particular type of structure created by an iterative, self-referential process. Their technical definition has to do with the strange fact that they have a fractional dimension, i.e., they are not two-dimensional, or three-dimensional, but have 2.3, 1.5, etc. dimensions. Fractals turn out to be an appropriate description of most naturally occurring forms (for example, mountains, clouds, trees, lightning). They've even been used to describe economic patterns (for example, variations in cotton prices). Their ubiquity and connection to "natural geometry" validate the sense that nonlinear dynamics are more normative than linear dynamics.

Fractal structure is a characteristic of chaotic phenomena though it is found in non-chaotic phenomena as well (Abraham and Shaw 1984).[2]

Self-Similarity and Scaling. Fractals also have an internal "microstructure" which exhibits the phenomenon of scaled self-similar layering. Finer and finer magnification of a fractal reveals smaller and smaller versions of the same structure at all levels. Hence fractals are infinitely complex — no matter how small a piece you take, it is an equally complex microcosm of the whole. Fractal self-similarity and scaling are particularly important because they repudiate two Newtonian assumptions as follows:

> *Reducing does not always simplify*. The KAM theorem finally resolved the three-body problem by showing that it leads to a fractal. The attempts to approximate the three-body problem via simpler curves couldn't work because smaller parts of a fractal are not simpler, they are equally complex.

> *Measurement is scale-dependent*. In fractals measurement depends on scale. The measurement you get depends on the size of your ruler and the scale of granularity you are willing to include. The world will not only look different to two observers at different scales, it will also measure differently.

The Breadmaker's Transformation: Recursive Mixing (Stretching-Folding). Fractals and the "order in chaos" appear to be a phenomenon of recursive mixing. The technical explanation of this is Smale's stretching and folding in phase space — also called the breadmaker's transformation. The stretching and folding done while kneading bread gives a concrete model of the process and the result. If you follow a particular spot of dough during kneading, the behavior will seem erratic, yet the process can still produce a whole which, like filo dough, contains finely structured order. The mathematical term "mixing" is used to define this process in which parts of the bread (i.e., points in the model) that were originally very close together become widely distributed throughout the pastry.

Universality. Sensitive dependence is the down side of Chaos because having the precise equations may not help prediction. Universality is the up side. It suggests that you can model the basic dynamics of complex systems with very simple equations. Apparently, interactive chaos tends to bleed systems of their complexity, effectively reducing many dimensions to a few. All equations of a particular universality class (no matter how complex) display certain universal qualitative and quantitative patterns of behavior. As Cvitanovic (1984) says:

> The wonderful thing about this universality is that it does not matter much how close our equations are to the ones chosen by nature; as long as the model is in the same universality class ... as the real system, both will undergo a period-doubling sequence. That means that we can get the right physics out of very crude models. (p. 11)

Universality provides a quantitative mathematical understanding of universal forms of behavior that hold regardless of the nature of the system — hence Chaos' reputation for working on systems as diverse as prices on the stock exchange, weather, populations control, fluid dynamics, pendulums, and heart beats.

The Geometry of Behavior. While Chaos ends the idea that determinism equals predictability, it does not imply an end to empiricism, experimentation, or verification. We can still predict events for limited time frames and under certain conditions.[3] More importantly Chaos' maps and methods provide very testable quantitative information about the patterns and structure of behavior. Thus, they allow empiricism to enter realms that are provably unbroachable via analytic methods. The approaches are just different. Specifically, they focus us on the geometry of behavior; they help us predict and verify patterns and transformations between patterns instead of focusing us on predicting specific events. As Crutchfield et al. (1986) state:

> The classic approach to verifying a theory is to make predictions and test them against experimental data ... [now] verifying a theory becomes a much more delicate operation, relying on statistical and geometric properties rather than on detailed prediction. (p. 57)

HOW CHAOS ALTERS THE NEWTONIAN SENSE OF THINGS

> Classical dynamics ... makes statements in terms of mechanics, such as positions or velocity of particles... The particles crossing the world on their lonely tracks do not interact with each other. Thus, classical dynamics becomes the idealized case of "pure" motion of a particle ... a thought model which nevertheless is useful for many considerations. But the "dirty" reality includes encounters, collisions, exchanges, mutual stimulation, challenges and coercions of many kinds.
>
> *Erich Jantsch (1980, p. 24)*

Thus far I've provided a whirlwind tour of what Chaos does differently and what it has found. Many popularized accounts can give a more thorough

Figure 2.7. Independent causality.

tour (Gleick 1986; Stewart 1989; Briggs and Peat 1989; Nicholis and Prigogine 1989). The important questions about Chaos, however, are "what does it mean?" and "why is it important?" This section begins to look at these questions, particularly from the perspective of how Chaos contrasts with classical mechanics.

Two Different Visions of Interaction

Physics started simple, with simple systems, calculus and a simple cause/effect model. The basic mechanistic scientific strategy was to hold everything constant, change one variable and see what the effect was. This is incredibly reasonable when one is first trying to get a handle on things. Still, in essence, this approach makes causality look like Figure 2.7.

Of course, causality never goes just one way. Newton's third law, "equal and opposite action and reaction," is a statement that mutual causality occurs in all interactions. So, the world is filled with more complex types of causality — mutual causality, circular causality, self-referential or recursive causality. Thus, causality actually looks more like Figure 2.8.

The interesting thing about the calculus-shaped view was that physicists acted as if they should and could figure out how to remove interaction effects from the models. Thus, as Prigogine and Stengers (1984) say:

> Any integrable system may be represented as a set of units, each changing in isolation, quite independently of all the others... Indeed, [classical science hoped that] through a clever change of variables, all interaction could be made to disappear... Generations of physicists and mathematicians tried hard to find for each kind of system the "right" variables that would eliminate the interactions. (p. 71)

Of course, one can never actually get rid of them. It's just that sometimes they are well-behaved in a Newtonian sense. But when they are not, these effects are impossibly hard to follow via the traditional way of looking at

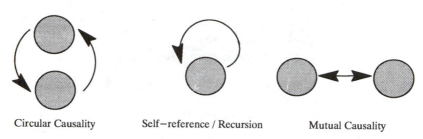

Circular Causality   Self−reference / Recursion   Mutual Causality

Figure 2.8. Interactive causality.

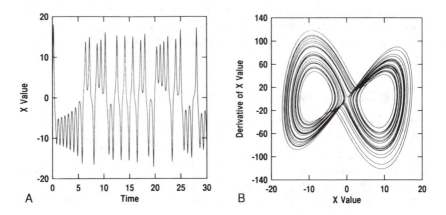

A   B

Figure 2.9. The Lorenz attractor, time series, and phase space (Sacks 1990, p. 359).

things. As we've seen, even the simple three-body interaction problem is hopelessly tangled. Chaos' single most important message is that interactions may only look messy because physics looked at them through its traditional tools. Chaos represents physics' budding awareness that interactions may result in something other than mess. As Figure 2.9 shows, the change of vision is striking.

Chaos produces a very unexpected picture of complex, interactive causality. Apparently, interdependent variables have the capacity to mutually affect themselves into an ordered flow that exhibits coherence and form. Interaction/interdependence has structure. Chaos opens the door to exploring this structure. Spurred by success in a wide number of fields, Chaos has become the pell-mell rush to uncover the interactive structure in various kinds of systems.

Characteristics of An Interactive World

Some basic characteristics of an interactive world are as follows:

Inseparability and Interdependence. Interaction, "affecting and being affected," means that you cannot separate the two variables, hold one constant and vary the other. For example, when a sled slides down an icy slope, friction and speed reciprocally affect each other: the faster the sled goes the more friction it generates, but more friction heats the sled runner which melts the ice which reduces friction and increases the speed. Similarly, nonlinear interdependent systems do not have the "modular virtue" — in engineering terms they cannot be broken down into component cycles. This inseparability/non-reducibility leads to the first ecological rule: you can't blithely expect to separate elements of a system. Interaction effects are important and nonlinear interactive systems are not decomposable.

Attraction. Interactive dynamics can create pull. "Attractor" is the name for a stable pattern of interactive flow. Conceptually, an attractor does "attract," i.e., it pulls behavior toward it. The whirlpool pulling in new water at the top and funneling it down through its form is an example of such attraction. Molecular mutual effect creates a dynamic that literally draws new molecules into the pattern of flow. The attraction that is visibly true in the whirlpool is mathematically true in more abstract systems. Interactive dynamics can pull things into its flow and in the process create forms and pattern.

Stability, Instability and Restructuring. Interactive dynamics can not only create a pull, but they can also be self-stabilizing. Thus, once an attractor (a dynamic) is going, it will tend to maintain its current pattern it springs back from small perturbations. Thus, you can stick your finger in the whirlpool and it will still keep its form and rebuild when you remove your finger. A self-stabilizing dynamic is said to have *structural stability*, which means it is resistant to change.

The structure that interactive dynamics produces can, of course, fall apart. For example, a spinning top holds itself up just fine — as long as the speed is maintained and the floor is smooth. If it slows or hits a rough spot, the self-stabilizing dynamic ends. The whens and whys of interactive stability and instability are a pivotal area of research.

In interactive dynamics instability may lead to a new form. Bifurcation diagrams, separatrixes, and basins of attraction are maps showing where one dynamic flow pattern transforms itself into another. Thus, interactive dynamics have a triple option to: exist, not exist, or change forms.

Notably, in interactive dynamics a change of form does not mean that the underlying process or equation has changed; the same process has just reorganized into a different pattern. Multiple attractor systems provide a concrete model of how one process can create many forms, for example, how an acorn growing into a tree is nevertheless one process.

Prior to Chaos, the concept of stability implied a single final state as in equilibrium or homeostasis or a repeated pattern such as the orbits of the solar system. Chaos' structural stability is a stability of a very different type. A system with structural stability may never repeat the same way twice (strange attractors) or may move back and forth between multiple distinct stable states. Such systems may even be in a locally stable pattern that is nevertheless part of an overall progression of states.

Feedback and Folding. The friction/speed example gives some sense of how interdependence between variables causes "feedback." One variable affects another which in turn affects the first. Nonlinear feedback is used to explain the curving back and folding that creates fractals and strange attractors and generally keeps the system bounded. Thompson and Stewart (1987, p. 236) explain how this works in the creation of the Rossler strange attractor from three simple equations: $x' = -y - z$; $y' = x + ay$; $z' = b + z(x - c)$.

> spreading is achieved with only linear terms. But if the full system of three equations were linear, the spreading would merely continue as all trajectories diverge to infinite distance from the origin. To confine the spreading action within a bounded attractor, the nonlinear term is required... Through the feedback of z to the x equation, trajectories are folded back and reinserted closer to the origin where they begin an outward spiral once more.

The incredible frequency of fractal geometry in nature attests to the foundational role that this "folding back" kind of feedback plays. It appears that nature tends toward recursive processes, ones that feed back and fold over, again and again.

The bounding effect of feedback is called negative feedback. But feedback can also go in a positive direction and cause explosive growth of one or both variables. Positive and negative feedback are behind the common

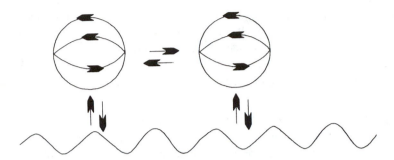

Figure 2.10. Symbolizing coupling (after Maturana and Varela 1987, p. 180).

notions of amplification and control and are very important in later chapters.

Coupling. The cuckoo clocks provide an example of another nonlinear phenomenon: coupling. In coupling, the interactions of two or more stable systems lead to the emergence of a *single higher system* (Peixoto's theorem, see Abraham and Shaw 1984). Essentially, in "acting and reacting," separate systems build a resonant frequency and come to act as one. This higher system is itself stable; small perturbations do not affect its long term behavior. Thus, interaction effects can lead to subtle types of co-joining (coupling) which provide a basis for the formation of "systems" themselves. Figure 2.10 shows the graphic sense of this in Maturana and Varela's representation of coupling.[4]

Shifts In The Newtonian Sense of How Things Work

Self-entanglement produces beauty.
James Gleick (1987, p. 23)

The following list looks at some of the unexpected ways interactive causality shifts our understanding of how things work.

The Importance of Internal Dynamics: Self-Generated Behavior. Strange attractors show order in chaos and Universality shows simplicity in complexity. Where does this order and simplicity come from? It is a product of the system's internal dynamics and nothing more. This order is self-generated, not imposed from outside. This simple observation entails a shift from the usual emphasis. In focusing on how one thing caused another, classical physics tended to overlook how things cause their own behavior. Chaos shows that a remarkable amount of ups, downs and abrupt changes are the result of internal dynamics, not the incursion of outside variables. While Chaos is certainly very interested in outside influences (called perturbations), it greatly increases our appreciation of internal dynamics and their role in "self-generated" behavior.

Global Order Arises from Local Activity. Interaction tends to make local behavior "messy"; it doesn't flow in nice smooth patterns. Yet, maps of the overall flow of interaction reveal fascinating patterns. The upshot is that interactive order is a different kind of order than what traditional approaches expected. It is not a local type of order. Rather, interactive order is a type of *global* order, order of the whole. Chaos suggests that seemingly erratic local behavior may be quite ordered from a global perspective.

Interestingly enough, this insight produces a nonmystical understanding of the old rubric "the whole is more than the sum of the parts." As Crutchfield et al. (1986) say:

> The interaction of components on one scale can lead to complex global behavior on a larger scale that in general cannot be deduced from knowledge of the individual components. (p. 56)

We get nonmystical holism. The whirlpool's form and the synchronization of the cuckoo clocks both show ordering of the whole created by interacting elements. Strange attractors and bifurcation maps reveal less visible forms of interactive holistic ordering. Once one of these dynamics is established, the various components act "as if" they were coordinated from some larger scheme. Yet, ordering of the larger scheme does not have to be attributed to some force outside the system. It can be the natural self-generated result of interactive dynamics.

This global order can be described as an *active* holistic ordering force, as the next section explains.

Global Order Phenomena Affects Local Behavior. Global order arises out of local behavior. But there's a corollary: not only does global order *arise out* of local behavior, but the global ordering flow also *affects* local behavior. Once global behavior is established it becomes active: it affects the very activity from which it arises. Thus, the whirlpool pulls new molecules into its flow and keeps the ones in the flow in line. Motion against the flow tends to be damped out.

One can understand how global order can affect the activity that generates it as something of a momentum effect. If you get a treadmill going, your walking will have created its momentum. But this momentum soon comes to affect your walking; you have to keep up the pace and may need to go faster to avoid falling down. You started it but now it runs you. The global-order phenomenon is "active" in a very real sense.

Top-Down and Bottom-Up Causality. There is one last interesting implication of global order that "arises out of yet feeds back onto" local activity: causality may appear to come either from the top down or from the bottom up. In fact, causality has both a bottom-up and a top-down component; it is effectively circular. Advocates of reductionism have long said that the "bottom" — the parts — are the only source of causation. Holistic approaches have long suggested that the top — the whole — is a source of causation. Chaos suggests that effects may be thought of as coming from either the top or the bottom and actually should be thought of as coming from both.

In practical terms this means we must suspend judgment regarding the original "source" of order. In fact, we should think of the system as being created *both* from the bottom up and from the top down; descriptions from either side alone are inadequate.

Local Action Embedded in an Ordering Context. There is yet another way of looking at this interesting local/global relationship. The global order effect leads us to an understanding of local action embedded in a pressuring and very structured *context*. As Diner (1986) says:

> Singularity is no more given in advance but generated inside a totality... This is the deep philosophy of Bifurcation theory and Catastrophe theory. The local properties get a real meaning only through their relations to the global properties. (p. 23)

Let me provide an example of the everyday reality of this idea. A male friend of mine was recently confronted by an alarming study. The study looked at life decisions made by males born at a certain time, in a certain place and with a certain ethnic background. It showed that virtually every one else in his cohort ended up making the same decisions he had made. The myriad of individual decisions that he struggled with in his own unique set of circumstances were made by all these men. In a very invisible way, each local decision was made in a context and the dynamics of that context exerted pressure in a very definite direction. From the global perspective, his unique decisions seemed almost foregone conclusions.

There's nothing magical about this invisibly ordered context. Yet, heightened awareness of context and specifically that the context may not be "just random" is a definite shift from the Newtonian conceptual scheme. In fact, let us take this one step further.

The Order in Randomness. The word "random" comes from an old English word *randon* meaning "disorder." It comes down to us today as haphazard, or chance and carries connotations of "without design" or "without order." Chaos suggests there may be order in random phenomena. In Diner's (1986) words, Chaos "establishes a link between mixing and the appearance of statistical laws." Thus, Chaos provides a more causal understanding of statistical laws. The following two quotations put it succinctly:

> We know that perfectly definite causal and *simple* rules can have statistical (or random) behaviors ... in a list of successive generated numbers there is such a seeming lack of order that all statistical tests will confer upon the numbers a pedigree of randomness. Technically, the term "pseudo random" is used to indicate this nature. One now may ask whether the various complex processes of nature themselves might not be merely pseudo random, with the full import of randomness, which is untestable, a historic but misleading concept. (Feigenbaum 1980, p. 50)

> Could it be that in Nature there are no such "genuine" random processes as we fancy them? (Chirikov, cited in Cvitanovic 1984, p. 933)

Order and Complexity. Chaos suggests order may be hidden in chaos and randomness and that simple rules generate complexity. Such a convolution of concepts has stimulated a reexamination of the terms *order* and *complexity* themselves. Where order and complexity once seemed apparent we now find we must look much more deeply. Complex erratic localities may be part of simple, orderly globalities. (The rubric of "order hidden in vicissitudes.")

In parallel with Chaos, several branches of mathematics have been pursuing such a reexamination of randomness, order and complexity. Much of the effort here is directed at precise mathematical definitions of these concepts. The goal is to find definitions that both support our common sense experience of these concepts and yet clarify their connection with chaotic phenomena as we have described them. The goal is to find ways to judge just what is complex, what is ordered and what that means. Explanation of this endeavor is beyond the scope of this book, however, Pagels (1988) outlines some of the basic ideas that I will present below.

As befits Chaos, the new definitions try to define order and complexity using concepts of iteration and process. For example, the number: 0.42857142 ... seems complex until we realize that it is 3 divided by 7. There is a very simple rule that will generate this complex-looking number. Similarly, Champernowne's number:

$$0.1234567891011121314151617181920212223242 5...$$

also appears complex until one realizes that it is simply the chain of integers written as one (i.e., 1 2 3 ...). Exercises like this suggest that one way to characterize complexity is by the length of the rule needed to generate it and the number of times that rule must be run. The pursuit of such definitions and their implications is the realm of *algorithmic complexity* theory. As with Chaos itself, the discoveries in this area are somewhat counter intuitive. They include such proofs as a phenomenon may be simple but we will not be able to prove that fact in any timely sort of way. (See Pagels (1988) and Rucker (1987) for readable overviews of algorithmic complexity theory.)

How Does All This Affect Our Image of Science?

> Ought we, for instance, to begin by discussing each separate species — man, lion, ox and the like — taking each kind in hand independently of the rest, or ought we rather to deal first with the attributes which they have in common in virtue of some common element of their nature, and proceed from this as a basis for the considerations of them separately?
>
> *Aristotle, in "De Partibus Animalium"*

Traditional science has been divided into two basic camps: determinacy and indeterminacy — those who had equations that allowed something like prediction and those who had only statistics. One was the ideal, the other what we did because we couldn't do the first (thank God normal curves work!). The two camps seemed disjoint, something like Figure 2.11.

Chaos shows us how to get from one camp to the other and starts to fill in the mid-ground. It also changes some fundamental assumptions hidden in the traditional sense of things. The separation between determinism and indeterminism is not just the result of practical difficulties. The Newtonian predictive ideal is a limited case and it is limited because of the nature of things. Chaos suggests a connection between interactive dynamics (technically, "mixing") and the emergence of statistical laws and forms. Thus, expanded understanding of interaction effects helps explain: why normal curves do work (and sometimes where they don't work); why Newtonian prediction is limited; and why Chaos fits in the middle. For example, if one body is very large compared to another (like the sun and the earth), the effects of the small one on the large one will be negligible — at least for long periods of time and under most conditions. Using traditional approaches and hoping for precise prediction on these systems is quite reasonable. In the middle ground when interactions effects are more vari-

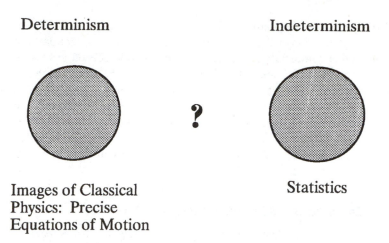

Figure 2.11. The traditional sense of science.

able, there is Chaos. One looks at the patterns produced by the interaction, how they change and which way things go depending on this parameter or that. At the far end, when interaction effects are massive and relatively equally bidirectional, one comes back to statistics. Normal curves work because they are the extreme-balanced pattern of interactive complexity. Thus, the expanded understanding of interdependence suggests a different picture of science, something like Figure 2.12.

This is one way that science shifts, but there is another, less obvious shift as well.

The Question of Questions

> If we ask whether the position of the electron remains the same, we must say "No"; if we ask whether the electron's position changes with time, we must say "No"; if we ask whether the electron is at rest, we must say "No"; if we ask whether it is in motion, we must say "No."
>
> *Robert Oppenheimer (1966, p. 40)*

Using interdependence as the center of science requires a change in the way we *think* about things and, specifically, it requires we change the *types of questions we ask*. This point is pivotal. I raise it now because it is virtually impossible to get a handle on the ecological revolution and its implications if one does not remember that it also implies a different way of thinking.

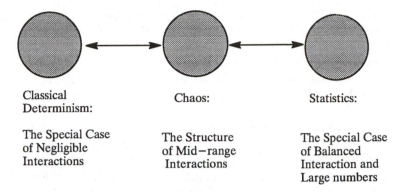

Classical
Determinism: Chaos: Statistics:

The Special Case   The Structure   The Special Case
of Negligible   of Mid–range   of Balanced
Interactions   Interactions   Interaction and
                                                       Large numbers

Figure 2.12. Science from the broadened view of interdependence.

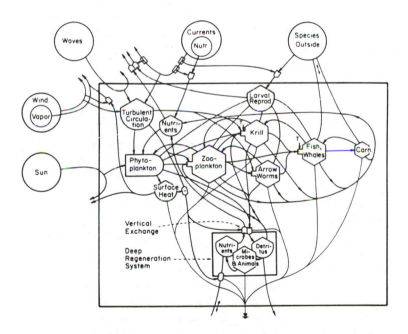

Figure 2.13. Sample ecomap (Odum 1983, p. 425).

Specifically, the traditional way of thinking about things tends to frame things in "either/or" terms (did "this" or "that" produce the effect.) This is not surprising if you remember that independent causality focuses on what "singular" thing produces an effect. However, in interactive causality "this or that" questions make no sense. In fact, they put the askee in a double bind because the actual answer is "yes/yes" (or "no/no" in Oppenheimer's approach).

Interactive causality requires how, when, where and how-much questions instead of either/or questions. If you try to explore a deeply interactive system with either/or thinking, you are likely to get a double-bind answer and this results in both anger and confusion. Is intelligence determined by heredity or environment? Yes. Did George start the fight or did John. No. In a certain sense, because Chaos helps us see and deal with interactive structure in more sophisticated ways, it becomes more feasible for us to think about things in the new way. Heredity or environment? Yes. But what a rotten question. Much better to ask: what's the structure of the hereditary dynamic, the environmental dynamic and their joint dynamic? Because such systems are likely nonlinear, it's quite possible that answer might be that sometimes heredity is a greater determinant and sometimes environment is.

From a Newtonian to a Nonlinear Ecological World

> Originally, the Greek word Chaos meant the infinite empty space which existed before all things ... in present usage, chaos means disorder... The technical Chaos I am going to speak about is nothing like total disorder... Chaos is not disorder. Chaos is not randomness. Chaos is simple... [it represents] a kind of global simplicity.
>
> *Michel Baranger, A Chaos Prime*

How does all of this relate to an ecological world? In a certain sense physicists found an ecological world the hard way — by following lines until they just couldn't be followed anymore. However, what they found is very much what an ecology portrays: a web of cause and effect that has coherence, hidden order, inseparability, and subtle connectivity. Thus (as Figure 2.13 shows), an ecological cause/effect map is very much a map of interdependence effects, of "affecting and being affected."

Chaos provides a hard-core physical understanding of the same image. It gives the ecological image greater depth (it isn't just biology) and some different details. For example, in physics' version, the world ecology probably has a fractal microstructure (scaled levels of self-similar microcosms in macrocosms) and it probably got that way through an infinite number of recursive breadmaker transformations (stretch and folding over and over again).

How does all this change the Newtonian sense of how the world works? Some of the ways Chaos changes the Newtonian vision are primarily of technical interest. Table 2.1 at the end of this chapter summarizes some of these shifts in scientific understanding.

Yet, we can also see some of the human dimensions of the shift in terms of world hypotheses. For example, organicism sees a whole developing through dynamics. Chaos sees these too. For example, Hegel's thesis-antithesis-synthesis vision of unfolding of world history is a type of organicism. It describes how the interactive dynamics of an idea and its opposite lead to new syntheses and how this basic process lies behind the developmental unfolding of world history. From the Chaos perspective such an idea is quite plausible. Does thesis-antithesis-synthesis describe the world's overall dynamic? Hard to say; there are certainly many more forms of dynamics at large (including linear ones). Still, such a thing is imaginable in an interactive world. Oddly enough, dialectics *is* a recursive process that fits a basic breakmaker's stretch-fold image of order through mixing.

Another example of Chaos' penchant for changing the standard scientific reaction comes from teleology, the doctrine that phenomena are shaped not only by mechanical forces but also move toward certain actualities. Originating in the philosophy of Plato and Aristotle, teleology was part of a world attracted toward ideal forms which existed beyond material manifestations. In Pepper's terms it is part of the formist world hypothesis (see Chapter 8). Mechanism has long considered teleology anti-scientific nonsense. As Rosen (1985) notes, teleology is the nearest thing to anathema in science. Yet attraction toward form is a perfectly "mechanical" aspect of Chaos. Here pull toward form is mathematical, precise, physical and not at all superstitious. Delattre (1986) even describes how the concept of basins of attraction allows a nonmystical form of final causation (e.g., end or goal of a system). "Final cause" does not have all the connotations that some philosophers have given it. For example, we don't know that final cause is fixed and immutable. Still, the essence of the original observation is confirmed. Formists were not simply fools, teleology is not all nonphysical nonsense.

These examples give a brief sense of how different the new physical view is from the old — and why it is both radically different and deeply familiar. Science is still science but this broader science is able to comprehend observations from views that mechanistic science labeled non-physical, superstitious, … etc.

Chaos provides a set of conceptual tools that are used throughout the rest of my discussion of the nonlinear revolution. Table 2.1 lists some of Chaos' alterations to Newtonian thinking. The next several chapters deal with results of nonlinear interdependent dynamics, moving from self-organization, to evolution, and finally to life.

NOTES

1. Calculus computes the length of curves by approximating them with smaller and smaller pieces of straight line (and taking the limit of this process). The full answer to "why calculus can't unravel the world" didn't come until the KAM theorem in 1962. It has to do with the fact that the solution to the three-body problem is a fractal and fractals cannot be approximated with simpler curves because smaller pieces of a fractal aren't simpler (see Appendix A). Note that this approximation aspect of calculus supports the idea that the way to solve all problems is by breaking them down into smaller pieces. Fractals set definite limits on the whole concept of "breaking things down."

2. Fractal dimensionality turns out to be an unexpectedly useful measure in a wide variety of situations. For example, the fractal dimension of 1/f noise in electronic systems allows the creation of appropriate chaotic filters. An example with more human interest is that images whose fractal dimension falls within the same range as naturally occurring phenomena (around 2.3) will generally be perceived by viewers as "natural" (from Mandelbrot 1990). There is a measurable basis for our subjective sense of what is natural and what is not. Fractal dimensionality also relates to people's perception of whether a sound is music or noise and even whether a sound is a particular type of music, say Western versus Eastern or Japanese versus Chinese.

3. You can of course still use the traditional approaches as well. The line is still a good tool and finding primary causes is still a wonderful thing. The difference is that you have more options and there is a growing body of information about when and where analytic approaches aren't very productive or simply won't work.

4. The coupling that works for mechanical systems works even more profoundly in biological systems. Maturana and Varela (1987) have described how coupling in living systems leads to the development of higher-order systems, from single-celled animals to multicellular animals to social systems. Like our clocks, as a biological system "acts on" and "reacts to" the other systems in its environment, it moves slowly toward stable patterns of activity. Once established these patterns of behavior become stable systems that resist perturbation.

Table 2.1. A Comparison of Newtonian and Nonlinear Thinking

If you use Newtonian thinking then:	If you use nonlinear thinking then:
Small effects can be treated as negligible	Small effects vary depending on context and can be determinative; in general small effects have greater import than before.
In principle, everything is predictable and controllable given a precise enough model and initial conditions.	No — everything is not predictable pragmatically or in principle. Prediction is possible for limited time periods and under certain conditions, but not in the general case.
In principle, change would appear smooth and controllable if you knew all the variables. Abrupt or erratic behavior is probably the result of the incursion of outside influences.	Smooth change is probably best thought of as imbedded in a larger process capable of much richer types of change (punctuated equilibrium); A system's normal internal dynamics are quite capable of causing abrupt and erratic behavior.
You need complex models to describe complex systems. Simple models lead to simple results.	Apparently not. Interactive dynamics tend to bleed systems of their complexity. You can often get the basic dynamics of very complex systems out of much simpler models (i.e., universality). Conversely, simple models often produce very complex results (e.g., bifurcations diagram).
One equation produces one pattern of behavior. A transformation of behavior means you need a new equation.	One equation can produce many different patterns of organization. Transformations of behavior are often part of the overall process.
An effective description of a system can always be built from its separately analyzable parts.	Interaction is important and interaction means inseparability; One can break things apart as an aid but separately analyzed components can never create a fully adequate description of the whole.
As you break things down they always get simpler.	When you break a fractal down, it does not get simpler. Much of the world's behavior is fractal.

cont'd

Table 2.1. cont'd

If you use Newtonian thinking then:	If you use nonlinear thinking then:
In the scientific method, what one does is hold everything constant, vary one variable and see the effect; You are looking for main effects; Eventually you want to develop equations of motion.	In Chaos interaction effects may be more important than independent effects. You need maps of how the system responds in different contexts and models of how it evolves, not solutions to equation of motion.
The bottom (i.e., the parts) are the only source of causation; reductionism is scientific, holism is mystical.	Causality may appear to come from the bottom-up or top-down; nonradical forms of holism and reductionism are compatible.
Order is visible at the local level (i.e., order is sequentially orderly) Order is constant and regular.	Global order may be hidden in local vicissitudes; overall order may house infinite variety and uniqueness.
Attraction toward a form is teleological nonsense.	Attraction toward a form is a well-understood result of interactive causality.

CHAPTER 3

Energy Flow and Self-Organization

> The physicochemical basis of biological order is a puzzling problem that has occupied whole generations of biologists and physicists ... the maintenance of order in actual living systems requires a great number of metabolic and synthetic reactions as well as the existence of complex mechanisms controlling the rate and timing of the various processes... *Coherent behavior* is really the characteristic feature of biological systems.
>
> Prigogine (1972, p. 24)

Chaos builds a general picture of interactive dynamics and its nontraditional types of behavior. The big message is that there is structure — patterning and coherence — hidden in nonlinear interdependence. But, really coherent behavior means life. How does one get from general patterning and coherence to the important stuff?

I am not going to discuss life in this chapter. What I am going to do is take the first few steps in that direction by outlining the findings of another branch of the nonlinear revolution, the branch dealing with energy flow — particularly far-from-equilibrium energy flow. This work starts by looking at the spontaneous emergence of physical shapes (forms) and ends up with a theory of "self-organization." Its ultimate quest is an understanding of how coherent identifiable "things," from whirlpools to societies, come about. It also produces a much deeper sense of how interconnected the overall earth-field is and has always been. It is the first major piece in the puzzle of an order-producing universe.

Note. Some references for this branch of the revolution are (an asterisk indicates a reference designed for a "popular" audience): *Prigogine and Stengers 1984; *Jantsch 1980; Morowitz 1968; Eigen and Schuster 1979; Roth and Schwegler 1981; and Csanyi 1989.

BASICS OF ENERGY FLOW

Thermodynamics is the science of energy flow and, in the final analysis, it is energy flow that produces order. To explain how this works, we need to establish some basic concepts of energy flow. This is important because despite energy's important role in modern society, people typically misuse the concept. For example, the common sense of "burning" or "consuming" energy is wrong, as is the idea that the energy content of a system is a measure of its ability to do work. It is worth correcting the nuances of energy flow because they affect the way we think about energy-flow systems and because hidden in the correct descriptions is an understanding of how energy flow creates ecologies and evolution.

The Energy-Flow Ecology

The concept of energy was developed during the nineteenth century through the observation that there was some "thing" that can be moved about and converted between many forms and in the process work can be done (gears moved, wheels turned, etc.). This dramatic insight laid the basis for modern technological society by showing how all motion is related to energy flow.

However, *by definition* energy is a quantity that is conserved; it can't be created or destroyed, only converted between forms. So you don't "consume" energy to do work. If we don't "consume" energy to do work, what makes things move? The correct wording is that "the *flow* of energy" makes things move.

Thus, the real question is: what makes energy flow? The answer is: energy concentrations (also called disequilibriums or gradients). Energy concentrations create a force that presses energy to flow toward equilibrium (i.e., even distribution). Concentrations create what Clausius called the "availability" to do work, that is, the potential to move things. What all this means is that it is the arrangement or *configuration* of a system's energy that determines its potential to do work, not the amount of its energy.

The correct understanding of energy is a key to an ecological understanding of energy flow. Conversely, the misperception that "energy" drives change supports the misperception that energy can be treated as an independent, self-contained entity. It can't. The very crux of what drives change has to do with distributions, or in other words, with the *relationships* between different concentrations in the field. Energy flow by its nature is a product of relationships between things.[1] It is a natural ecology.

A simple example will show how the three elements of an energy flow system — field, forces and flows — form a very tightly bound nonlinear ecology. A bathtub full of warm water represents an energy concentration if the room is at a cooler temperature. The interior of the room, including all the matter and energy in it is called a *field*.[2] The uneven distribution between the water and the room produces what is called a *field potential*. This potential represents a *force*, a pressure to flow. As long as there is some path by which energy can flow, that force will spontaneously produce a flow of heat from the bath water to the room. The flow *drains* the concentration until the temperature of the room and the bath water are equal. At this point all flows stop and there is no further change; the potential or availability is minimized. And all this happened because there was an uneven distribution of energy.

Where is the energy flow ecology? Note that forces and flows co-effect each other: the more force, the faster the flow, but because the flow reduces the energy concentration, the faster the flow the less the force. Hence force and flow are interdependent. A force may also generate multiple flows. For example, the coziness of a nice warm room may be drained by a crack under the door, a poorly insulated window and slow conduction through the walls. All these flows are interdependent because they drain the same disequilibrium. Forces and flows form an interactive causal web.

The warm room being drained by three flows gives us a simple sense of the energy-flow ecology, but energy's multiform nature leads to an even stronger form. A field may have multiple forces and flows and these reciprocally affect each other *even when forces and flows are of different energy types* (Onsager 1931). Thus, a temperature gradient affects electrical flow and electromotive gradient affects heat flow. Chemical, electrical, mechanical, etc. ... energy force-flow systems are a web of interdependence effects between forces and flows of all types!

You can get a sense of the incredible ordered connectivity of the energy-flow ecology from recent work on the evolution of the oceans and atmosphere (Holland 1978) and even of the biosphere as a whole (Gaia hypothesis, Lovelock 1979). If you think of energy as a thing that you can burn, you miss the interdependence of energy-flow phenomena. You miss the embracing and active nature of the energy-flow field.

SELECTION

Before leaving this general tour of energy flow, let me note one last important feature: selection. Selection provides the first step toward order-production. Most of us are familiar with selection of species in biological evolution. Selection of forms also exists in energy flow and is an important part of the evolution of forms nonliving forms and probably living forms as well.

Selection in energy flow systems is obvious, people just don't tend to comment on it. For example, the warm room being drained by a crack under the door, a poorly insulated window and slow conduction through the walls has three different flow paths all trying to drain the same concentration. Does the same amount of energy flow through each path? No. If the crack under the door is large, it will probably drain the disequilibrium before either of the other two paths have much of a chance to get started. The *force distributes energy to each path in accordance with its capacity* (how fast energy can flow through it).

This differential allocation of energy is a form of selection. And though it doesn't seem very interesting in the example of the warm room, it turns out to have important implications. The warm room is not very far from equilibrium, so the flow does not produce order; it is still in a linear range. However, farther away from equilibrium, above a critical threshold, the flow becomes nonlinear. Here selection becomes part of the process of driving new patterns (forms) of flow into being and generating new forms out of nothing which is what self-organization is about. The next section takes a look at such self-organization.

Before leaving, let us emphasize selection and self-organization's connection to Chaos. The "allocating" of energy to one path or another is a result of the deep interdependence of energy flows and forces in the field. It is a web of interdependence effect. Far-from-equilibrium force/flow systems are nonlinear. Self-organization occurs in far-from-equilibrium systems, or in other words, in nonlinear interdependent systems.

SELF-ORGANIZATION

Self-organization researchers are interested in the emergence of new "entities". In physics if one is interested in the emergence of new "entities" or "things," one starts by looking at the emergence of coherent motion and one studies it in the simplest physical systems possible. Perhaps the simplest case of the emergence of coherent motion is the emergence of turbulence in a fluid. So, let me take the bull by the horns and outline the basic process of "spontaneous emergence" as seen in the onset of turbulence in an apparatus called a Benard cell.

The Benard cell is an apparatus consisting of a flat box with fluid in it. You add heat to a metal plate in the bottom of the box. The experiment involves observing what happens in the fluid when different amounts of heat are supplied. I will go through this experiment with excruciating detail, partly to introduce terminology and partly for reasons that will become clear in the next section.

Note. In physics, the change from incoherent to coherent behavior is called a *symmetry break*.[3] If you add a small amount of heat to a Benard cell there will be a uniform transfer of heat occurring slowly through conduction. This symmetry is broken when larger amounts of heat are added.

Order Through Fluctuation

With no heat supplied, the fluid in the Benard cell is at equilibrium. The fluid's molecular motion is incoherent,[4] characterized only by random (stochastic) collisions. It is statistically homogeneous (on average all locales are similar). Still, it is not actually homogeneous. Small collections of relatively hotter molecules will occur and move apart. The fluid is filled with local inhomogeneities, called "brief statistical fluctuations." Systems in this incoherent, statistically homogeneous, near-equilibrium range are the traditional focus of thermodynamics.[5]

The fluid remains incoherent when a small amount of heat is added. Random molecular collisions spread the heat and the system moves slowly to equilibrium. However, if large amounts of heat are added (i.e., larger disequilibrium), the balance of forces changes. Heat is still spread by collisions and collections of hot particles still occur, but the steeper gradient creates field conditions that are primed for a new type of behavior. Hot collections are lighter than cold collections. Super-heated collections will occasionally extend from the hotter lower layers into the colder upper layers. If a collection is hot enough, its buoyancy will be greater than the viscous drag of the surroundings and it will move upward. The collection becomes a small parcel that moves some distance as a whole before its heat dissipates into the surroundings. Above a critical temperature, some random parcels' buoyancy completely overcomes drag and dampening forces and the parcel rises all the way to the top of the cell. In the process, it will pull up other, relatively hotter, bottom molecules in its wake (vacuum effect). When it reaches the top the parcel loses its heat to the outside environment and begins to sink back downward, pulling cooler molecules after it. Seeded by the original collection, the region erupts into a coherent

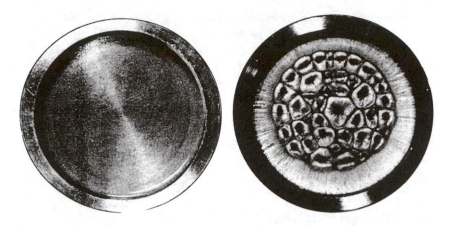

Figure 3.1. Rolls in Benard cell from the top (Swenson 1989a, p. 197).

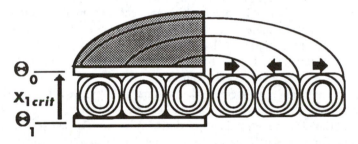

Figure 3.2. Rolls in Benard cell from the side (Swenson 1989a, p. 197).

circular motion. Figure 3.1 shows a before and after picture from the top. Figure 3.2 shows this motion from the side.

In nonlinear terms, the emergence of the circular flow equates to the emergence of a new attractor (see Chapter 2). The field conditions have driven the nonlinearity's potential for structuring into coherent motion, a new form, a new stable pattern. Order through fluctuation means that under critical conditions, a small fluctuation (a small difference) seeds a bifurcation and the emergence of a new attractor. The symmetry break corresponds to a bifurcation, a qualitative change in form. Figure 3.3 shows the relationship of attractors, flow and bifurcation.

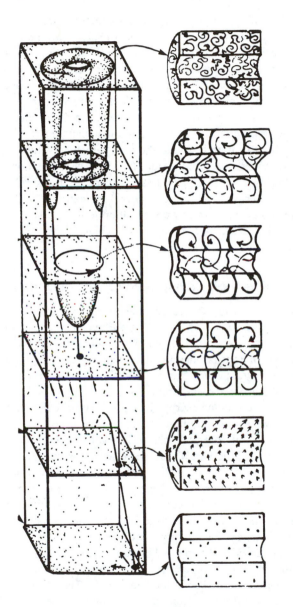

Figure 3.3. Attractors, flows and bifurcations (Abraham and Shaw 1989, frontispiece).

Speed and the Importance of the Self-Feeding Cycle

The Benard cell in all its simplicity gives us a number of insights into how natural order production works. Note the role of selection. The example of the warm room being drained by three paths shows selection's preferential treatment of faster paths. The faster the path, the more energy it receives. Above a critical disequilibrium, this preferential treatment is what causes a new flow. The small, minutely more efficient path (the parcel) pulls in energy which makes it move faster which, in turn, pulls in more energy. Upward motion starts which causes a momentum which transfers heat more efficiently which pulls more heat into the flow which adds more momentum. The cycle moves faster and faster. The flow becomes nonlinear; it begins to amplify itself. Once triggered, the flow maintains itself by pulling in and circulating energy — hence the term *self*-organizing. The fluctuation actually creates a new path. In self-organization terms the new flow triggered a self-feeding cycle — also called a circular relation or a positive feedback loop.

The On-Board Potential: Staying Away from Equilibrium

Also notice that it is a naturally occurring energy pocket that seeds a new, more efficient way for energy to flow. It is the parcel's energy difference (being hotter relative to its surroundings) that provides the initial conditions for movement; which transfers energy faster; which pulls energy into itself; which accelerates motion; which amplifies the flow and triggers the circular relationships that make it self-sustaining.

Thus, there is a quirk in the energy-flow story. The circular flow carries and sustains its own energy buildup. The collection of hot molecules that seeded the flow is a little energy buildup. It was this energy buildup that triggered the flow, i.e., the parcel rose because it was hot relative to the surroundings. Further, the flow's motion helps preserve and even increase the buildup. As the parcel moves it generates friction and drags in more energy from hotter regions which keeps the internal energy difference from dissipating. Thus, the circular roll system keeps itself away from equilibrium. It is a self-organizing, far-from-equilibrium system.

Another way to describe the energy buildup and its role in self-organization is to say that the attractor embodies an "on-board potential" (Swenson 1989b). which is the source of its being and growth. The energy buildup is a potential, i.e., its difference from the surrounds creates a force or a potential to do work. The self-organized flow contains an on-board "force" that sustains the organized motion. The apparent function of the organized

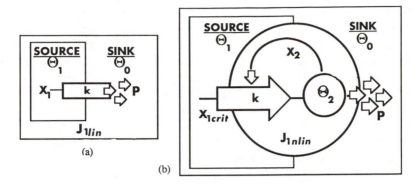

Figure 3.4. Linear and nonlinear flow (Swenson 1989a, p. 197).

motion is to increase the rate of the energy transfer process. But this means that the motion, the growth of the attractor and acceleration of flow are related. Once the attractor emerges, the on-board potential acts as an amplifier: it causes the attractor to grow in size and speed as part and parcel of accelerating the energy transfer process. Figure 3.4 shows the generalized thermodynamic picture of this process.

All of this is important because one of the notable things about living systems is that they carry around and maintain their own energy buildup. Maintaining an energy buildup is what metabolism is all about. Thus, from a very crude perspective, the on-board potential which generates a flow to keep itself around in the Benard cell, is a precursor to the much more highly organized version of the same thing in living systems.

The Same Pattern: Examples and Isomorphies

The strange thing is that this same pattern of self-organization and order-through-fluctuation holds in many places. A tornado is a real-world example of order-through-fluctuation and self-sustaining flows. Tornadoes emerge when small, naturally occurring wind-shear effects are amplified into a massive self-feeding flow — and this amplification occurs under conditions of very steep disequilibriums and severe constraints on energy flow. A cold, dry, low pressure moving in one direction and a warm, moist, high pressure flow moving in opposition produce strong disequilibrium conditions. Tornadoes generally occur when various pressures (constraints) force the energy differences into close proximity and block less catastrophic equalization of the gradient. In the United States, the Rocky

Mountains create such a constraint physically. The mountains both block regress of the cold dry air and drive the warm, moist air upwards in the atmosphere towards colder regions and greater energy imbalance. Small shear fluctuations are then amplified into the self-sustaining flow. Its torsional winds accelerate transfer via "highly convective pumping" (Byers 1974, p. 395). And, when the tornado does erupt, it carries an on-board potential in the form of a very low-pressure center.

Nor is order-through-fluctuation limited to tornadoes and whirlpools. The reason for going through all this detail is that same basic elements of transformation are seen in all sorts of systems. Thus, as Prigogine (1972, p. 24) notes: "We have investigated systematically the behavior of nonlinear chemical networks of biological interest... The surprising result was that in fact they share most of the properties of hydrodynamic instabilities."

Chemical disequilibriums that trigger change via order-through-fluctuation are responsible for a variety of important biological change patterns. For example, Turing (1952) suggests a chemical diffusion basis for morphogenesis — "a possible mechanism by which the genes of a zygote may determine the anatomical structure of the resulting organism" (p. 37). He notes that chemical concentration and depletion points set the stage for differentiation of a cell in a particular location but the change is "triggered" by "random disturbance." Lintilhac (1974) similarly describes differentiation in plant cells as a result of mechanical stressors creating instability with specific change triggered by random variations in strength.

The observation that there are common change patterns across levels and types of system is very long standing. Certainly it was well-established in the mid 1800s as described by Spencer (1862) in his *First Principles*. It also forms the basis of Von Bertalanffy's (1968) more mathematically based General Systems Theory. In general systems' terms, there are *isomorphic* patterns of change that hold across all forms of system. Yet, the simple fact is that similar patterns make sense because energy flow is energy, whether chemical, mechanical, electrical, thermal, ..., etc.

The Concept of Dynamic Entities: Prototypical Selves

> All is process. That is to say "there is *'no thing'* in the universe." Things, objects, entities, are abstractions of what is relatively constant from a process of movement and transformation. They are like the shapes that children like to see in the clouds.
>
> *David Bohm (1972, p. 42)*

Self-organization theory attempts to build a physical picture of the origins of new "things," prototypical entities. We're now in a position to see what this work was driving at.

Part of what makes us able to label something a "thing" is organization — organization that makes it distinct from the surrounds. Thus, in self-organization terms, even the Benard cell rolls are prototypical "entities." The molecules in the collection stayed together longer than mean-free-path collision times; their correlated movement made them identifiable over time (albeit a short time by our standards). The emergence of the attractor corresponds to the emergence of a new "thing" in the field. It is visibly identifiable as a "thing" because of its organized motion and it is structurally stable as a result of its dynamic energy relationships with the field. It carries its own on-board potential which helps it remain distinct from the field.

If we put these elements together we see that this definition of an entity is a type of matter/energy configuration; it is a combination of field, flow, matter and the co-effecting relationships that hold them together. It does not have a static set of material components nor is it the product of a fixed energy field. An emergent attractor is a dynamic, flow-based, relationship-based definition of both what "entities" are and how they work. Thus:

> it is not the components of a hurricane or dust devil that persist in time since they are continuously replaced by the transport of matter and energy across the entity's boundary; it is the nonlinear relationships between elements that persist (Swenson 1989b, p. 4)

This concept of a dynamic entity is one of those things that has both obvious and non-obvious implications. For example, a molecule is not a solid "thing" but a whirling dynamic system of atoms — and atoms are a dynamic system of smaller particles, etc. Yet, the concept of a dynamic entity also holds for the "thing" that we call our body and the "thing" that we call society — and what is obvious for molecules is not nearly so obvious for these. A great deal of philosophical verbiage has been spent on the idea that "society" is a ubiquitous "they" which nevertheless can't be pinned down to some one or more particular individuals. Similarly, we can identify our body but the material that makes up our bodies recycles such that every few days we consist of an entirely new set of molecules ... molecules rotate through our bodies just as in a dust-devil.

The images of nonlinear dynamics provide new ways of conceptualizing such beasts. An attractor attracts new matter into its form whenever matter falls into one of its basins of attraction. So, an attractor supports both the idea of an organized coherence and flow-through. Attractors have a topological boundary as well and thus can be thought of as having a surface while nevertheless being very dynamic. Interestingly, such a dynamic surface is "open" while nevertheless functioning as a boundary. Matter that falls into one of the attractor's basins of attraction will be drawn into the system. Matter that falls just outside a basin will be excluded by the flow (the flip side of "not being drawn in"). Attractors, basins of attraction, and topological surfaces provide a model for analogous behavior in human and biological systems.

A lot of the self-organization literature focuses on the emergence of these islands of relative autonomy under far-from-equilibrium conditions.[6] However, nonlinear interdependence's ability to cause *self*-organization and *self*-maintenance need not be thought of only in terms of little islands of relative autonomy. Interactive structuring through energy flow can also lead to the formation of cycles and networks. Such networks and cycles — particularly those that result from chemical dynamics — add some important elements in the movement toward life. Awareness of these more general self-organizing and self-maintaining flows increases awareness that life is a result of, and embedded in, a larger process of energy flow structuring.

Better Living through Chemistry

In the section on isomorphies, I quoted Prigogine (1972) as follows:

> We have investigated systematically the behavior of nonlinear chemical networks of biological interest... The surprising result was that in fact they share most of the properties of hydrodynamic instabilities. (p. 24)

This quotation continues:

> with the additional important feature that the variety of the regimes beyond instabilities is much greater in chemical kinetics. (p. 24)

So, though there are commonalities, chemistry's difference also makes a difference. This difference is what moves the structure of interdependence toward life. Of course, chemistry too is a great candidate for Chaos because interaction, stability/instability, and small seeding differences describe the basic elements of most chemical reactions. In chemistry, the self-feeding cycle form of interaction is called *autocatalysis*. Autocatalytic reactions produce an output (i.e., a chemical product) which is also a reactant in the reaction. Thus, autocatalytic reactions like the Belousov–Zhabotinsky reaction shown in Figure 3.5 re-feed themselves.

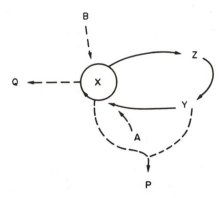

Figure 3.5. Cyclic organization (Jantsch 1980, p. 33). The Belousov–Zhabotinsky reaction starts with $A = B= [BrO_3]$, produces intermediate products $X= [HBrO_2]$, $Y = [Br]$, and $Z = [2Ce^{4+}]$ and end-products P and Q. Intermediary product X reproduces autocatalytically (the step marked by the arrow in a closed circle) and thereby holds the whole cycle in motion; it decays continuously into Q so that the system is globally stabilized.

The autocatalytic self-feeding cycle has the same relationship to speed as the self-feeding cycles described earlier in this chapter. It has the same ability to pull in energy and thus is likely to be "selected" as the following quotations from a serious book on evolution (Csanyi 1990) note:

> Among synthesis reactions, autocatalytic reactions have the greatest reaction rates. It is easy to demonstrate that if other conditions for their existence also are given, in a steady-state chemical system these reactions will predominate.
>
> ... A kind of "selection" automatically starts among the various types of reactions in the system. All changes tending to increase free energy's storage are incorporated into the system and become a stable part of it. From energy-preserving reactions the ones having greater capacity will be *selected*. These are autocatalytic reactions since their rates can exponentially increase in time. (p. 41)

These are the usual elements of self-organization. What's different? The most important difference is that chemical reactions involve the creation and destruction of different stable chemical complexes — and this means variety. The permutations and combinations of their interactions with other complexes in different chemical contexts is tremendous. The Benard cell's variety came in the form of little heat collections. In chemical systems variety comes in relatively stable movable forms of new-yet-changeable complexes. The number and types of interactions are larger, the number and types of stable dynamical complexes are larger. Thus, as Prigogine (1972, p. 24) notes:

> In chemical kinetics nonlinearity may arise in a practically unlimited number of ways through autocatalysis, cross-catalysis, activation, inhibition, and so on.

One of the results of this variety is the capacity for self-feeding *reaction networks*. Here the cyclic organization of the Belousov–Zhabotinsky reaction spreads over larger regions of time and space. Both large-scale and micro-scale reaction networks play important roles in life and the origins of life. At both levels, the same self-feeding acceleration of flow is observed. Thus, as Eigen (1979) says:

> The Bethe–Weizsacker [carbon] cycle ... contributes essentially to the high rate of energy production in massive stars. It, so to speak, keeps the sun shining and, hence, is one of the most important *external* prerequisites of life on earth. Of no less importance, although concerned with the *internal* mechanism of life, appears to be the Krebs or citric acid cycle. (p. 3)

Figure 3.6 shows the carbon cycle and Figure 3.7 shows the Krebs cycle.

Chemistry being what it is and nonlinearity being what it is, if you can form one cycle you can also form cycles of cycles. This particular type of reaction network, called a hypercycle (Eigen 1979), has the desirable feature of being both faster and more stable than lower types of cycles. Hence, its desirability from a selection point of view. Thus:

> On the basis of King's (1977) investigation it also can be stated that in a sufficiently large steady-state system, with conditions adequate for various reactions, the different autocatalytic reaction chains may interlock and produce increasingly greater autocatalytic complexes... Matsuno (1978) ... found that the probability of forming cyclic processes was rather high, and these were especially stable kinetically. He also proposed that *compartments* spontaneously emerge within the reaction networks, which have a tendency to develop self-preserving organizations. (Csanyi 1989, p. 42)

As the last sentence notes, the tighter the feedback loops, i.e., the more self-feeding, self-affecting it is, the more self-regulating the system becomes. This is fairly obvious if you imagine an already self-feeding cycle "**A**" which produces reactants that are inputs to an already self-feeding cycle "**B**" which, in turn, produces reactants that are inputs to cycle "**A**." Each supplies the other. The behavior of each affects the behavior of the other; together they are a more self-regulating whole. The more self-

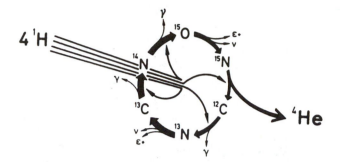

Figure 3.6. The carbon cycle (Eigen 1979, p. 3). The *carbon cycle*, proposed by Bethe and v. Weizacker, is responsible, at least in part, for the energy production of massive stars. The cyclic scheme as a whole represents a catalyst which converts four ¹H atoms to one ⁴He atom, with the release of energy in the form of γ-quanta.

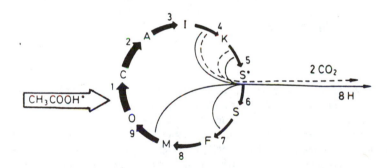

Figure 3.7. The Krebs cycles (Eigen 1979, p. 3). The *tricarboxylic or citric acid cycle* or *Krebs cycle* is the common catalytic tool for biological oxidation of fuel molecules.

regulating the system, the longer its possible life span. Thus, as Eigen (1979, p. 5) says, "the hypercycle is self-reproductive to a higher degree."

Csanyi (1989) provides a summary of the whole process and some of its unexpected implications (italics are his):

In an open chemical system material cycles "energized" by the energy flows through the system would begin ... in these systems only cyclic chemical

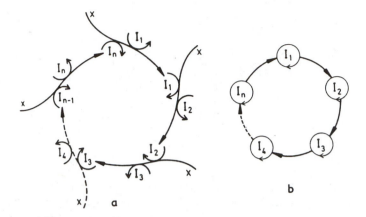

Figure 3.8. The catalytic hypercycle (Eigen 1979, p. 5). A catalytic hyper-cycle consists of self-instructive units, I_i with twofold catalytic functions As autocatalysts or, more generally, as catalytic cycles the intermediates I_i are able to instruct their own reproduction and, in addition, provide catalytic support for the reproduction of the subsequent intermediate. The simplified graph (b) indicates the cyclic hierarchy.

reactions can exist for an extended time because any others quickly use up their supply of reactants compounds (p. 47). King (1982) ... found that if a reaction network includes at least two bimolecular reactions, complete *chemical reproduction* may emerge ... such a cyclic chemical network is not very complex, and King (1982) provides reasonable proof of its *spontaneous appearance* (p. 47). With the spontaneous appearance of reproductive chemical networks, [new] selective processes ... also emerge. This selection is not Darwinian or competitive, which is well known in biology. The reproductive chemical network (RCN) ... will select those processes that will not destroy the system... Reactions that fit into the RCN without destroying its cyclic reproductive organization can be incorporated, while others, which can effectively obstruct reproduction, will destroy it (p. 48). The appearance of this kind of selective mechanism will make the RCN very sensitive to its environment (p. 48). The organization of RCNs is a reproductive organization by definition. It is the organization of *being*; therefore, it precedes any other kinds of organization. Any organization that cannot maintain itself is only temporary and irrelevant to evolution. (p. 49)

Through chemistry, self-organization produces increasingly more complex and increasingly more stable dynamical organizations. These organizations become selective and sensitive to their environment. Interactive structuring begins to take on much more lifelike forms.

THE ENERGY-DRIVEN ECOLOGICAL WORLD

The following quotations summarize this chapters most important points:

> We shall find that the flow of energy is a self-organizing principle at both the macroscopic and the molecular level.
>
> *Morowitz (1968, p. 5)*

> Molecular organization and material cycles need not be viewed as uniquely biological characteristics; they are general features of all energy flow systems.
>
> *Morowitz (1968, p. 454)*

> Huge material cycles characterize the developed biosphere and ... living organisms are [also] composed ... of material cycles. It is increasingly clear that the most important characteristic of life is the complex network of joint material cycles.
>
> *Mizutani and Wada (1982, cited by Csanyi 1989, p. 41)*

Chaos provided tools and showed us that there was structure in interdependence. Adding energy flow to our model lets us apply this structuring into the real world. It gives us a first understanding of the spontaneous emergence of self-organizing, self-sustaining order and coherent dynamical selves. It gives us cycles and networks, global and microscopic. It shows us that concepts such as selection and replication — which traditionally only apply to living systems — actually have their roots in nonliving physical systems. Replication is one possible result of cycles and networks.

The energy-flow ecology also deepens our awareness of the web of interaction/interdependence. The field is a ubiquitous, all-encompassing and interconnecting unity. You don't have to go looking for connections, you are embedded in them. The energy-flow ecology gives us a few new rules, for instance: critical gradients, order through fluctuation, isomorphies, and selection with its affinity for speed and self-feeding cycles.

All of this begins to make producing order and structure seem remarkably commonplace and natural. All of this is the background material for life and evolution.

NOTES

1. A social example may help clarify the importance if seeing energy flow as driven by uneven distributions. A simplistic version of social upheaval is that "poverty causes unrest." But people with little material means do not revolt if the entire culture is similar (e.g., aborigines). Conversely, people with more than aborigines can imagine seethe in the face of large buildups in one segment of society compared to another. Thus, it is not poverty per se that sparks social unrest but unevenness of distribution. Like energy, poverty causes revolts (motion) only because of relationships between elements of the field.

2. Technically, a field is a region of space in which you have defined certain quantities at every point. Thus, an energy-density field has the energy density defined at every point. A field represents the *distribution* of the quantity under question.

3. There is a technical definition of symmetry here having to do with translational symmetry: if you move from point A to point B in the system, things look essentially the same — i.e., you find the same temperature, direction of heat flow, velocity distribution, etc. This symmetry is broken when larger amounts of heat are added.

4. Incoherence is defined technically as molecular motion having no correlation greater than mean-free-path collision times.

5. Just as classical mechanics was built around calculus and calculus-approachable systems, classical thermodynamics was built around equilibrium and near-equilibrium situations. Retrospectively, both fields were somewhat over-shaped by the characteristics of their first successfully-approached systems.

6. In making a case for dissipative selves pulling themselves up against the forces of equilibrium, there is a tendency to over-focus on autonomy and forget the role of the field, that is, the role of the distribution of energies in the overall region. I mention this because this overemphasis on the "self" in "self-organizing" goes against the ecological sense of things and creates a distorted sense of how things work. Comments such as "dissipative structures do not require any outside drive to maintain their form" (Jantsch 1980, p. 100) are intended to highlight the "self" part of the equation but create an impression that "selves" do it all by themselves, the field doesn't play any role. The idea that selves arise regardless of the field not only makes a mockery of the physics but also blocks full appreciation of the deep ecological nature of things: fields give rise to relatively autonomous selves because such selves serve the field; self and field are never actually separate. Chapter 5 discusses these ideas.

CHAPTER 4

The Revolution in Evolution

> The view is spreading that the evolution of life is a necessity, and the physical and chemical processes leading to its emergence can be experimentally reproduced.
>
> *Csanyi (1989, p. 26)*

Self-organization and chemical networks set the stage for life. The last 20 years of physics tells us that there is order in interactive chaos. Yet, there are still two big pieces missing in the order-building puzzle. First and foremost, life still isn't explained. Living systems have some very important characteristics that nonliving, self-organized systems don't have — for example, the ability to respond functionally to information about the environment (i.e., bacteria moving toward light). How does the nonlinear revolution explain these differences? Secondly, there is no overall theory of evolution. What drives it? Why does it seem to have a progression towards ever-increasing levels of complexity? This chapter deals with the second of the two missing pieces, an overall theory of evolution (the next chapter discusses life).

Until now I've been describing things that, if not well-known, are nevertheless pretty well established. This chapter (and the next) dabble in more murky waters. There is a striking amount of empirical observation. There are some definite Newtonian limitations on thinking that can be overturned. And, although there is no established theoretical winner, there *is* a strongly emerging outline of the thermodynamics of evolution that is highly consistent with the rest of the nonlinear revolution. It is this outline that is my primary interest. To build a picture of it, I will attack the Newtonian limitations, describe the data, and present a version of the outline based on what I believe is a plausible approach to the material, Swenson's (1989–90) Principle of Maximum Entropy Production (MEP).[1]

Note. Some references for this branch of the revolution are: Ulanowicz (1986), Weber and Depew (1985), Morowitz (1968), Wicken (1987), and Brooks and Wiley (1986).

EVOLUTION AND THE SECOND LAW

So, what drives evolution? The very unexpected suggestion is that what drives evolution is the second law of thermodynamics, i.e., producing entropy. This is indeed a radical shift in interpretation with even more radical implications for our view of how things work. Where before we had a general sense that ordered complexity came about, this part of the revolution gives an overall theory of *why* there is an inexorable push toward increasing levels of ordered complexity. Three things become linked — the growth of complexity, increasing efficiency, and the acceleration of change. These elements form the basis of a general theory of evolution, from molecules to civilizations, as one overall process that exhibits isomorphic patterns of change. The message: evolution is inexorable, not improbable; it includes more than just species and it is going on right now.

The Unnaturalness of Order

Most of us were raised scientifically with the idea that life started as some initial accident and has evolved since then through natural selection. You may notice that postulating life as an accident is unusual in science. Science normally prefers postulating probability, not improbability. Further, as the opening quotation notes, a growing body of work suggests that life was a probable event not an improbable event. So, you may ask, what's the problem? Even if we don't know exactly how it started, why not imagine life was probable?

The answer to this question can be put in a single word: entropy. The common interpretation of the second law of thermodynamics (entropy always increases) portrays order as improbable. The universe goes in one direction and order struggles uphill against it. Since the second law is often held to be the single most well-supported scientific principle, this interpretation has put some pressure on biologists studying evolution.

> The view that the universe is running down into a condition where its entropy and the amount of disorder are as great as possible has had a profound effect on the views of many biologists on the nature of biological phenomena. (Morowitz 1968, p. 2)

It is now over one hundred years since the introduction of the theory of
evolution in biology and the second law of thermodynamics in physics.
Each of these principles has been a unifying and heuristic theory within its
own science. Yet, the relationship of biology to physics has disclosed a
slight antagonism between evolution and increasing entropy (Morowitz
1968, p. 2).

One of the things the nonlinear revolution helps us see is that order is both
natural and quite ubiquitous — even outside of biology. So, how does this
ordering fit with the second law's common interpretation?

The Second Law and Improbable Order

First let me comment on entropy and the second law. As explained in more
detail in Appendix B, entropy has a very generic definition that can be used
across different types of system, from quantum to information theoretic. So,
like energy, entropy appears to be a "thing" that comes in a lot of diverse
forms. Yet, the diversity of form — energy to information — is much harder
to deal with in entropy. Are energy-related and information-theoretic
entropy related? Are they physically related? Such questions are central to
the changing understanding of evolution and life. Asking how one gets from
energy to information is just like asking how one gets from physics to
psychology or from body to mind. Thus the question "what is entropy" is
not at all trivial.

For most of this chapter I will be talking about entropy produced in
energy flow situations, energy-related entropy. Each time energy flows or
is converted between forms, some percentage of it is irretrievably lost in
microscale dispersion. Entropy is a measure of work potential lost as a
result of that dispersion. Increasing entropy (the second law) represents a
fundamental limit on our ability to follow and control energy.

How does this relate to disorder? Energy-related entropy is usually
described in terms of work potential lost to microscale disorder, i.e., heat.
Maximum entropy is reached at equilibrium and is described as "the state
of maximum disorder." Yet, the word "disorder" here is actually a substitute
for the word "random." Maximum entropy equals maximum probability
distribution, essentially maximum randomness. Yet, as Bohm (1972) notes,
the word "disorder" is misleading:

> Very often the quality of randomness has been equated with what is called
> "disorder." But if one thinks for a moment he will see that disorder, in the
> sense of the total absence of any kind of order whatsoever, is both a logical
> and a factual impossibility... It is a source of confusion to equate random-

ness with disorder, or even to say that disorder can exist in any context
whatsoever ... what we have to do is to describe the order and analyze the
order rather than to avoid the question by calling it disorder. (p. 20)

The common language used to discuss entropy is part of the reason why the
second law and order have seemed so at odds. Insights from nonlinear
dynamics help us see why it is worth changing the language. We should say
that each time energy flows or is converted between forms some percentage
of it is irretrievably lost in microscale *dispersion*, not disorder. (This distinction will have more important implications in the next chapter.) From
the budding nonlinear perspective, it is best to leave "maximum entropy"
as "maximum randomness" but, if more has to be said, it should be something like "maximum randomness equals maximum complexity" or "highly
mixed" — disorder should be left out of it. The behavior is the same in
either case, but the perceptual differences are very important. Structure is
at odds with disorder but not with well-mixed complexity.

The major technical reason that the second law has been equated to
increasing disorder and infinitely improbable order is Boltzmann's H-
theorem. In attempting to give thermodynamics a mechanical basis,
Boltzmann showed how the second law could be explained via the
mechanics of random collisions. The H-theorem showed how the state of
maximum entropy and maximum "disorder" (i.e., randomness) is also the
most probable outcome of random collisions. From this perspective the
flow toward maximum entropy is only the natural progression of probabilities and, hence, movement toward order is infinitely improbable. As
Boltzmann (1886) said: "molecules moving at the same speed in the same
direction is the most improbable case conceivable ... an infinitely improbable configuration."

Now obviously order is not infinitely improbable. The Benard cell
shows that. So, where's the confusion? The H-theorem only describes
behavior at or near equilibrium — this is spelled out in its assumptions.
Spontaneous order is infinitely improbable near equilibrium. Apparently,
order is compatible with increasing entropy in the far-from-equilibrium
case.

To sum up, the second law does not mean that order is improbable and
its association with disorder is misleading at best. The traditional *interpretations* (as opposed to definitions) were made before physics could
approach the chaos of interaction, and sound similar to interpretations in
pre-Chaos mechanics.

BACK TO ENERGY: THE EVOLUTION OF ORDERED FLOWS

What in the ever-loving blue-eyed world do these innocuous comments on thermodynamics have to do with [evolution]!

Anonymous manuscript reviewer
The American Naturalist, 1979
(cited in Ulanowicz 1986)

The above quotation should say "ecology" instead of "evolution" but the sentiment is the same. This section returns to discussion of driven energy flow for a short story about evolution as increasing complexity and increasing efficiency.

Disequilibriums create a motive force that press energy to flow via interactions between material elements of the field. Consequently the flow of energy is always faced with resistance — the inertia of various time-space constraints. There is always a tug-of-war going on between inertial resistance and the motive force. The balance between the two determines what type of flow occurs.

This force/inertia tug-of-war is analogous to Newton's second law $\mathbf{F} = \mathbf{m \cdot a}$. However, Newton's law is linear; its tug-of-war changes proportionally as the force increases. In the nonequilibrium case, the war is linear near equilibrium and nonlinear when the system is far from equilibrium. In the nonlinear range small changes in force may result in a large affect on inertia. Thus, it is the far-from-equilibrium realm where order-through-fluctuation is likely to occur.

As we saw in the Benard cell, if the motive force is small the flow will proceed by random collisions, the classical near-equilibrium range. If the motive force is high, it moves ahead in the force/constraint war. It provides a constant pressure that accelerates energy flow by accelerating the activity of the particles — random collisions occur faster and faster.

But there are limits to how fast any particular type of dissipative interaction (in this case random collisions) can transfer energy. When the limits are reached, there is a dissipative shortfall, an energy buildup, and a growing tension. Force and limitation reach an impasse. If the motive force is above a critical threshold, it will break the time-space constraint holding the form of the current flow in place and force a new form of flow into being. If the force is very large, the process will occur again — the force will again accelerate activity and energy flow until it reaches the form's limits; a crisis will occur and a new, more efficient form will come into being. We see this in boiling water. We turn up the heat full-blast. First, small bubbles form,

Structure	F (erg s^{-1} gm^{-1})
Milky Way	1
Sun	2
Earth's climasphere	80
Earth's biosphere (plants)	500
Human body	17,000
Human brain	150,000

Figure 4.1. Acceleration over cosmological time (after Chaisson 1987, p. 254). If order is driven into being as a product of dissipative efficiency, then in Chaisson's words, "what is important is the **rate** at which free energy enters a system of some given size... The operative quantity used to specify the order and organization in any system is the flux of free energy density, denoted here by the symbol F." F is an energy flux (i.e., per unit time) "density" (i.e., per unit mass). This table shows the free energy flux density through various systems. Note that living systems require substantially larger values of F to maintain their order.

then a string of bubbles up the side of the pan, and then gradually larger bubbles and undulations until a full rolling boil erupts.

Under massive disequilibriums, there is a recursive growth/limitation/transformation cycle of dissipative evolution. Each time the force exceeds the flow's limits (a condition called *incommensuration*), a crisis ensues and the field drives a more efficient flow into being. Each successive form comes into being, accelerates the dissipation and reaches its limits. There is a shortfall, new field conditions, and the emergence of a new, yet-more-efficient form. Under massive incommensuration the motive force's pressure continually accelerates energy flow by recursively breaking constraints and opening new paths of flow.

So, you say: this is fine for boiling water; what does it have to do with evolution? First, note that the earth being between the sun and the cold sink of space is in a very massively incommensurate field. The universe itself, expanding from the big bang, is a massively incommensurate field. So, these fields should exhibit accelerating dissipative evolution tied to increasing complexity. And they do (see Lotka 1922; Pettersson 1978; Chaisson

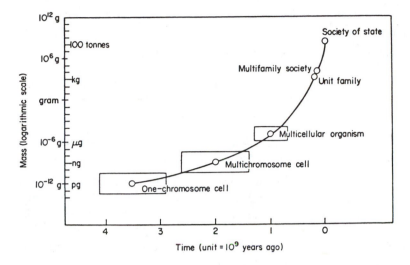

Figure 4.2. Acceleration over biological time (Peterssen 1978, p. 202). One of several forms of evidence for a general long-term acceleration during most of biological and social evolution is the estimated mass and the time of first appearance, of a series of progressively more complex integrated natural entities. The larger areas of uncertainty are plotted as rectangles.

1987; Odum 1953; Morowitz 1968), over both cosmological and biological time (see Figures 4.1 and 4.2).

What? Biological Evolution?

> Many people feel that things are changing faster, nowadays, than during the time of their parents or grandparent. It may give cause for concern (Tofler 1970; Erlich and Erlich 1970; Meadows et al. 1972) ... hitherto, this acceleration of change has seemed a purely human phenomenon, confined to our own lineage ... however, there is evidence, from long before man, of a general long-term acceleration during the greater part of biological and social evolution.
>
> *Pettersson 1978, p. 201*

Accelerating energy flow seems plausible for cosmological time (plasma to planets) but not for biological time (bacteria to civilization). Yet, acceleration of energy processing is a long-established principle of life. For example, Lotka (1922) says:

> Boltzmann [pointed out] that the fundamental object of contention in the life-struggle, in the evolution of the organic world, is available energy. In accord with this observation is the principle that, in the struggle for existence, the advantage must go to those organisms whose energy-capturing devices are most efficient... In every instance considered, natural selection ... operates [so] as to increase the total mass of the organic system, to increase the rate of circulation of matter through the system, and to increase the total energy flux through the system. (p. 147)

Ecologists in particular discovered accelerating flow long ago when watching ecological succession. Over their life times, ecosystems move through a succession of dominant forms, from grasslands to shrubs to pines to oaks. Each successive form uses more energy flow per unit time than the previous (evidenced by metabolic rates). The evolution of life on early earth gives a clear sense of how this "succession" works biologically. As Figure 4.3 shows, the relationship between succession and accelerating rate of flow holds over the early evolution of life on earth.

The early atmosphere of earth had very little oxygen. The story of increasing energy flow in early life is very much the story of increasing oxygen content because oxygen allows much more sophisticated forms of metabolism that occur at much higher rates. Thus, Figure 4.3 is given in terms of increasing oxygen levels (%PAL, present atmospheric levels). Because early earth had little oxygen, the first dominant forms of life were anaerobic bacteria (i.e., non-oxygen users) whose form of metabolism was fermentation. This is how Swenson (1989b) explains the acceleration:

> Living systems emerged by increasing the rate of chemical reactions... Limitation on ... anaerobic fermentation was transcended and gradient degradation accelerated by the emergence of photosynthetic bacteria that could attract solar gradient directly and metabolize most of the end products of the fermenters... This expansion was limited, however, by the dependence of these bacteria on ... H_2 and H_2S... This limit too was overcome by a symmetry-breaking event that occurred when protocyanobacteria acquired the ability to split water molecules and get their hydrogen from H_2O. This greatly accelerated the rate of gradient degradation by effectively coupling the sun to a virtually unlimited electron source for carbon reduction while at the same time releasing [oxygen] O_2 into the atmosphere and dramatically increasing the chemical disequilibria and reactivity of the entire system. This led ... to another major symmetry-breaking event ... an immediate consequence of the shift to aerobic biochemistry was remarkable increase in efficiency of glucose degradation (18 times as much ATP per mole) over

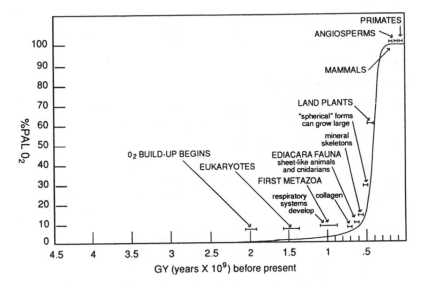

Figure 4.3. Acceleration in metabolic rates (Swenson 1989b, p. 51).

anaerobic fermentation and the ability to build internal membranes (sterols are necessary) both of which were necessary precursors to the emergence of eukaryotic cells which are orders of magnitude bigger than prokaryotes, and themselves necessary precursors to the emergence of complex multicellulars... Ultimately increased levels of O_2 lead to the emergence of increasingly dissipative forms (e.g., "spherical" forms ... with increased volumes, homeotherms, etc.) including the emergence of the human brain, perhaps the most oxygen-dependent organ on earth. (p. 51)

Like dissipative evolution in boiling water, the key here is the cycle: each phase improves, reaches its limits and creates new conditions. Those new conditions, in turn, spawn a more complex, faster metabolizing successor. As in dissipative evolution, the common measures of succession are acceleration of energy flow, growth of complexity, and increasing efficiency.

So the energy observations provide strong evidence for an overall energy-related evolutionary process that holds from molecules to man. As Lotka (1922) continues:

the influence of man ... [also] seems to have been to accelerate the circulation of matter through the life cycle. The question was raised whether in this, man has been unconsciously fulfilling a law of nature, according to which some physical quantity in the system tends toward a maximum. This is now made probable; and it is found that the physical quantity in question is of the dimensions of power, or *energy per unit time*. (p. 151)

Does Order Serve the Second Law?

When we left the second law interpretation puzzle, order was not improbable and not necessarily incompatible with entropy increase, but nothing was said about how order and entropy increase fit together. Of course, the interpretation debate moved on:

> Those who have approached the problem of the relationship between the second law and evolution have come to a variety of conclusions. Lotka (1924) essentially synonymized the second law and evolution because both were concerned with the history of irreversible changes. This attitude was shared by other workers of the early twentieth century. Others such as Bridgman (1941) and Schrödinger (1945) sensed a potential conflict between the second law and evolution, because while the direction of change in the universe should be toward disorder and increasing entropy, the direction of change in evolution seemed to be toward greater order and decreasing entropy. Schrödinger (1945) explained this apparent contradiction by suggesting that the very existence of living systems depends on increasing the entropy of their local surroundings. Thus, there can be a balance — decreased entropy representative of life compensated for by increased entropy of the universe as a whole. The second law is not violated but only locally circumvented at the expense of a global increase in entropy. (Brooks and Wiley 1988, p. 7)

Note that in Schrödinger's interpretation order is "permitted," but it still appears to be going against the flow. In this interpretation, life is often spoken of as creating an "entropy debt" or as producing "negentropy." Thus, in the negentropy interpretation order is still a fairly unnatural aspect of the system. From the nonlinear perspective order seems to be a very natural part of things. But to be able to see it that way, one always seems to have to go back to the far-from-equilibrium energy scenario.

In fact, the one thing on which most researchers agree is that the far-from-equilibrium scenario is key to the entropy/order interpretation puzzle. So, let me add more fuel to the interpretive fire. Entropy is not really measurable and not even very well defined in the far-from-equilibrium situation. Worse, from the definitions we do have the one thing we know is that it definitely does not follow the same rules as at equilibrium. Thus, as Morowitz (1968) notes:

Schrödinger rather poetically worded his argument in terms of negentropy ... we find it more useful to concentrate on the energy aspect of the argument. For nonequilibrium systems, it is often difficult to define entropy, while energy and energy flows are often more accessible quantities. (p. 19)

So, this is how things stand. We know how order looks from the energy flow story, we know that the second law holds overall, and we know that we really don't know how to interpret entropy increase in the far-from-equilibrium situation. Extending the near-equilibrium impression of entropy to the general case seems analogous to extending the Newtonian impression of mechanics to the general case but we have little theoretical foundation for a new far-from-equilibrium interpretation.

For now I will present a plausible interpretation, Swenson's (1989a, 1990) interpretation of the thermodynamic story of evolution. I use it because is parsimonious. It fits and expands the energy-flow story while bringing a very naturalized order under the umbrella of the second law.

MEP: The Accelerating Ecology of Ordered Flows

Extending the understanding of entropy to the far-from-equilibrium case is very important to understanding biology and the kinds of chemical evolution discussed in Chapter 3. One approach to the far-from-equilibrium case (following Onsager 1931, see also DeGroot and Masur 1969) is to use energy flow's connection to creating entropy to talk about entropy *production*. The idea is that entropy is produced when energy flows. Thus, the rate of entropy production is connected to the rate of energy flow.

Swenson uses this approach to reinterpret acceleration of energy flow rates in terms of entropy production. He suggests that we can explain what's been said so far about the evolution of ordered flows, reach other insights, *and* make order part of the second law — simply by adding a rate factor to the original second law. This is quite an elegant twist. The second law says only that entropy always increases. Swenson's Principle of Maximum Entropy Production (MEP) says that entropy always increases (i.e., is produced) *at the fastest possible rate*. Entropy production increases as fast as the time-space constraints and the motive force (disequilibrium) allow — so the acceleration of energy flow reflects a rate aspect of the second law.

Adding a rate factor makes the energy-flow selection principle (described in Chapter 3) a basic statement of maximum entropy production — i.e., a system takes the fastest route possible in order to produce entropy as fast as possible.

> The [flow] that drains the force the fastest, the one with the fastest rate, consumes the greatest amount of resource, and likewise the next fastest drains the next greatest amount... By this selection process the system as a whole ... spontaneously chooses the assembly of actions that maximizes the rate of entropy production for the system as a whole given the constraints ... [thus, the law of maximum entropy production] enters spontaneously and naturally into the world wherever multiple pathways occur. (Swenson 1990, p. 3)

MEP also ties the second law to an ecological perspective because it is a statement of entropy production for the field as a whole, not for one particular path or part of the whole. This turns out to be an important perceptual shift. A great deal of work in the far-from-equilibrium case has been centered on entropy production in those little islands of self-organization. The focus has been on their ability to *minimize* entropy production internally by exporting entropy externally (see Prigogine 1980). This approach, focused on the emergence of a self in the field, doesn't show how and why the self is *part* of the field. Both aspects — the self as "pulled away from the field" and the self as part of the field — occur, but only the field perspective can explain both. As I shall discuss in a minute, MEP's view of the self as part of the field helps explain phenomena such as the growth cycle of selves and their relationship to the whole.

MEP also changes the image of order. From MEP's perspective, the field prefers orderly flows because order is a more *efficient* producer of entropy — i.e., coherent motion transfers energy faster than random motion. The more coherent or structured the interactions, the faster the rate of entropy production. Under massive disequilibrium, the field forces higher and higher levels of ordered flows into being in the drive to maximize entropy production. Here, order production serves the second law. If the system breaks the symmetry then it creates a new structure which becomes a more efficient producer of entropy. Thus, there is incentive to break symmetry. The field prefers self-organized, symmetry-breaking flows. Increasing flow, increasing efficiency and increasing complexity are all part of increasing entropy production.

Finally, MEP leads to a General Theory of Evolution:

> The explication of emergence and its relation to the second law of thermodynamics leads to a general theory of evolution whose fundamental claim is that the generalized behavior observed even in simple fluid experiments is universal in nature and isomorphically observed in all nonlinear transformation of matter/energy including the emergence of life on earth and the rise of civilization No longer the exclusive province of selfish genes and populations of competing replicators, evolution can be reconceptualized

as a generic change process operating across levels from inanimate to animate, from molecules to civilization. (Swenson 1989b)

The next several sections present the General Theory of Evolution perspective on dissipative and biological evolution.

Attractors, Entities and Dissipative Surfaces. I've described the emergence of order in the Benard cell in terms of the emergence of a new attractor and a new dynamic "self." The visibly coherent behavior of the separate rolls is the result of a dynamic and reflects a pattern of flow guided by an attractor of that dynamic. It is an entity because it is visibly coherent and can be said to have a boundary corresponding to the attractor's boundary. The General Theory of Evolution ties these ideas to dissipation by suggesting that the new attractor brings into being a new dissipative surface. Correlated behavior, an attractor, and existence of a surface all become related features. Generalizing the idea of a dissipative surface allows the idea of energy being transferred through dissipative collisions to be generalized. Thus, the little parcel of hot molecules rising as a whole generated friction, a type of dissipative interaction that could not have taken place until the surface defined by this collection came into being. These generalizations turn out to be of surprising utility, as the next section outlines.[2]

Efficiency and the Surface/Volume Battle. Haldane (1954, p. 323) once remarked that "comparative anatomy is largely the study of the struggle to increase surface in proportion to volume." The dissipative surface concept allows Swenson to tie this long standing biological observation to the story of energy flow and efficiency.

Energy is transferred by surface contact. The bigger a form's dissipative surface the more energy it can transfer and the more entropy it can produce. Yet, the attractor and its surface are supported by the on-board potential. The bigger the attractor's volume, the larger the space over which the on-board potential is spread, the less efficiently it sustains the flow. There is a dissipative bureaucracy rule: the bigger a form gets, the less efficient it gets. As the attractor grows, it produces more and more entropy, less and less efficiently (because the surface grows by the radius squared and the volume grows by the radius cubed — a 2/3 power ratio).

Under incommensuration, decreasing efficiency is a problem. Producing lots of entropy is not enough; the field requires acceleration. Division is one way for the field to increase its efficiency. And we see this behavior in the Benard cell: under enough force, one large circular flow cannot dissipate the gradient efficiently enough and the rolls split horizontally into two rolls.

Splitting (prototypical replication/differentiation) increases overall entropy production (doubles the surface) and increases the efficiency of that production (halves the attractor's volume).

Yet, splitting will not be the only result of the surface/volume battle. The field seeks to increase both the efficiency of ordered activity and the volume filled by it. It can only increase volume and efficiency through new ways of correlating or coupling entities — or, as Ulanowicz (1986) puts it, "adding structural relations." If big forms divide and then couple back together, they can get bigger still — because they have more surface they can have more volume. This appears to be the path through which life has developed — from cells to multicellular animals to collections of multicellulars (see Maturana and Varela, 1984, described below).

The surface/volume battle explains in energy terms why the world consists of coupled parts and why single forms can't become infinitely large. The object of the game is not just to produce more or get bigger — efficiency is the key. Past a critical threshold, increase in size must be accompanied by an increase in complexity — more efficient forms of relations. Growth, division and coupling/correlating all fit into the natural process of maximizing entropy.[3]

Cooperation and Competition. The General Theory with its tie to efficiency and growth of complexity also provides a very different perception of competition and cooperation. As the Benard cell shows, attractors come into being to the extent the field can support them. Even in the Benard cell these entities compete for resources (i.e., energy) and balance out each other's ranges. The more efficient the cell, the more energy it pulls in to itself. Because of efficiency oscillations like the surface/volume battle, this competition moves the system toward a balanced set of similarly sized cells that fill the volume, as Figure 4.4 shows.

Note, however, that the self-organizing act that gave rise to these little competing entities in the first place involved the *correlating* of activity. The quantum jump in efficiency was created by an essentially cooperative phenomenon, a "coming together" of previously uncoordinated entities into an energetically more efficient form. It involves atomisms "working together" in a new way. In entropy terms, competition and cooperation are both sides of the survival issue. (Though from this perspective competition has more to do with immediate personal survival and cooperation has more to do with increasing efficiency for long-term survival.)

What is poetically true for Benard cells turns out to be a growing idea in biology. Margulis (1970, 1981, 1982) has articulated this same principle — the co-joining of separate forms into a new, more mutually advantageous

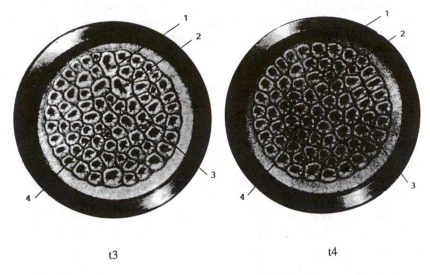

t3   t4

Figure 4.4. Competition for resources in Benard cells (Swenson 1989a, p. 197). Two time slices (t3 and t4) of the Benard Cell show selection, cooperation, and competition in the field over time. Each cell qua macro-state selects its microstates so as to maximize its entropy production while the cells themselves are progressively constrained microstates at the next higher level network. Such multiple levels of constrained maximization function to maximize the global mass specific entropy production for the entire field. Comparison of t3 (1) to t4 (1), and t3 (2) to t4 (2) show two oversize cells dividing into four smaller ones (see discussion in text on decreasing efficiency with increasing size). Comparisons of t3 (3) to t4 (3) shows one irregular four-sided cell and one smaller three-sided cell combining and dissolving their common sides to form a six-sided, maximally efficient hexagon, and t3 (4) to t4 (4) shows the competitive exclusion of a smaller cell by a larger one with a faster rate.

the phenomenon in terms of parasitism and symbiosis but the basic idea is that two sets of independent entities evolving into "relationships of mutual dependence" is the "driving force in the evolution of cellular complexity" (Dyson 1987, p. 12). For example, she notes that the main internal structures of eukaryotic cells (for example, mitochondria) did not originate within the cells but reflect a long standing coupling between previously independent organizations. Similarly, symbiotic relationships between lichens and photosynthetic algae may reflect the way land plants came into being. Lichen, which survive in a wide range of environments (wet to dry, being. Lichen, which survive in a wide range of environments (wet to dry, hot to cold), enfold and protect the algae, which in turn produce food for the cooperative. The coupled consortium results in a new entity that is more efficient than either separately.

The large amount of work supporting Maturana and Varela's theory of autopoiesis (see Varela et al. 1974; Maturana and Varela 1980, 1984) is also of the same vein. Here the concept of coupling is extended both through computer modeling and also through the historical record to describe the patterns of coupling that give rise to various levels of being. Thus, the coupling of single-celled animals eventually led to multicellular animals, the coupling of multicellulars led to communities (colonies, herd, families, etc.) and so on, up to the highly evolved coupling of societies and civilization.

Ulanowicz (1986) provides a more sophisticated description of this growth of coordinated organizational complexity in terms of *ascendancy*:

> increase in network size and organization, therefore, translates into an *increase in ascendancy*. The word ascendancy was chosen for the dual interpretation it affords. The overt connotation of domination or supremacy reflects the advantages of size and organization. To win out over other systems (real or putative), an entity must have a propitious combination of size and organization. Size alone will not guarantee success, as was the case with Goliath. Conversely, it is difficult to imagine, even in this day of powerful and sophisticated weaponry, that a small but highly developed state such as Luxembourg could by itself long fend off the hostile advances of a superpower. The intention here is to use the word ascendancy exercised by the combination of size and organization (p. 103). Growth is seen to be an increase in total system throughput; and development is a rise in the average mutual information [relations] of the network flow structure... The ascendancies of systems with autonomous development are dominated by terms involving the internal (cyclical) transfers (p. 136).

This last fits the ecological sense of things. The growth of complexity involves increasing the number and coordinating effect of interconnections among elements of the network. However, unlike the usual mechanistic sense of things, "coordination" does not mean "control" but rather reciprocal feedback relations. This "self-organizing" sense of coordination and complexity becomes important in later chapters.

Chance and Necessity in Order Production. The General Theory suggests that under incommensuration, the growth of higher and higher levels of ordered complexity is inexorable, not improbable. When flow can no longer accelerate, a crisis will ensue, and the crisis will be resolved with acceleration — at least from the field's point of view. This may of course mean either new structural relations, splitting or extinction from an entity's point of view. There is a put-up or shut-up aspect to dissipative evolution.

One way or the other, the field will accelerate. Although resolution is inexorable, the seeding is accidental. The field spawns new complexity via order through fluctuation. Some randomly occurring event in the right place, at the right time seeds a new attractor. Increasing the level of complexity is a process accomplished by chance and driven by necessity. The chance aspect, of course, fits the genetic mutation story of biological evolution. The physics of evolution, however, converts this "all accident" version to the story of an active searching field. It fits the sense of Cyril Stanley Smith's observation of history, "that historically necessity has not been the mother of invention; rather necessity opportunistically picks up invention" (cited in Jacobs 1984, p. 222). Swenson's stronger statement of this is that "the field searches the space stochastically." From this perspective, the field seeks to increase efficiency. It discovers faster ways by spawning a tremendous amount of diversity some aspect of which will seed a new efficiency appropriate to the context. Here diversity, inhomogeneity, and error may all play a role in increasing efficiency.[4]

Order through fluctuation also results in the "frozen accident." The fluctuation itself has elements of chance and necessity. Certain of its characteristics are critical, and yet many other characteristics are irrelevant. Both the relevant and irrelevant are built into the new order. Thus, though one always gets cells in the Benard cell, the pattern of cells never happens the same way twice (the ordering, sizes, seeding sites, etc. are all unique). Similarly, Pattee (1982) notes that:

> the genetic code which maps the codons to the amino acids is very likely arbitrary to some degree ... there appears to be no physical or logical evidence why the same phenotype could not in principle be produced by gene strings in a very large number of different genetic languages. (p. 331)

This notion of "frozen accident" becomes particularly important in the next phase, the creation of levels in a scaled universe.

Niches, Levels and the Scaled Universe. The accelerating field is very opportunistic; it sponsors new efficiencies whenever the field conditions afford it. A lot of efficiency accrues from filling niches: small efficiencies arise to drain small local gradients. Yet, the field is also capable of a transformation of levels, the creation of a level of being at a new scale of measure (space or time). For example, the Benard cell's molecular correlation is described on a scale of 10^{-8} cm and 10^{-15} sec before the transformation and on the order of 1 cm and 0.5 sec afterwards. Such changes of scale fit well with the cosmological record (plasma to planets) and relates to Chaos' fractal sense of things. Recursive micro/macroscale transitions would produce a scaled fractal universe.

The notion of scale plus attractors provides an interesting sense of the solid-yet-sparse nature of reality (e.g., how we can be made up of molecules with lots of space between them and yet experience ourselves as solid). Things look very different to observers at different scales and there is no absolute metric. A molecule approaching a cell membrane would experience the membrane much as we would experience approaching a city on a highway: no solid surface, just increasing numbers of houses. Similarly, human history, effectively an eternity for us, hasn't achieved even a mayfly existence in geologic time.

The Societal Example

So, this is the General Theory of Evolution. There is also evidence that its patterns apply to the human systems as well. Carneiro's (1967, 1970, 1987) description of the evolution of hierarchical civilization shows a remarkable similarity to the pattern outlined for dissipative evolution including: symmetry breaks in the face of constrained flow to the adding of structural relations and new levels and even the surface/volume battle. Carneiro, of course, was writing without any reference to or knowledge of dissipative evolution.

Carneiro suggests that *force* (resource need) and *limitations* on flow (environmental constriction) were the critical factors in the emergence of early hierarchical societies. The areas where most hierarchical societies originated (the Nile valley, the Tigris-Euphrates valley, the coastal valleys of Peru) have one major characteristic in common: they are all areas of circumscribed agricultural land. Natural boundaries sharply delimit the space people can occupy. Carneiro notes that in areas without constriction, war is generally about revenge or prestige, not about land. The defeated are neither evicted nor subjugated; they may flee but usually do so just to avoid further attack. Without constriction, war serves to disperse villages over a wider and wider area (much like random collisions).

Under constriction, however, the motives for war change from revenge to a desire for land — and the frequency and importance of war increase. Once the habitable area is filled, war collisions begin to take a different form. If a defeated village is allowed to remain on its land, instead of being exterminated or expelled, it is politically subjugated. It becomes a subunit of a larger political unit controlled by the victor. From this perspective the emergence of hierarchical political units was not the result of war per se, but the result of constriction on flow that changed the field conditions and thus changed the face of war, its goals and its outcomes.

Subordination meant the emergence of a new form of political unit, one with significantly different forms of internal structure. Individuals who were successful in war were assigned the task of administering the new areas. Besides maintaining law and order and collecting taxes, they also mobilized work forces to build roads, irrigation works and fortresses. In the process they set up structural relations that transformed a group of small collectives into one integrated political unit.

The new form resulted in increased efficiency and increased ability to grow. Subjugation generally involved the payment of a tax or tribute — and this could only be done by having each village produce more food than it had produced before. Carneiro notes that subjugation squeezes out an "untapped margin of food productivity." The new administrative social classes were sustained by the increased productivity extracted through taxes. In turn, the new integrating relations allowed these more complex political entities to concentrate and direct resources, which allowed them to expand their domains further. The net result was increasing levels of ordered complexity. "Villages were succeeded by chiefdoms, chiefdoms by kingdoms, and kingdoms by empires."

Yet perhaps the most striking of Carneiro's findings is that the pattern of growth and extension of societal organization also follows the surface/volume (i.e., 2/3 power) ratio described earlier. The plot in Figure 4.5 shows how the structural complexity of a village increases as approximately the 2/3 power of its population (structural complexity is calculated by the levels and number of structural units present).

Carneiro summarizes the implications as follows: "the contention is that if a society does increase significantly in size, and if at the same time it remains unified and integrated, it must elaborate its organization" (1967, p. 239). He notes that villages whose populations grow beyond the 2/3 ratio either split into two relatively equal-sized villages with no change in social structuring or a new form of structuring emerges which extends the amount of population a village can sustain.

Carneiro also notes that this contention is quite different from the idea that societies become more complex just by growing larger; coherence/complexity of structuring is different from size alone. Nor is it true that as societies grow larger they *invariably* become more complex.

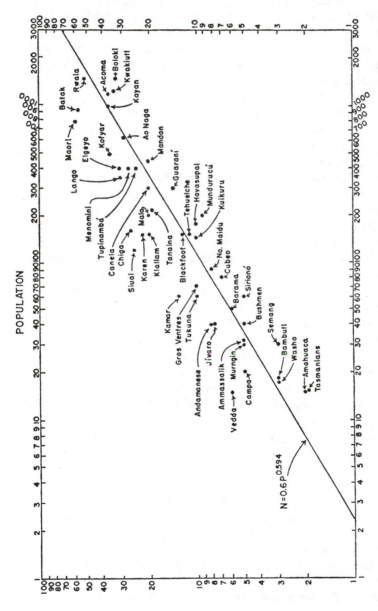

Figure 4.5. Organizational complexity vs. Population size (Carneiro 1987, p. 116). The plot shows the relationship between structural complexity and population size for 46 villages plotted on logarithmic coordinate paper. The regression line shown was fitted by eye and produces a line described by the equation $N = 0.6P^{0.594}$, where N is the number of organizational traits and P is the population size

Apparently, societies can fail to achieve more integrative structuring and this implies they will not be able to hold together a larger size.

The really interesting point is that the same size/complexity ratio holds across systems from the physical to the biological to the societal and that this fits an entropy production scenario as well. I'll discuss some possible explanations for how and why this should be in the next chapter. For now, that such ratios fit is enough to give one pause.

THE ORDER PRODUCING UNIVERSE

The following quotations summarize the chapters most important points. First, quotations from the thermodynamics of evolution:

> We are led to a vision of the fundamental unity of all processes.
>
> *Ulanowicz (1986, rear cover)*

> the concepts of growth and development are removed from the confines of ontogeny and portrayed via a new, quantitative principle as elements of larger scale ecological, economic, and social systems ... Darwinian notion of fitness thereby acquires a new meaning as the ability of a species to play a coherent role in the web of ecological processes.
>
> *Ulanowicz (1986, rear cover)*

This chapter makes the idea of energy flow pressures producing order much more serious — it changes it into evolution. Ordering and growth become fully naturalized. Order production serves the second law through its relationship to efficiency. The rules that govern the emergence and evolution of order become more refined: critical gradients; recursive cycles; tradeoffs between size and complexity; structural relations; cooperation and competition; timing. Far from improbable or simply accidental, under incommensuration order production, the growth of complexity and the acceleration of change become inexorable. The vision is of a directed, active, order-producing universe and this is a radical departure from the classical vision.

Yet, of all of the implications that this work holds, I believe Ulanowicz's comment summarizes the most important: "fitness ... acquires a new meaning ... the ability of a species to play a coherent role in the web of ecological processes." This is the most radical departure from classical vision and it is the deep implication of the ecological vision. The revolution in evolution gives it a physical basis.

Now, by way of tying this chapter to the next, let me describe some of Herbert Spencer's (1862) early observations on "general" evolution, the molecules to mankind type.

Spencer defined evolution as a "change from an indefinite, incoherent homogeneity, to a definite, coherent heterogeneity; through continuous differentiations and integrations." Spencer also recognized another process, "dissolution" (now generally called "devolution"), which he saw as the opposite of evolution. In dissolution there is a breakdown of structure, yielding a relatively simple form of order or organization. Thus, dissolution undoes what evolution has done. Spencer noted however, that in the history of the universe, evolution has predominated over devolution. Despite breakdowns of structure that have occurred here and there, now and then, the cosmos today is far more complex than it was when it began.

He also notes that three great stages may be distinguished in the evolution of the universe. During the first, matter was aggregated and reaggregated into more and more complex inorganic structures. Protons, neutrons, and electrons united to form atoms and atoms united to form molecules. There then came a time when certain types of molecules began to combine and recombine into more complex structures have such novel properties as locomotion, metabolism, and reproduction. Life had begun.

The first living organisms were exceedingly simple. They consisted of no more than a single cell. But these single cells eventually became the building blocks for larger and more complex organisms. What had been *wholes* at a lower level of life became *parts* at a higher one. Cells were organized into tissues, tissues into organs, and organs into large multicellular organisms. Through this increase in the complexity of organic forms, larger, more varied, and more successful kinds of life evolved and spread over the earth.

Finally, certain species of animals began to form aggregates — societies — which Spencer fittingly called *super-organisms*. The constituent elements of societies were not fused together into an indissoluble unit, like tissues in an organ, but retained their physical individuality. Still, they were able to coordinate their activities by behavioral means in such a way as to enhance their changes of survival. Social life conferred a great advantage on a species in the struggle for existence.

The next chapter begins to explore how it might be possible to get to the top two levels of evolution given the base we have built so far. This is a very delicate issue which opens the door to large amount of philosophical debate — particularly concerning teleology and vitalism. The advent of Chaos, however, does change the mix of arguments as I will discuss Chapter 9. For now let me add one last apropos quotation from friend Ulanowicz:

> One can choose (as indeed, many do) to adhere conservatively to the strict, reductionist view of nature and to continue paying homage to Laplace's demon. Or one can proceed boldly to talk ... about principles of organization that extend beyond molecular mechanisms, all the while treading deftly through a conceptual minefield planted with vitalism and teleology. (1986, p. 4)

NOTES

1. Note that Odum's (1988) Maximum Power Principle is essentially a formulation of the same principle from a different perspective — a fact that adds credence to both. I use Swenson's formulation primarily because I find its direct connection to the second law more parsimonious than introducing a whole new (albeit related) principle. But this is primarily matter of preference.

2. In the simplest sense these surfaces are defined by the relative motion of two portions of the field. Relating the concept of surface to attractors allows the possibility that the attractor's topological boundary can define the surface more accurately.

3. The balance between the efficiency of a particular system versus the efficiency of the whole field also helps explain certain classic life-cycle patterns. Growth, maturation, and decline reasonably follow from the efficiency limitations on any given form which is nevertheless embedded in a continually demanding field.

4. The field's use of chance and error is born out in biological stories as well. For example, Deneubourg, Pasteels and Verhaeghe (1983) describe how ants maximize their ability to find food by a natural "accident" method. Scout ants leave a pheromone trail to food but some percentage of ants fail to follow the correct pheromone path and may start other paths that yet others will follow. The net result of these accidents is a combination of good servicing of beaten paths to known food plus a fanning out in areas likely to contain more food. Natural accidents help ants search the food-space much more efficiently than would straight control. "Accidents" are the rule, not the exception (at least with ants), and it is important that things are this way.

CHAPTER 5

Life and the Origins of Information

A cell is a stable system ... because its chemical
reactions are controlled.

Csanyi (1989, p. 33)

To live is to cognize.

Maturana and Varela (1980)

So far I've talked about the nonlinear revolution in terms of interaction
networks, self-organization, and the view of evolution as the accelerating
growth of complexity in an order-producing universe. And though the
nonlinear version of evolution suggests that life was most likely a probable
part of the overall acceleration of energy flow, what I've said so far about
energy flow doesn't speak much to life's more distinctive aspects — like
responding to information, being able to persist in a wide variety of environments and to search out the means for its subsistence. Life still seems
to be a horse of a different color. How does energy flow produce the
amazing thing that is life? How can we possibly understand the qualitative
difference that life represents as part of the same continuum?

These are the questions this chapter addresses. Like the thermodynamics
of evolution, there is a plethora of speculation about the origins of life but
no fixed answers. My goal here is not to establish the answer to the origin
of life but to reexamine the question using the nonlinear ecological sense
of things. (Hereafter, I will use "ecological" instead of "nonlinear.") This
perspective finds the sentiments given in the two opening quotes to be the
pivotal issues of life.

WHAT IS LIFE?

When Schrödinger (1944) asked, "What is Life?" (in a book of the same
title), his primary concern was "what is the biochemistry of replication?"

This latter question spurred a new generation of molecular biologists to seek answers. This is very important because now we have a much better understanding of the basic chemistry of living processes. So, though we still don't know what life is, we're better prepared to look at the question.

Dyson (1985) points out that the thrust of Schrödinger's concern reflects a past and continued bias — i.e., life effectively equals replication. As Dyson notes (p. 5) "in popular accounts of molecular biology as it is now taught to school-children, life and replication have become practically synonymous." Yet, as we've seen, there are forms of replication (e.g., Csanyi's replicative chemical networks) that no one seems to mistake for life. Geneticists usually point out that it is not replication but reproduction that counts, i.e., it ain't over until the RNA makes copies that reproduce the whole system, not just itself.

Dyson points out, however, that this distinction is only another example of over-focus on replication. Note, for instance, that metabolism is taken for granted. Metabolism is that set of complex processes that keep the cell's on-board potential (see Chapter 3) alive and well. From the ecological perspective, metabolism is just as foundational as replication because without an on-board potential there is no identifiably coherent collection of molecules (i.e., a proto-cell) to reproduce. Cell metabolism is particularly important because it manages to sustain that coherence *much* more potently than the simple mechanical maintenance of on-board potential in, for example, the Benard cell. Systems like the Benard cell are "slaves" to their local gradients, i.e., if you block the immediate energy source they immediately slide back into oblivion. This is not true of a biologic cell. Such cells manage to "skate" across local gradients, that is, their potential-preserving mechanisms let them persist long enough that they have relative independence from these mass-driving gradients. In a very real sense, metabolism is what allows a cell to be a cell rather than just a blip on the screen of some local gradient.

So, at least part of what is interesting about life is the coupling between replication and metabolism. Yet, there is another very important niggling detail — function. One of the most important characteristics of higher life is its ability to respond functionally to information about the environment. Thus, in order to live for the periods of time that distinguish life from blips, even a cell must be able to move toward (or alternatively, to attract) other gradients that will allow it to survive. Even metabolism requires gradients with which it can exchange matter and energy. So, what is really interesting about life is the coupling of replication, metabolism and function.

Notice that this is a very ecological way of looking at things. Usually each of these things is considered separately. Some scientists worry about how replication came to be; some worry about how metabolism came to be. And, at a much higher level, experimental psychologists worry about the relationship between structure and function. But, if you worry about these things separately, you miss the fact that the most important thing about life is that these things are very much interconnected. Any one of them without the other doesn't really get you life.

So, following Pattee's (1982) argument, the important thing about life is the functional coupling of these three. This functional coupling forms what he calls the *semantic closure loop*. But before trying to understand what this means let me provide some background by looking at how metabolism and replication might have become coupled.

COUPLING, CELL FRAMEWORK, METABOLISM AND REPLICATION

To get a cell, you need a cell framework, metabolism going on inside and replication. There are theories about how each of these elements came about. These theories make it clear that any of the elements could have emerged on its own and then either spontaneously generated or coupled to the other elements. Oparin (1957) suggests how a cell framework may have originated when oily liquids mixed with water to form coacervate droplets which then provided a stable framework for housing metabolic cycles. Eigen (1981) demonstrates spontaneously generated replicative mechanisms, by showing that "a solution of nucleotide monomers will under suitable conditions, give rise to a nucleic acid polymer molecule which replicates and mutates and competes with its progeny for survival" (Dyson 1985, p. 9). And Cairns-Smith (1982) describes spontaneous mechanisms of coding and metabolic control by showing how irregularly distributed metal ions in clay microcrystals could have operated like genetic material in early cells, directing the synthesis of enzyme molecules and thus guiding metabolism. In short, all of these elements could easily have emerged on early earth by the same energy-driven nonlinear processes that I've described so far.

Margulis (1970, 1981) has already provided support for the idea that the major steps in life involved the coupling of previously disjoint forms into a new, more advantageous unity. So, the first ecological shift is to imagine the origin of life as a series of proto-life systems coming into being and coupling instead of the usual single event sense of the origin of life. Dyson

(1985) uses this idea to present a particular double-origin hypothesis of the emergence of a metabolizing-replicating life. I reproduce Dyson's thesis (below) for two reasons. First, it shows some of the characteristic nonlinear emphases noted in previous chapters (I highlight nonlinear points with italics). And secondly, it gives a concrete theory of how the chemistry of metabolism (proteins and enzymes) becomes tied to the chemistry of replication (nucleotides and RNA). Dyson's double-origin hypothesis focuses first on the metabolic part of the puzzle. It proposes:

> that the original living creatures were cells with a metabolic apparatus directed by enzymes (proteins) but with no genetic apparatus. Such cells ... lack[ed] the capacity for exact replication but could grow and divide and reproduce themselves in an approximate *statistical fashion*. They might have continued to exist for millions of years gradually diversifying and refining their metabolic pathways. Amongst other things, they discovered how to synthesize ATP, adenosine triphosphate, the magic molecule which serves as the principal *energy-carrying* intermediate in all modern cells. Cells carrying ATP were able to function more *efficiently* and prevailed in the Darwinian struggle for existence. (1985, p. 13)

Thus, in Dyson's rendition, the self-sustaining energy-flow relationships are the platform to which genetics were added. This energy-flow platform actually provides a natural bridge to genes and replication. To show this he notes the strange fact that two molecules ATP and AMP have almost identical chemical structures but have totally different though equally essential functions in cells. ATP is the universal energy carrier. AMP is one of the nucleotides which make up RNA; hence it functions as bits of information in that genetic apparatus. To get from ATP to AMP, all one has to do is remove two phosphate moieties. Dyson suggests that the primitive cells had no genetic apparatus, but because of ATP's energy-carrying function, they were saturated with molecules like AMP. According to Dyson, excessive concentrations of ATP would create "a dangerously *explosive situation*," and in some cell carrying an unusually rich supply of nucleotides, an *accident* might occur. With help from preexisting enzymes, the nucleotides might produce an RNA molecule which then continued to replicate itself. Such an accident would amount to nucleotides doing the Eigen experiment on RNA synthesis three thousand million years before it was done by Eigen. It would also imply a metabolic system that added replication to itself as a result of an accident related to its energy-flow processes.

Dyson's intriguing hypothesis may or may not be exactly the way life happened. Still, though no one knows the exact sequence, it is fairly clear that you can get naturally occurring metabolic activity coupled with naturally occurring replicative activity through processes that fit the basic interactive dynamic scenario. Now let's look at Pattee's even more intriguing perspective on things.

LIFE AS AN INFORMATION PROCESSOR: SYMBOL-MATTER DYNAMICS

> I describe the simplest living organism, the cell, as a symbol-matter system — an observable case of how a natural representation using a word-processing format constrains the real-time behavior of a material organism... The exercise is motivated by the belief that if we expect to get anywhere with the mind-body problem at the brain level, then our concepts must at least be adequate ... to explain the symbol-matter relation in single cells where it all started.
>
> *Pattee (1982, p. 325)*

Thanks to Schrödinger's question and molecular biology, we now have an exquisite understanding of the biochemistry of living systems. We know about DNA carrying a code and RNA being a copier and we know that the wonderful result of their interaction is the creation of proteins that are the basic fodder of life — used in everything from cell structure to metabolism (i.e., generating usable energy). So, we have a code, a code processing system and a wonderful result of the two.

Pattee makes two points: 1) that most approaches take for granted that code, processor, and result each fit the other; and 2) that if you take *getting* these things to have this relationship as the real crux of life, then you radically transform your understanding of the whole process from cells to psychology. The result of looking at things this way is a very different understanding of why life *is* a horse of a different color. Life is different not because it replicates or metabolizes per se. The miracle of life is that it uses metabolism and code-processing to create a system that preserves functional information — it is a single, inseparable symbol-matter system that preserves functional information. Let me explain how this works.

We talk about genes as codes rather blithely. Have you ever thought about what makes a code a code versus just an irrelevant pattern? Part of the answer had better be that it is readable by someone or something which, in turn, means that it has an effect. In other words, the meanings of terms like "code," "reading," and "writing" (or "copying") are interdependent; hidden in back of them is the assumption of an effect (hopefully a functional effect). There is a very special interdependent code-reader-effect relationship, or, as Pattee calls it, a symbol-matter-function relationship. In essence you can't have one without the other. This fundamental interdependency becomes very clear at the cellular level and making it concrete at the cellular level adds clarification at higher levels.

The Cairns-Smith theory provides an example of a symbol-matter-function relationship in a very simple form. It's a particularly good example because it does not use DNA/RNA whose nature as a code is already overly reified, and because its physical relationship to function is clearer.[1] The point here is that to be a "code" a thing must be readable by a "reader," that is, a system designed to interact with the code and to be affected by it in a way that has implications for the code-reader system's own long-term existence. Dyson (1985) summarizes the Cairns-Smith theory as follows:

> The theory of Cairns-Smith, is based upon the idea that naturally occurring microscopic crystals of the minerals contained in common clay might have served as the original genetic material before nucleic acids were invented. The microcrystals of clay consist of a regular silicate lattice with a regular array of ionic sites but with an irregular distribution of metals such as magnesium and aluminum occupying the ionic sties. The metal ions can be considered carriers of information like the nucleotide bases in a molecule of RNA. A microcrystal is contained in a droplet of water with a variety of organic molecules dissolved in the water. The metal ions embedded in the plane surfaces form irregular patterns of electrostatic potential which can adsorb particular molecules to the surfaces and catalyze chemical reactions on the surfaces in ways dependent on the precise arrangement of the ions. In this fashion the information contained in the patterns of ions might be transferred to chemical species dissolved in the water. The crystal might thus perform the same function as RNA in guiding the metabolism of amino-acids and proteins ... directing the synthesis of enzyme molecules adsorbed to its surface. (p. 32)

Here the ions act as code and *particular* adsorbed molecules are readers, they "pick up information" (i.e., are affected) and then have an effect, i.e., catalyze reactions. Notice there are two basic parts to the story. First there is code processing — a code and a code-recognition/copying mechanism. Then there is effect — some code-effected (or in Pattee's terms, code-constrained) part of the system causes a physical change to the rest of the system. In living cells RNA plays the role of middleman, the code-constrained executor of effect. After getting the genetic code instructions, RNA goes back out into the rest of the cell to interact with enzymes and serve as a template for making proteins. This second part of the cycle does not involve code-processing. Pattee (1982, p. 333) says:

all primeval perception or pattern recognition and selective action is mediated by enzymes or enzyme-like molecules. This is the case for the cell's sensing of the external environment, for sensing between the cells, and for intracellular recognition of patterns. At [the] molecular level the recognition-action process is generally pictured as a conditional physical template matching of the enzyme with a target structure, such that if the fit is good enough, a change of shape is induced in the enzyme causing specific ... physical actions to occur in the target structure, usually involving a specific chemical reaction. This mechanical strategy also appears at many higher levels of aggregation (e.g., ribosomes, microtubules, membranes, and so on). I do not see in any of these molecular or aggregate conditional pattern-recognizers and action-executors any dependence on string processing during their actual functioning. At the same time, I do not see any example of a functioning structure that was not syntactically constrained by strings during the initial synthesis of the parts.

There's an important addition code-processing and physical effect: the symbol-processing side of things ends up guiding metabolism in a way that *adds survival value*. When something manages to do this — i.e., code processing with survival-enhancing effects — it has really become life. Pattee's basic point is that code, code processor and effect all go together; life implies a *functional* interdependence among these elements. The semantic closure principle is a statement that symbol-matter-function must form a functional, logically connected (i.e., closed) interdependency before we call it life. What is functional? Selection answers that question over time.[2]

Semantic closure has a number of implications. One has to do with the co-effecting relationships the different elements have with each other. The symbol system is a tightly coupled self-organized system. The gene is not an abstract code (symbol) that is independent of the system. The hardware that's necessary to utilize the symbols (like the ribosomes) are themselves symbolically described, matched to the coding scheme and created by the system. Semantic closure includes the sense of a closed network of causes, each element matched with and constrained by the others.

Semantic closure also implies control. The opening quotation notes that a cell is stable because its chemical reactions are controlled. Controlling those chemical reactions is exactly what the cell's symbol-matter dynamic does. The self-organization component of nonlinear dynamics tends to highlight self-feeding flows, i.e., positive feedback. But for a system to preserve and persist, negative feedback or control is equally important.[3] Life includes greater self-control. Thus, in the process of closing the loop life increased its autonomy. It became a more substantial "self" than the dynamic selves I've been talked about so far.

Pattee's perspective suggests that the origin of life may mark the beginning of "codes," "readers," "information," and "meaning." And all of this may also be related to self-organizations achieving greater autonomy and self-control. Closing the semantic loop life truly became a horse of a different color because a living systems preserve "learning" through symbol-dynamics. That did not exist before life.

THE ORIGIN OF LIFE IN ENERGY-FLOW TERMS

Swenson (1990b) provides an explanation of how Pattee's symbol-dynamic system fits with MEP and the driven energy scenario.

The most obvious difference between living and nonliving systems is that nonliving systems are slaves to their local gradients; if you turn the heat off in the Benard experiment, the self-organization "dies." But when you remove local potential from even the simplest living systems (say, bacteria), their activity tends to increase. Possessing an on-board potential gives ordered flows the first component of self-organization but this component alone doesn't go very far. The emergence of life represents a flow with two very new components: 1) relative arbitrariness with respect to local field potentials (I'll call them mass-driving gradients); and 2) major activity governed by non-local potentials, what are called kinematic or information-based gradients.

What is an information-based (kinematic) gradient? Bacteria find desirable resources by perceiving and acting on a trail of observables — that is, fine-grained gradients *related* to molecules they consume. These are called information-based gradients. The General Theory suggests that living systems are still governed by potentials, the difference is that they are governed primarily by finer-grained gradients with a level indirection. The activity of living systems is tuned to potentials of "higher-order" fields (Swenson 1990b).[4]

Swenson postulates that replicative activity provided the basis for life's relative independence of mass-driving gradients and growing dependence on kinematic gradients through the addition of *rate-independent* constraints to flow. The molecular compounds necessary for replication, including necessary amino acids and nucleic acids, arise naturally and spontaneously by the same mechanisms already described and were demonstrably abundant on early earth. DNA chemically/mechanically interacts with messenger RNA, whose subsequent mechanical activity produces a copy of the

DNA base-sequence code. However, this simple, naturally occurring chemical/mechanical interaction has a component that is arbitrary with respect to the local mass-driving forces — the sequence of the code. The copying process is driven by the local gradients, but what is copied, the sequence of the code, is relatively independent of the local potential.[5]

Hence, with replicative activity selection starts acting on systems that have a rate-independent component. In energy terms, replicative activity is likely to be selected in general because it is autocatalytic (i.e., it increases its own rate because it outputs compounds that are inputs to its own process). If the code's rate-*in*dependent configuration happens to affect rate-*de*pendent activity in a way that enhances continuation (i.e., moves toward closing the semantic loop), the system is likely to be selected because it persists, it serves energy flow by pulling in more energy over a longer time. Like the Benard cell's hot collection persisting for increasingly longer distances, we can imagine replicative systems with accidentally "functional" codes continuing for increasingly longer periods of time. Non-living self-organizations that happen to respond functionally to appropriate kinematic potentials further expand their potential for continuation. Through energy selection, such organizations begin to "hook" into kinematic fields. Life and its sensitivity to kinematic fields co-evolve. Symbol-matter dynamics with its relative independence of mass-driving gradients opens the door to self-organizing systems focused on information-based kinematic potentials — life.

In this scenario, replicative symbol-matter interaction is also intertwined with the progressive emergence of "perceiving-acting systems" (Gibson 1979). The cell's semantic closure, its symbol-matter-function, need not be thought of only as internal metabolic maintenance. Response to "the outside" is also a survival function that must be accrued. If this semantic loop is closed, perceiving, acting and functionality become the critical selection complex. The three evolve together because it is their inseparable interaction that effects efficiency and hence selection.

This is the energy-flow scenario for life and the origins of information. Swenson suggests a similar scenario for the emergence of language and the origins of meaning — second-order semantic closure and the emergence of the symbol/*meaning* dynamics.[6] Thus, as Swenson (1990b) notes, the emergence of culture and the creation of language entailed another qualitatively different form of behavior, "second-order kinematics" or *flows about flows.* Where genetic coding was arbitrary with respect to mass-driving potentials, language codings are arbitrary with respect to first-level kinematic potentials: you speak independently of the sense experience that you speak about.

Where genetic coding's symbol/matter interaction is fixed in the processor's physical structure, language allows symbol/*meaning* interactions that can be efficiently transmitted to other systems. The learning that results from selection on symbol/meaning interactions can now survive, multiply and be tested orders of magnitude more rapidly than genetically coded information which is limited by mutation rates. Symbol/meaning coupling leads eventually to the rate-independent words on this page that effect (constrain) a reader:

> Second-order kinematics provided a new creative substrate which as the emergence of life had done before, opened the door to the accelerated expansion of dissipative space otherwise inaccessible. In this way, the explosion in mass communication and globalization going on at present is but a new phase of matter that is part of the same evolutionary order-building behavior started some 4 billion years ago. (Swenson 1989c)

In each case a dynamic that is relatively independent of one level's driving gradient allows the emergence of a totally different type of being with distinctive, qualitatively different behaviors. There is a bifurcation of being — a qualitative change that is on a continuum with previous forms, a hair's breadth away, and yet is discontinuous with its predecessors as well.

Figure 5.1 shows Schneider's (1991, p. 238) image of the result.

THE CHANGE IN PHYSICS' METAPHYSICS

This chapter can be summarized quite simply: life too is an inseparably integrated phenomenon. It is interwoven internally and with the environment. It represents both a continuity and a discontinuity with what went before. Its emergence represents the interplay of three things: energy flow, function and information. The coupling of these three produced a horse of a very different color, a new phase of evolution.

This chapter also ends my outline of the nonlinear revolution. As promised, it started small with structure in interactive systems and ends with a vision of an order-producing universe in which life and consciousness are a natural unfolding of a process that is still going on. "Galaxies, stars, cells, ecosystems, civilizations, hydrodynamic structures and cognitive states in brains are all examples of coherent macroscopic states of matter in motion that came into being by the progressive attraction of some subset of accessible microstates from some much larger set of initially accessible microstates" (Swenson 1989a, p. 188).

I started with classical physics' metaphysics and its inability to imagine certain things, particularly how order emerged and how things are fun-

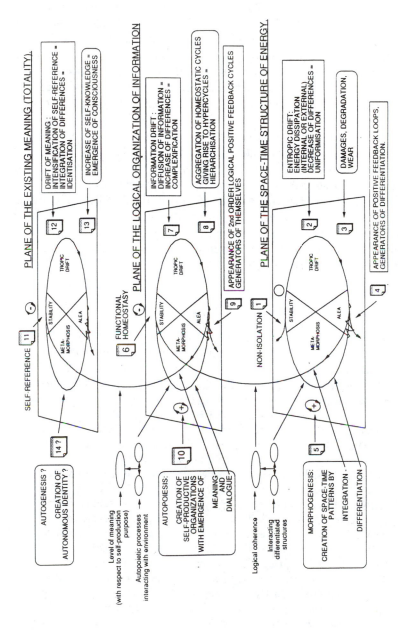

Figure 5.1. Levels of energy, information and meaning (Schneider 1991, p. 238).

damentally interconnected. The last three chapters have attempted to build a sense of just how much and how unwittingly mechanistic thinking has been shaped by its unseen metaphysics. Being able to see and explore the structure of interdependence, finding how common order production is, radically changes the mechanistic view of the world. We find ourselves to be an interwoven part of an unfolding order-building process. Even life, information, and meaning appear to be logical parts of this order-producing universe.

The outline is still speculative. Yet, the perfect correctness of all the theories is not the primary issue here. What is important is the overall and growing consonance that these and similar theories reveal. New tools, new insights, new frameworks, new perspectives — we stand only at the beginning. I would not be surprised if one or more of the theories reported here are inaccurate, I would be very surprised if the overall thrust was not confirmed. My claim for the evolving ecological perspective stands on the consonance of the themes and, in fact, their overall consonance with commonsense — life is not an anomaly, the universe produces order.

NOTES

1. Pattee makes the point that the structural aspects of RNA and DNA also play a part in their symbolic function, but this is much more complex than the symbol-matter interaction in the Cairns-Smith model.

2. The idea that symbol-matter-function must form a functionally closed loop and that selection is the great and ever-present arbiter of functionality presents a new twist on the problem of radical relativism. Radical relativism says that human beings only have "constructions" of reality, not contact with the real thing, and that, hence, no one can really substantiate the claim that their construction is better or more correct than another. In short, there are only different views, not better and worse views. This is the message of the classic movie *Rashomon*. There is no way to tell if one person is right and another wrong and there probably isn't any right or wrong, just different views and self-deception. It is a very debilitating vision because it denies the sanity of conviction. However, if selection is the arbiter and selection is based on efficiency not just randomness, then in some sense there *are* better/worse constructions. It is also quite possible that we have an ability to sense better versus worse constructions as, for example, in the sense of "beauty" or "elegance" in science (see also the footnote in Chapter 4 about Mandelbrot's discovery that fractal dimensionality as a measure of people's subjective sense of "naturalness"). Thus, constructions can be "judged" not because we "know" in some "provable" way but rather because we have the ability to sense better (more

consonant?) constructions. Constructions improve with time because selection keeps constructions honest; dysfunctional constructions, individual and societal, detract from our ability to survive.

3. Life is a complex blending of both positive and negative feedback mechanisms. The question is not which is more important but how do the two relate.

4. It's worth noting that Swenson did not invent this term and the idea is not without support. There is an entire discipline of Ecological Psychology that works with kinematic fields and their effect on living system, particularly human beings. See Chapter 8 for further discussion.

5. Genetic material itself is remarkably stable, hence the reliability of preserving the code. However, when I say the sequence is independent of the gradient, I am not referring to this kind of stability but to the fact that the gradient doesn't play a directive role in setting the sequence.

6. This fits with Jaynes' (1976) description of the co-evolution of language and consciousness. Second-order kinematics could be seen as describing the emergence of *consciousness*, language and the origins of meaning. This is worth contemplating and has a number of supporting sources.

Reprise: The Learning Universe

The oneness of all life means that the same streams of life energy runs through all the veins of the universe. It is this stream which binds all life together making them one, each being governed by its own particular laws which it must obey. So while there are higher forms of life in other worlds and human life is the highest form on this planet, mineral life, plant life, animal life, human life and other world life are one in their essence. A realization of this Oneness should do much to eliminate discrimination, especially against colour, race and caste.

From "Essentials and Symbols of the Buddhist Faith"

The nonlinear revolution offers a lot of food for thought. By way of ending, this chapter offers: 1) a summary of the changes the revolution suggests; and 2) a unifying vision of the nature of the universe in the evolving ecological view. First, the unifying vision.

THE WORLD AS A LEARNING SYSTEM

We can put nonlinear insights into a more unified and more human-accessible vision by realizing that order production in the universe is the paradigmatic learning process. Learning is induced by problems. In the simplest framing, the universe is faced with the problem of how to reach equilibrium as fast as possible given inertial resistance — the constraints of space and time. It learns in that it configures and reconfigures itself toward greater and greater efficiency and thus with each iteration it performs some activity better. Learning is not intentional because, like a baby growing, the goal need not be in mind. Each stage is a current-best solution that works until the things it cannot do, the efficiency it cannot achieve, creates a critical shortfall. Its learning proceeds (i.e., more-efficient states are achieved) through a combination of structure and stochasticity. Structure embodies previous learning but also current limitations. At each stage the field uses random non-average fluctuations to search the current space-time level stochastically (Swenson 1989b, 1990b).

Humankind's more conscious learning and planful activity is the latest result of the universe's learning process. In first-order flows, such as the Benard cell, learning involves re-configuration at the level of bulk-mass geometry. Since learning is embodied in structure, learning is limited by the system's general physical shape. The emergence of first- and second-order kinematic flows represents a dramatic increase in efficiency whereby more and more mass is driven by finer and finer flows. In second-order flows, such as bacteria, re-configuration produces tighter coupling internally and a different kind of coupling externally. Learning accumulates faster as systems extend over time and over more complex fields. In third-order flows, such as culture and science, the flow turns back on the field. Learning moves beyond the individual's life time and is turned back on the environment. What is learned is how to restructure the environment itself. And in the process, the field's differentiated aspects (human beings) have become more intentional and planful, i.e., rational.

SUMMARY OF NONLINEAR ECOLOGICAL CONCEPTS

By way of ending, let me summarize what I think are nonlinear ecological science's the most important conceptual changes:

Chaos attractors, bifurcations, the Butterfly effect (chaos), universality, stability/instability, coupling, scaling, fractals.

Energy. The matter/energy field is deeply ecologically interconnected, gradients (uneven distributions) drive change, it is relationships between things, not things in themselves, that drive change.

Self-Organization. Order through fluctuation, selection through efficiency, amplification through the self-feeding cycle, networks form at global and microscopic levels.

Evolution (the Order-Producing Universe). Inexorable acceleration related to growth of complexity and increasing efficiency, the cycle of change (new/acceleration/limit/transformation), competition plus cooperation, stochastic searching, levels and niches, the frozen accident, the unity of Being.

Life and Learning. Life and the origins of information are related. Life, mind, and body are inseparable. Life and evolution are about learning.

Part III:

Human Dimensions of the Ecological Universe

CHAPTER 6

Power

> The worst of all possible misunderstandings would be that psychology be influenced to model itself after a physics which is not there any more, which has been outdated.
>
> *Robert Oppenheimer (American Psychologist 11:127, 1956)*

This chapter looks at forms of the ecological view arising in various fields other than physics. Why name this chapter "Power"? because power comes from a model's ability to help us navigate the world. The ecological shift allows us to incorporate and handle aspects of the world that could not really be addressed from the mechanistic vision. The ecological model is more powerful than simple mechanism.

Writing this section is a bit difficult because there has been such a mushrooming of what I would call nonlinear ecological observations. One need only peruse *Scientific American* over the last 3 or 4 years to get some idea of the revolutionary impact Chaos has had. And then, of course, there is much more that is not billed as Chaos but is nevertheless part of the same underlying change. For example, there is the dissipative system and non-equilibrium thermodynamic work of Prigogine and his co-workers (see Nicolis and Prigogine 1989). Similarly, Margulis and Maturana and Varela also use ecological thinking and nonlinear concepts though they may not use these terms. Pribram's (1976) holographic paradigm arising out of his work in neurophysiology is of the same mold as is the Gaia hypothesis (Lovelock 1979).[1]

My goal then, is not to review the entire arena but just to give a sense of the emergence of these new ideas and the depth of their impact. To do this I will focus on the concepts and not the technical extensions of nonlinear dynamics into various fields. (There is a list of selected readings in different fields at the end of this chapter.) I will use economics as my core example because it provides a nice mid-ground field: more quantifiable and physically substantiated than fields like psychology and less standardly physical

119

than fields like biology. Besides, a chapter entitled "Power" should talk a lot about economics.

ECONOMICS #1: POSITIVE FEEDBACK

The following quotations are from W.B. Arthur's "Positive Feedback in the Economy" (*Scientific American*, February 1990). This article describes how economic theory is affected by a relatively simple change — the ability to address the more complex dynamic of positive feedback (increasing returns). It discusses in economic terms the ideas of critical conditions, seeding by random fluctuations, frozen accidents (he calls them "locked-in accidents"), multiple equilibria, evolution and cooperation.

> Conventional economics texts have tended to portray the economy as some-
> thing akin to a large Newtonian system, with a unique equilibrium solution
> preordained by patterns of mineral resources, geography, population, con-
> sumer tastes and technological possibilities... Given future technological
> possibilities, one should in theory be able to forecast accurately the path of
> the economy as a smoothly shifting solution to the analytical equations
> governing prices and quantities of good. (p. 99)

Conventional economic theory is built on the assumption of negative feed-back or diminishing returns. In this theory economic actions create a nega-tive feedback that leads to a predictable equilibrium for prices and market shares. Negative feedback tends to stabilize the economy because any major changes will be offset by the very reactions they generate. Thus, high oil prices of the 1970s encouraged energy conservation and increased oil exploration, precipitating a predictable drop in prices by the early 1980s. Such negative feedback implies a single equilibrium point for the economy and a "best of all possible worlds" sense of things. Thus, according to conventional theory, the equilibrium marks the "best" outcome possible under the circumstances: the most efficient use and allocation of resources. Unfortunately, as Arthur notes, this "agreeable picture often does violence to reality."

Arthur's work stresses "physical systems that consist of mutually rein-forcing elements" and which produce "positive feedback economics." The addition of positive feedback, "increasing returns", makes for a very dif-ferent picture of economics. For example, positive returns have the pos-sibility of many possible stable ("equilibrium") points with no guarantee that the particular economic outcome selected will be the "best" one. In fact, once random economic events select a particular path, the choice may become locked-in regardless of the advantages of the alternatives. And, of course he notes small perturbations are important and possibly determinative events:

> Small events ... are often averaged away, but once in a while they become all-important in tilting parts of the economy into new structures and patterns that are then preserved and built on in a fresh layer of development. (p. 99)

He provides several specific economic examples of positive feedback and lock-in determined by small events. For example, the VCR market started out with two competing formats, VHS and Beta, emerging at about the same time, for about the same price, and with roughly equal market shares. Early on, the two market shares see-sawed for a variety of reasons: external circumstance, "luck", and corporate maneuvering. But, as demand built up, a positive feedback or "increasing returns" situation suddenly forced a lock-in. Video stores originally stocked both formats but this required high inventories. VCR owners choose format based on their best guess as to which format would be most available. As inventories grew, the pressure to stock only one format grew. As the number of VCR owners grew, the perception of which format would be most available created an accelerating cycle of "the format that is perceived to have more, gets more." At some point the synergy of the feedback loop tilted in favor of VHS recorders leading it to take over virtually the entire VCR market. Arthur notes that a similar series of events locked virtually the entire U.S. nuclear industry into light water.

This simple example does not fit traditional economic expectations. Arthur notes that it was impossible to tell at the outset which format would win. Further, the fact that Beta was considered technically superior indicates that the market's choice did not represent the best economic outcome.

Arthur also explores why economic theory has largely ignored something as obvious and commonplace as increasing returns. He cites the affect of traditional physical theories, computational complexity and also the human factor:

> Orthodox economists avoided increasing returns for deeper reasons ... "Multiple equilibria," wrote Schumpeter ... "are not necessarily useless, but from the standpoint of *any exact science* the existence of a uniquely determined equilibrium is ... of the utmost importance ... [multiple equilibria] is a chaos that is not under analytical control." ... increasing returns would destroy the familiar world of unique, predictable equilibria and the notion that the market's choice was always best... When Hicks ... surveyed these possibilities he drew back in alarm. "The threatened wreckage," he wrote, "is that of the greater part of economic theory." (pp. 93–94)

Arthur's response is that the new physics and mathematics offer new ways of handling increasing returns:

> Increasing returns should be modeled ... as dynamic processes based on random events and natural positive feedbacks, or nonlinearities... Making it work call[s] for a nonlinear random-process theory that did not exist in [earlier times] ... we can determine the possible patterns or solutions of an increasing-returns problem by solving the much easier challenge of finding the sets of fixed points of its probability function ... increasing returns are no longer a chaos that is not under analytic control.

Interestingly enough, Arthur also notes that in a world with increasing returns, government policies should emphasize interventions which stress cooperation not competition:

> Conventional ... policies are appropriate for the diminishing returns parts of the economy, not for the technology-based parts where increasing returns dominate. Policies that are appropriate [for the increasing-returns sector] ... foster strategic alliances, enabling companies ... to enter a complex industry that none could tackle alone. (p. 98)

In Arthur's view economic theory also shifts its emphasis away from prediction toward steering the economy. The issues become determining when changes between patterns are possible, what patterns are beneficial and where and how to dislodge locked-in structures. He argues that with the acceptance of positive feedback, economic theories begin "to portray the economy not as simple but as complex, not as deterministic, predictable and mechanistic, but as process-dependent, organic and always evolving" (p. 99).

ECONOMICS #2: THE GROWTH OF COMPLEXITY

Arthur's work adds a new type of dynamic to economic theory. Jacobs (1969, 1984) provides an economic understanding of the growth of complexity.

Jacobs' work, spread over two decades and two books, provides a more strongly ecological model of economic theory. Her analysis of the growth and development of city economies shows the importance in the economy of what Ulanowicz (1986) would call structural relations. Cast in nonlinear ecological terms, her work shows that in an economy, as in thermodynamics, structured self-organization is an engine that drives flow in a field. The power and efficiency of that engine comes from the complex reciprocal functioning of its various parts and these are best understood as having grown or developed, not as having been planned.[2]

Jacobs notes that traditional macro-economic theory is centered around the operation of national economies and assumes certain relations between measures of those economies. For example, price levels and unemployment rates are traditionally conceptualized something like a seesaw with prices sitting on one end of the board and unemployment rates on the other. In this image prices rise and unemployment falls during times of expansion and prices fall and unemployment rises during recessions and depressions. Unfortunately, in the 1980s a new economic problem called stagflation — rising prices and rising unemployment — came into being. Stagflation makes the seesaw image absurd.

> [Price and employment have been linked in a certain way.] Break that link and the entire chain of [seesaw] reasoning disintegrates to nothing... [Even] Marx, who supposed he had so little in common with the supply-side economists of his time, had this in common: his theory also outlawed stagflation. [In traditional theory] overproduction ... mandates *both* un-employment and falling prices, a point Marx himself made over and over... Remove the twin consequences of overproduction and Marx's reasoning collapses. But leave them in and stagflation cannot happen. (1984, p. 23)

The problem is that, since in theory stagflation shouldn't even exist, traditional economists have no idea how to combat stagflation without intensifying unemployment on the one hand, or inflation on the other. As Jacobs says, the puzzle of stagflation has not only destroyed the mechanistic sense of smoothly running, manageable economic life, "it has destroyed the very intellectual foundations upon which all schools of macro-economic theory rest" (1984, p. 9).

As with other mechanistic conceptualizations, the major problem here seems to be oversimplification. Jacobs suggests that in this case the problem centers on use of a macro-scale view that ignores the importance of micro-scale structuring.

> In the face of so many nasty surprises ... we must be suspicious that some basic assumption is in error... Macro-economic theory does contain such an assumption. It is the idea that national economies are useful and salient entities for understanding how economic life works and ... that national economies and not some other entity provide the fundamental data for macro-economic analysis. The assumption is about four centuries old, com-ing down to us from the early mercantilist economists who happened to be preoccupied with the rivalries of European powers for trade. (1984, p. 29)

Jacobs' thesis is that cities and regional economies provide a much better tool for economic analysis than do national economies. Her approach is to describe the way self-generating economic engines grow in a city's relative micro-scale context and to contrast self-sustaining and self-generating economic engines with other types of economies.

She starts with a very simple observation of the growth of economic complexity: economies grow naturally by adding new work on to old. Our remote ancestors did not expand their economies much just by doing more of what they had already been doing, they expanded by adding new kinds of work. Each kind of new work was added logically and "naturally" to a specific bit of older work. And in the process work diversified yet also stayed integrated.

Jacobs emphasizes that this simple and well-integrated growth pattern creates a self-sustaining economic system which is vastly more stable, resilient and *self*-generating than are other types of economic systems. She also notes that historically cities are the place where such adding new work to old proceeds most vigorously. Cities have more different kinds of divisions of labor than villages, towns and farms and thus they contain more kinds of work to which new work can be added. Thus, cities not nations make the best unit of measure for natural self-sustaining economies.

The growth of the Japanese bicycle industry provides a concrete example of Jacobs' self-generating economic growth: After World War II bicycles had become enormously popular in Japanese cities. Japan's economy was also suffering severely from Western imports including bicycles. Because bicycles were expensive, repair shops sprang up to keep them in good working order. Because imported spare parts were expensive, after a while repair shops began to make replacement parts themselves. In the beginning repairmen tended to specialize in one kind of part; such small steps kept the process feasible and built expertise. Eventually groups of bicycle repair shops were doing most of the work involved in manufacturing entire bicycles. The next step was taken by bicycle assemblers who bought parts, on contract, from repairmen. Eventually the bicycle industry broadened into the motorcycle industry and from there to automobile manufacturing.

This whole process makes perfect sense. Far from being costly to develop, bicycle manufacturing in Japan paid its way right through its won development stages. Moreover, the work of making appropriate production equipment was added to the Japanese economy gradually and in concert with the development of bicycle manufacturing. The Japanese got much more than a bicycle industry. They had acquired a pattern for many of their other achievements in industrialization: a system of breaking complex manufacturing work into relatively simple fragments, in autonomous shops. The method was soon used to produce many other goods and is still much used in Japan. Parts making became a standard foothold for adding new work. Sony, the enormous manufacturer of communications equipment, began, at the end of World War II, as a small-parts shop, making tubes on contract for radio assemblers.

The "building-on-old" form of structural growth has all the characteristics of a self-sustaining ecology. The relationships are reciprocating and thus are more resilient, mutually supporting and generative. They result in a complexity of ecological niches that increases diversity and thus helps sponsor greater creativity as well as more efficient utilization of resources. They generate a network of flows with other economic entities which increases a city's own economic resilience. And the integrated forms of relations pay for themselves as they grow.

In ecological terms, the economic flow through the system must be designed to feed back into the system's ability to generate itself — it must include structural growth not just activity. This point is also found in physics: moving fast is not enough; the trick to survival is increasing efficiency by increasing the ability to self-generate. Rapid activity that does not include rapid structural growth leads to collapse.

Thus, for Jacobs, the critical issue in a healthy economy is the soundness of these reciprocating internal structural relations for generating and expanding the means of production. She contrasts this type of economy with others, for example, supplier economies that live off exporting raw materials that pay for their imports. Such supplier regions may have a lot of activity and may even be "rich" in terms of money but because they lack internal self-maintaining and self-generating structural relations they remain economically fragile. Even transplanted economies (e.g., a plant that relocates) do not necessarily represent a developmental improvement. Until and unless the plant becomes broadly reciprocally integrated into the local economy, it represents an economically fragile windfall.[3]

The simple yet profound upshot of the notion that health is a function of sound structural relations is that the traditional measures of economic health are misleading.

> The orthodox notion that a country's "basic" capital is the land and the labor poured into the land is obviously incorrect... A country's basic wealth is its productive capacity ... inescapably a country's economic development depends on its own work... No form of financing, however lavish, can help an economy develop if people within its own cities are not adding new

kinds of work to old ... the same rule applies to highly developed
economies too: if they do not continually create organizations to supply
capital for new work in their cities they too must stagnate and then their
wealth must inevitably begin to dwindle, even though very slowly. (1969, p.
219)

There is something so obvious about Jacobs' focus on the importance of the
structural relations and their fundamental role in generating economic
health that it's sometimes hard to see why this is revolutionary. Yet, it is.
Seeing the connections, the complex relations as fundamental is not the
mechanistic way; hence, mechanism's common distortions — economies
are viewed as simple mechanisms that can be manipulated, transplanted,
and bought.

She also notes that blindness to the role of fine-grained reciprocating
relationships and the role of city/local economies versus national is the
source of much confusion in how we think of economics in general. Failure
to see such distinctions are directly responsible for many wildly expensive
economic debacles in backward countries. As she says:

Carried away by the power of money to finance great capital undertakings,
many people seem to think of such investments as being development itself.
Build the dam and you have development! But in real life, build the dam
and unless you also have solvent city markets and transplanted industries,
you have nothing. (1984, p. 105)

The Volta Dam in Ghana, one of the world's great hydroelectric projects, is
a classic example of Jacobs' point. The Volta Dam was built as a way to
supply factories with power. Yet, despite the extraordinary cheapness of the
power, almost no power "users" have materialized — apart from an
American-owned aluminum refinery, whose promised participation supplied the original justification for the dam. In theory the dam was supposed
to promote irrigated case cropping. But this scheme proved so impractical
that it was dropped. The 80,000 people whose traditional village subsistence economies were wiped out to make room for the dam were resettled
on soil so poor that more than half found they could no longer feed
themselves. These drifted away — most of them, it is believed, to become
landless paupers.

The Marshal Plan is another example. This plan was advertised as a way
to transform stagnant economies into developing self-generating
economies. The consequences of those groundless promises are appalling:
In countries that have remained stagnant, the people became angry and
disillusioned. In countries that provided money, people became cynical
about the worth of aiding. And behind it all, the international banking

community now tries to stave off collapse. Worse, under the illusion that their development would justify and carry the costs; backward countries assumed vast unpayable debts. These debt-carrying charges eat into poor countries' earnings to the extent that "some desperately poor societies have been working, in effect, for virtually nothing except the honor of [being] promoted for a brief decade from 'backward' to 'developing'" (1984, p. 9).

The insidious aspect of the traditional approach which focused on national economies and struggled with how stagflation could occur, is that it houses an overly simplistic understanding of how to grow and sustain economies. Jacobs' analysis, with its more complex understanding of healthy self-generating internal relations versus mere activity, provides an explanation of how stagflation can exist. High activity does not mean economic health. Structural fragility may lie beneath it.

Jacobs' analysis with its very different understanding of the growth and sustenance of city economies also suggests that a very different approach to managing economies. Her ideas in this area are the most thought-provoking. The most intriguing of these is the idea that planning and controlling are perhaps the wrong images altogether.

She uses Boston's "computer miracle" as an example. Boston had been a creative city for two centuries, but at the beginning of the 20th Century it was stagnating. The popular approach was to attribute the difficulties to factors beyond the region's control: cheaper labor, foreign competition, etc. A man named Ralph Flanders, however, had a different interpretation. He reasoned that Boston's trouble was "low birth rate of enterprises." So he formed a venture capital firm to stimulate Boston's business birth rate and this is what grew into Boston's computer alley.

Now notably Flanders and his colleagues had no preconceived ideas whatever of what they were doing. Certainly the last thing that entered their heads was to build a high-tech city, for the good reason that no such thing existed. Flanders and his colleagues weren't scientists or technologists themselves, they weren't trying to control or mastermind or second-guess the people they were financing. They were merely giving people a chance to create their work, whatever it might be and whither it might lead. And this ties to a subtle but key point to an evolving ecological economy — they cannot be planned or controlled: As Jacobs notes:

A Japanese anthropologist, Tadao Umesao, observed that historically the Japanese have always done better when they drifted in an empirical, practical fashion: "Even during the Meiji revolution, there were not clear goals; no one knew what was going to happen next".... "the aesthetics of drift" ... [has also] worked better for Western cultures than "resolute purpose" and "determined will." In its very nature, successful economic development has to be open-ended rather than goal-oriented, and has to make itself up expediently and empirically as it goes along. For one thing unforeseeable problems arise. The people who developed the automobile couldn't foresee acid rain ... economic development [is] a process of continually improvising in a context that makes injecting improvisations into everyday life feasible. We might amplify this by calling development an improvisational drift into unprecedented kinds of work that carry unprecedented problems, then drifting into improvised solutions, which carry further unprecedented work carrying unprecedented problems. (1984, p. 221)

Jacobs' work presents a clear picture of the unfolding ecological nature of economic growth. Economic life develops and expands through a process of open-ended drift. Like biological evolution, it is a unfolding process whose purpose we cannot see until the end. It has order but not the order of "challenge" and "response" to be found in military thinking. "Industrial strategies" to meet "targets" using "resolute purpose," "long-range planning" and "determined will" expresses the military kind of thinking. Behind it lies a conscious or unconscious assumption that economic life can be conquered, mobilized, bullied. and directed. Economic growth and development rarely fits this assumption.

I have a personal story regarding the veracity of "economic drift". Over 12 years, Data General, the computer manufacturer for which I work, has had two company-saving innovations arise outside of, behind and in some ways in spite of, upper management's focus. The first time is documented in the Pulitzer Prize winning book, *Soul of a New Machine* (Kidder 1982). The story is formula. The company put its money on a specially formed off-site operation staffed with the creme de la creme. Meanwhile a rag-tag development group, without support and scrupulously hiding from management directive, emerged with a technically innovative new computer. The company then embraced the successful renegades, making them the new elite. But the story continues after Kidder's book. Six years later, a new renegade group, again outside of management directive and ironically arising from the remnants of the unsuccessful off-site elite, pulled off a new coup, an innovative new operating system which is now embraced as the company's hope. One is reminded of Ralph Flanders. In evolving economic systems, management may be better off facilitating than directing. This would be quite a shift in approach, yet, perhaps it is imaginable.

Jacobs work, started more than two decades ago and published in 1984, is quite prescient. The growth of complexity and rapid pace of change has forced many industries to seek "empowerment" solutions. Empowerment inside a large company is a catch word for local initiative addressed to local problems and not burdened with the overhead of upper-level intervention. The goal of these efforts? To allow "open-ended growth," to let the system "make itself up expediently and empirically as it goes along," to "give people a chance to create their work, whatever it might be."

ECONOMICS #3: EMERGY AND ECOLOGICAL ECONOMICS

Economic systems were conceived of as ecologies even before Jacobs. Odum, a well-known ecologist has extended ecosystem networking, modeling and energy-flow concepts to such economic ecologies. Howard Odum provides models for analyzing the health of an economic ecology in terms of energy flow principles.

The second law suggests that every time energy flows or is transformed some potential is lost. Yet in ecosystems (biological or economic), energy flows up as well as down the hierarchies. Thus, sunlight is successively transformed from light to plant to herbivore to carnivore, and so on. As energy goes up the hierarchy, larger and larger quantities of low-quality energy are transformed into smaller and smaller quantities of higher-quality types of energy. At each stage, work potential is degraded, but at the same time a smaller quantity of higher quality potential is created. For example, it takes four joules of coal to make one joule of electricity.

The interesting upshot of this is: "A joule of porpoise work and a joule of sunlight are located in different parts of the energy transformation hierarchy. So more sunlight [service] is comparable to less porpoise service" (Odum 1988, p. 1135). Odum extends these and other rules relating energy transformation and hierarchy to economic systems, providing measures of the work done and work potential stored at various places in the hierarchy. Thus, we can measure how much work went into creating everything from peanut butter to adult human beings — and how much potential that product now represents and how it is being used. The result is the ability to see the hidden costs, the wastes, the flow of energy in the system and whether or not the system feeds back to sustain or just dissipate. Such analyses, called "Emergy analyses," provide a much more revealing picture of economic vitality and cost/benefit than money (either prices or profit/loss).[4]

PSYCHOLOGY: ECOLOGICAL PSYCHOLOGY

As I've covered a lot of economics, I'll try to be brief about psychology. There is indeed a great deal of work using Chaos as a way to reconceptualize various specialty areas: for example, Langs (1989) in Freudian theory, Koerner (1989) in behaviorism, and Rossi (1989), May and Groder (1989) in Jungian theory.[5] Psychology readily lends itself to nonlinear ecological analogy because it is already so pattern-, interaction-, and systems-based. For example, co-dependence is a form of coupling; Feidler's stages of group development could be couched in terms of bifurcations and growth of complexity; and Family Systems is a coupled ecosystem theory.

But there is also a specific discipline of "Ecological Psychology" which warrants mention. This discipline is making remarkable strides in understanding "perceiving-acting systems" (see Gibson 1979, mentioned in Chapter 5) and takes a strong, rigorously defined ecological position. It gives a more solid sense of how *physical* nonlinear ecological principles are applied and represents a significantly different tack from traditional perceptual approaches.[6] It specifically notes scale dependency of measures and focuses on relationships and organism-environment inseparability as follows:

> Perhaps the fundamental conception of ecological realism concerns the logical dependence of organism and environment ... each component of an organism-niche system logically conditions the very nature of the other. Such a claim demands that organism-niche systems be the irreducible units of analysis. (Turvey and Carello 1981, p. 315)

Kugler and Shaw (1990) provide an example of ecological psychology in their model of how African termites construct their nests. Their focus is on how goal-directed work (nest-building) emerges as a intertwined process of the insect/environment ecosystem.

African termites periodically cooperate to build nests that stand more than 15 feet in height, weigh more than 10 tons and persist in excess of 300 years. The task involves the coordination of more than 5 million insects. This feat is particularly remarkable because each termite works independently of the others. The task evolves through an interactive process of termites depositing wastes with pheromones and reacting to the pheromones. The result is a recursive series of building modes as follows: random depositing — pillar construction — arch construction — dome construction — random depositing — ..., etc. Each level of organization arises out of a lower level and involves the coupling of behavior of the entire insect/environment ecosystem as described below. Figure 6.1 shows the building stages.

Each spring the termites become sensitive to pheromones in their waste. When the pheromone gradient reaches a certain threshold, a termite responds by depositing more waste which, of course, contains more

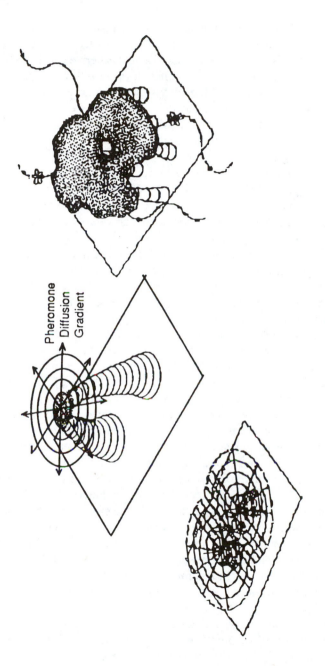

Pheromone
Diffusion
Gradient

Figure 6.1. Termite pillar, arch and dome construction (Kugler and Shaw, 1991).

pheromone. At first there are small, randomly distributed deposits at the nest-building site and only few insects deposit waste. However, deposits accumulate and above a critical threshold a new pattern emerges with more termites depositing more waste. Termites begin to follow the pheromone gradient to its highest point before depositing. A pillar of waste begins to form at this high point. The pillar building continues for a while until another qualitative change occurs. Since deposits started randomly, there are likely to be multiple pillars in a region. As the pillars grow, eventually the pheromone gradient patterns of two pillars overlap. The overlap shifts depositing such that the two pillars tend to grow toward each other (each pillar's high point shifts toward its neighbor because of its neighbor's pheromone contribution). The result is the formation of an arch. Once the arch meets yet another change occurs: there is now only one high point. The result is the formation of a dome.

Now, this description is rather one-sided — it sounds like pheromones control insects. This image, however, ignores the termite's role in causing the pheromone gradient in the first place. The pheromone gradient affects the termite and the termite affects the pheromone gradient. The interaction is a circular coupling, not a unidirectional control.

From the termite's perspective the process involves a cycle of action — perception — action — perception etc. The image of one-way control also obscures the fact that it is the termite's nature as an kinematically (fine-grained gradient) driven system that causes the whole action in the first place. Were termites not alive and did they not respond to fine-grained stimuli like pheromones, the perceiving-acting cycles would not exist nor would nest building be necessary. Pheromones are not a primordial cause but part of a tightly coupled multi-leveled ecosystem of interaction.[7]

The termite example shows how activity that produces a functional product and that is driven by information involves a lawful (if complex) coupling between living and nonliving systems. Perceiving and acting is not pasted on top of a mechanical body with the emergence of a brain, but woven into the structure of living systems and their relationships to the environment. The end result (the nest) involves relationships between season (spring), termite sensitivity levels, pheromone diffusion patterns and probability distributions of random waste deposits. The whole activity is awesomely interwoven; no doubt the result of a long history of evolution and selection.

Ecological studies of perceiving-acting in higher beings (like humans) extend this integrated reciprocal-interaction sense of perceiving-acting. For example, Turvey (1990, 1991) describes how people accurately determine the shape of an irregular object suspended from a rod, which they cannot see or touch. All they do is shake the stick. An algorithm for computing this shape would require a tremendous amount of tensor math, differential calculus and computation time — if it could be computed at all, given the sensitivity such calculations might have to initial conditions and the fact that computers always have finite precision. The difference in living systems is a cascade of integrated action-reaction cycles. Living systems do not have an algorithm into which they feed initial conditions and then run. Rather, starting with some information, they act; the field changes; they react; the field changes again, etc. The cascade of action/reaction cycles allows for correction and variation as the cycle proceeds. It also allows vastly increased computational/reaction speeds. Thus, ecological behavior is not the controlled result of a fixed, hard rule but a dance of mutually effecting (or, more technically, "mutually constrained") activity.

This integrated reciprocal-interaction understanding results in a very different framework for learning and behavior studies, which, indeed, changes even *the types of questions and answers that make sense*. The following quotation explains why ecological psychology does not use the classical notion of "stimulus-response":

> What's the stimulus for a response when you're about to hit a car in front of you? The car? The moving car? The whole scene? What specific *stimulus* prompted the *response*? Did it *cause* the response? Actually, the ecological reply is that the rate of change of the optical flow field [a relational measure] tau ... was less than 0.5, specifying a hard collision. All animals studied adhere to this tau < 0.5 rule: birds landing on branches, diving for fish in water, etc. (Barry 1991)

In psychology as well as in physics, interaction-centered thinking requires a new logic; the question is not "this or that" but "what relationships" and "how."

Ecological psychology gives a rigor to the notion that relationship, interaction/coupling and embedding are the fundamental dimensions of perceiving-acting systems. Still, there is more to psychology than the low-level perceiving-acting that termites do. Such behavior patterns are highly constrained; the interactions and their result are essentially always the same. Thus, my next discussion, from Greeley (1990, 1991) moves the question of physical dynamics and ecological relations to the higher realms of human behavior — the world of philosophy and intentionality.

PHILOSOPHY AND PHYSICAL DYNAMICS

> Science is what the universe says to itself when the universe gets
> old enough to speak.
>
> *Robert Artigiani (1991)*

So, now for something completely different. Let's not talk about termites, economics or anything else remotely physical. Let's talk about that most lofty of all human activities: philosophy. Specifically, let's talk about the possibility that philosophical questioning might be the central dynamic by which human knowledge systems evolve increasing levels of functional complexity. The work described here adds some evidence that philosophical questioning is part of real-world dynamics and that it fits the nonlinear dynamic sense of things.

Now for the hard part, the substance that goes with these fine thoughts. Dr. Greeley has found what might be a chaos-like pattern woven into the structure of philosophical dialectics. In trying to figure out what dynamic might produce this pattern, she then discovered that very diverse theories of intentional behavior — from existential psychology to neurophysiology — describe a common pattern of behavior. She uses these two findings to support a particular perspective on the nature and purpose of the most profound form of intentional behavior — philosophical questionsing. This perspective is, of course, an ecological one. From this perspective, philosophical questioning is not about the acquisition of knowledge per se or even the refining of knowledge per se. It is about learning and continuing to learn. In this view, the important thing about philosophical questioning is that we grow and change as a result of it. Thus, the important thing about the dialectical process is *the process itself*. Grounding such ideas in interactive dynamics creates an ecological perspective on some long standing philosophical debates about what science and learning are all about.

Here is how the story goes. Dr. Greeley has been interested in philosophy for years and is particularly interested in Socrates' dialectics. She was also particularly interested in what made the dialectic work — what is important about it. Through the years she had noticed that dialectical discourses by Socrates and others contained small diversions in the text. Thus, the speaker would have a brief digression not related to the content of the discourse — a story, an emotional release, a moment to collect from confusion. For example, Socrates in *Euthydemus* (cited in Greeley 1990, p. 80):

> And Dionysodorus whispered softly to me again, "Here's another, Socrates, just like the first." "Good heavens," I said, "really I thought that first one of yours a fine question!" "All our questions are like that Socrates — no escape!" "Now," I said, "I can see why you have such a reputation among your pupils!"

Interested in how the dialectical process worked, Greeley was first curious about whether these little diversions — she calls them "philosophic spacings" (PS) — played some role in the process, a break to regain one's wits or to let things sink in, perhaps. While investigating this thesis, Greeley discovered the Chaos literature. It occurred to her that though these spacings appeared to be randomly distributed, perhaps (a la Chaos) they might have structure and, if so, perhaps the structure might give some clue as to the role the pauses played. So she applied Chaotic techniques to find if the PS distribution in the various texts was structured or random. Her early results do show a three-dimensional pattern, even across a 2500 year span of different texts and authors (see Greeley 1990, p. 168). The nature and basis of this pattern are still unknown.

Thus, there is apparently a pattern to philosophic spacings which implies an underlying dynamic. The next questions are: what is the nature of this dynamic, and what role does it play in the dialectical process? The attractors (patterns) themselves are relatively mute on what the dynamic might be, so Greeley went to other sources to investigate descriptions of the types of dynamic that might be going on. Perhaps the structure of pauses was "attentional," a by-product of the neurophysiology of focusing on and processing information. Still, if they did tie to the dynamics of philosophical questioning, *intentionality* was the logical choice.

First a word on intentionality — a very complex topic. Intentionality is behavior which is focused on an end or toward a future direction. The notion of an attractor attracting behavior provides a causally explainable model of such "moving toward" but explaining goal-directed behavior in higher systems requires something more than the notion of attractors. Kugler and Shaw's termites are "intentional" systems in a crude sense, i.e., they are information gathering-processing-using systems that *pursue an end goal* ... a nest. But termite intentional behavior is deeply locked in; it's more like stored-then-recited evolutionary lessons. Human beings, on the other hand exhibit a qualitatively different, higher-level type of intentionality — directed generative learning and self-change. Greeley's work addresses this type of intentionality. Understanding philosophical dialectics requires exploring intentional dynamics.

Descriptions of intentional dynamics are found everywhere from existential psychology to neurophysiology. What Greeley (1991) discovered is that you can see common themes in these theories even across this wide gamut. The commonalities in their most general form are: 1) the process goes in a direction, it "seeks"; 2) it centers around interaction between things; 3) it proceeds through a "cascade" of states or forms that are best thought of as reorganizations of changes of states; 4) it has a backward or Gamma loop which means that the process goes in one direction, *reorganizes* and goes out in a different direction. Reorganization refers to the fact that the system changes as a result of interaction.

The overall cycle of intentionality is: seeking (intention) — reorganization — extension (outward cycle, the application or result of the reorganization.[8] Interaction is part of both sides of the cycle. The name Gamma loop highlights reorganization's role as the pivot point. During reorganization the process "turns back around" and the original intent becomes reoriented and moves out again in a new direction. The Greek letter gamma, γ, has such a turn around loop and Greeley uses it to diagram the reorganization stage in each cycle of intentionality. She uses three theories: 1) Rollo May in existential psychology; 2) Skarda and Freeman in neurophysiology; and 3) Kugler and Shaw in ecological psychology — to demonstrate her point.

Skarda and Freeman's work in neurophysiology of the olfactory lobe is the first example of Gamma loop behavior. Greeley quotes their work as follows: (I've added bracketed comments to highlight Gamma loop elements.)

> Chaos in the brain arises when two or more areas of the brain, such as the bulb and the olfactory cortex ... excite one another strongly enough to prevent any single part from settling down [[interaction]]... Competition between the parts ... increases the sensitivity and instability of the system, leading to chaos... Because various factors maintain great sensitivity, a very small signal — a whiff, a whisper, a glimpse — can trigger a massive collective state change in the neural system [[reorganization]] ... input to the system continually destabilizes the present stable state and necessitates a convergence to a new form of behavior [[redirection]]... We hypothesize that convergence to an attractor in one system ... in turn destabilizes other systems [[cascade of states]] ... leading to further state changes and ultimately to manipulation of an action within the environment. (cited in Greeley 1991, p. 18)

Greeley diagrams the neurophysiological version of this process as shown in Figure 6.2.

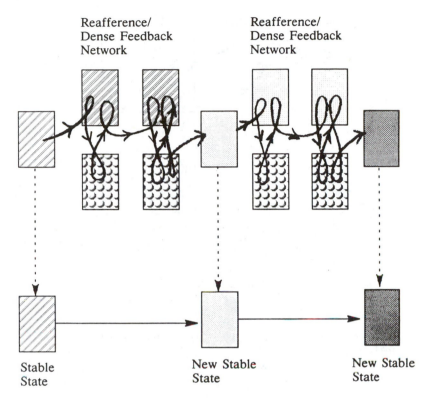

Reafference/
Dense Feedback
Network

Reafference/
Dense Feedback
Network

Stable
State

New Stable
State

New Stable
State

Figure 6.2. Skarda and Freeman's theory of intentional behavior (Greeley 1991, p. 20).

I discussed Kugler and Shaw's work on termites as intentional, i.e., end-seeking systems. They describe themselves as *ecological psychologists*. In ecological pyschology terms, each level or element of a system represents a complex interior which is affected by complex interiors by other levels. It's easy to imagine that a series of cross-scale transactions amount to a cascade of reorganizations, each complex interior affecting and being affected. Greeley's diagram of Kugler and Shaw's process is shown in Figure 6.3.

This leaves the most interesting case, Rollo May's (1969) work in intentionality from an existential perspective. Greeley provides an sample of May's work as an example (I've added boxes to note various commonalities):

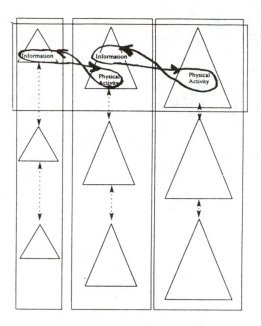

Figure 6.3. Kugler and Shaw's theory of intentional behavior (Greeley 1991, p. 20).

our intentionality object-nature and subject-nature are brought together [interaction], and in our experiencing both, we already change both [reorganize]. Consciousness creates in the same sense that it conceives its knowledge; but this is a continuous, reciprocal, attracting, counter-attracting, responsive relationship between subject and object [cascade of interactions]. Both intentionality and Eros presuppose that man pushes toward uniting himself with the object not only of his love, but his knowledge. And this process implies that a man already participates to some extent in the knowledge he seeks and the person he loves. (May 1969, cited in Greeley 1991, p. 20)

Greeley's diagram of May's theory is shown in Figure 6.4. This diagram shows several elements — Eros, the Daimonic, and Ideal forms — whose definitions can be interpreted in nonlinear ecological terms. Eros is "that which gives form to the Void." It is the process of forming form. The Daimonic is part of Eros, as follows:

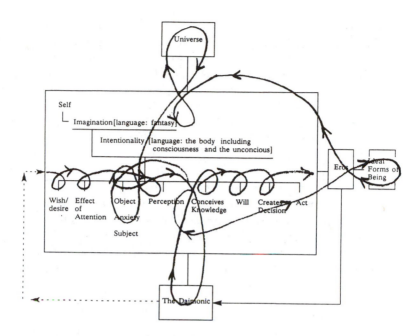

Figure 6.4. May's theory of intentional behavior (Greeley 1991, p. 20).

we initially experience the Daimonic as a blind push ... an impersonal dynamic ... it arises from the ground of Being rather than the self as such. Its the urge in every being to affirm itself, assert itself, perpetuate and increase itself.

The Daimonic's blind push is really part of Eros drawing us. The purpose of the draw is to connect the self with the ideal forms of Being — Truth, Beauty, the Good, the Noble. The Daimonic blindly pushes wish and desire proceeding by an uncharted path, it oscillates between the various forms and states. It may go forward and then come back to the wish and desire to be refueled. It goes, collects, reformulates and returns — and then returns again collecting and changing into something else. And all of this is the process by which Eros transforms the self and moves it toward union with the Ideal.

Using the ideas of top-down and bottom-up causality described in Chapter 2, we can construct a nonlinear ecological description that shows remarkable consonance with May's description. Top-down/bottom-up causality refers to interactive dynamics' holistic potential — you get a global-order phenomenon that arises out of and acts upon the very interaction of the parts that construct it. Top-down/bottom-up causality provides a physical, mechanical description of a thing that pushes, pulls and at the same time coheres and orders itself through the process of interaction. This sounds remarkably similar to the relationship among Eros, the Daimonic that May describes. Thus, Eros would be the overall process including the pull and the Daimonic would be the push and the interaction of elements. The evolving universe also strives to unfold into higher and higher levels of ordered complexity and many people describe this as the pull of a global attractor(s) — ideal forms of Being? Finally, the universe goes in an overall direction but in the process it follows an uncharted path: it goes in cycles, it oscillates, reformulates and moves to different levels. It bubbles up, pops and bursts back. It does all these different amazing things internally while nevertheless going as a whole in a general direction.

In sum, we have three theories of intentionality coming from wildly different discourse that all house similar cascading interactive dynamical descriptions. Seek and interact, change, go out, seek and interact, change, go out — a repeating cycle of Gamma loops. Now, one more interesting observation. The Socratic dialectic itself can be diagrammed as an intentional seek-change-go-out flow: an inductive process followed by a reorganization and an extensional flow, the deductive side. Figure 6.5 shows Greeley's sense of the dialectical the cycle.

Now, what does all of this get us? A stronger sense that intentionality is at heart an interactive, dynamical sequence whose recursive seek-change-go-out cycle moves us forward. And this sense supports the perceptual change that I mentioned before — that the role of the dialectic is to help us grow, to evolve, to change ourselves by well-constructed interaction.

Like the other ecological shifts, in some sense seeing dialectical questioning as a way to evolve through interaction seems obvious, not a big deal. Yet it turns out to be an important shift in perception. Dr. Greeley, like others, argues that the Socratic dialectical model that came down to us through Plato is missing something. In Robinson and Meyers terms, "philosophical questioning died with Socrates" (cited in Greeley 1990, p. 325). What does this mean and why is it important? I'll talk about what it means in the next section but its importance is easy to describe. Our model of science is based on the model of questioning that came from Socrates through Plato and then modified by Aristotle. What's missing is important because it speaks to our understanding of what science and learning are all about. The interesting possibility is that Plato's model is missing the same thing that mechanism is missing: an awareness that we are embedded in the

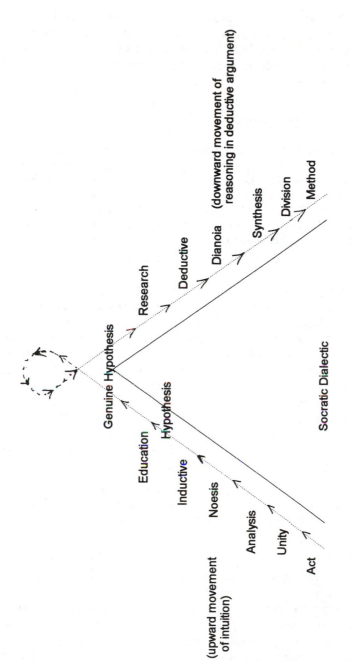

Figure 6.5. The Socratic dialectical cycle (Greeley 1990, p. 233).

process, that the point of the process is to change us. In short, what is missing is an evolving ecological awareness. This difference can be seen in the difference between the Socratic and Platonic visions: a focus on growth, evolution and change versus a vision of acquiring a static objective truth that can be held on to.[9]

DIALECTICS AS EVOLUTION

> The problem is that, in many cases for many systems, there may simply be no such thing as a truly independent variable. Out here in the real world, the phrase "*in*dependent" may often be oxymoronic. The very notion of independence reflects the world of Platonic idealism, a pure world populated by separate discrete *things* each with its essence, floating suspended in a sea of laws, rules governing the relations between these autonomous entities.
>
> *Jon Koerner (1988, p. 118)*

The question of what changed from Socrates to Plato to modern science is a source of unresolved ambiguity that many scholars have examined. Dr. Greeley's exploration of intentionality as evolutionary dynamics puts these old arguments in a new light. The translation of dialectics from Socrates to Plato to Aristotle included a shift of focus — from the dialectical *act* (Socrates) to the *method* (Plato) and finally to *logic* alone (Aristotle). Hidden in this shift was a loss of the real purpose of the process — from changing the learner to acquiring knowledge. And this shift is exactly the difference between an ecological and a mechanistic understanding of learning and knowing.

Greeley notes that the key to Socratic dialectics is the dynamic dialectical process itself. As Greeley writes:

> it is the *act, not the method*, of the dialectic that is central to it. It is the act of the dialectic whose consequences must then be tested for authenticity, that is at the crux of the Platonic dynamical philosophy. (p. 231)

Now why should it be so important to emphasize that it is "act," not "method"? This is a subtle distinction to those not schooled in philosophy. But this difference makes all the difference and — in all its obscurity — represents an important key to the ecological shift.

In creating his dialectics, Socrates changed an earlier Sophist method of discourse — designed for arguing for the purpose of winning an argument — into a method of arguing for the purpose of learning. And in the process he created the quintessential model for philosophic questioning and learning in Western civilization. Yet, science did not get its model of the dialectic directly from Socrates but from Plato via Aristotle:

> Aristotelianism, the philosophy that all is unfolding exactly as it should be, is teleologically based, [it suggests] that the moral man facilitates the unfolding of the world by methodically and logically ... describing and discovering relationships which bring harmony through understanding ... relying on the logical *method* and *not the act* of the dialectic. (p. 235)

Notice how, in this view, man stands outside the world and facilitates. Man helps the world unfold by method. Man affects the world, not himself. This method-centered view was invented by Plato. Aristotle elaborated it by separating the logical method from the dialectical activity. And herein lay a change, for as Robinson and Meyer (cited in Greeley, p. 235) say:

> [Aristotle, separating the logical method from the activity, isolated] it from the source of its inspiration, [changing] dialectic from the highest intellectual activity to a dubious game of debate ... the Aristotelian theory of syllogism can be viewed as the completion of the movement initiated by Plato: by supplying formal criteria of justification, Aristotle has made science totally independent of questioning ... [this form of the dialectic] no longer bearing the slightest resemblance to the Socratic dialectic. (pp. 235–236)

Why should separating logic and method from activity make such a big difference? In ecological terms, the separation is deadly because it is *in the process of acting* that human thinking evolves. Separating logic and method from activity is deadly because you cease to think the point is learning (i.e., changing oneself, evolving) and instead begin to think that the point is acquisition of knowledge ... out there, immutable, separate, objective, final, absolute, etc. You get all the deadly sins of science so clearly seen in Positivism at the beginning of the century.

Greeley's description of intentionality as cascades of interaction and change provides a *reason* why the act itself is crucial. And in that reason we see the ecological versus the mechanistic perspective. Humankind is not applying a method to a separate universe. Humankind is embedded in an active universe. Our special generative learning is but the latest phase in that universe's increasing efficiency. We evolve better knowledge relations with the world because of our increased independence and flexibility but we are still part of that world. In a sense our generative learning is part of the universe's method of improving itself through us (hence the opening quotation).[10]

THE PRAGMATIC ECOLOGICAL THINKER

> Philosophy of science in the twentieth century has until recently been dominated both by physics and by a particular interpretation of physics... Mayr notes that the philosophical accounts of physics "do not apply to, are irrelevant to, are not true of, and have no equivalent in" biology, yet he does not see ... that biological theory and fact *conflict with* these philosophical interpretations of science stemming from physics... To be explicit, there are two separate and conflicting philosophical interpretations of science, and — lying behind them — two separate cosmologies... Both interpretations claim to apply to all of science.
>
> *Radnitzky and Bartely (1987, p. 7)*

The Newtonian interpretation of physics has dominated science. Western thinking is riddled with a wide range of its assumptions and images. Only now — with the ability to *do something better* — do we really stand a chance of growing beyond it. So, one final quotation by way of conclusion:

> The group was gathered in the late afternoon at an enormous round table in the Grand Salon, and [Archibald] Wheeler had just delivered a brilliant exposition of his interpretation of quantum mechanics. [Karl] Popper turned to him and quietly said: "What you say is contradicted by biology." No one present meant to suggest that the reported facts of physics and biology were in conflict — nor even that physical and biological *theory* conflicted. Rather, it was meant that Wheeler's *interpretation* of physics was incompatible with fact and interpretation in the life sciences. Behind Popper's remark ... was yet another contention: *that the interpretation of physics that had been presented did not apply to physics either.* (Radnitzky and Bartely 1987, p. 7).

NOTES

1. Work arising from the Gaia hypothesis provides perhaps the most beautiful articulations of bio-chemical-thermal-mechanical networking and the coherent evolution of the biosphere. Unfortunately, Gaia usually frames these observations in terms of homeostasis and self-organization for the self's own sake rather than in terms of stable self-organization emerging as part of an evolving universe. Still, the basic vision is the same.

2. Jacobs' analysis is particular fascinating because, although it is a sophisticated description of Ulanowicz's "growth of structural relations," she developed it without the insights of nonlinear physics. She is a good example of the idea that physics is not the source of the ecological change.

3. The same is true for economies that are overdependent on a single industry as, for example, Detroit and automobile manufacturing.

4. Odum adds this note for economists: "Some people confuse Emergy concepts with the technocrat movement of the 1930s, which used energy as the basis of value and proposed to pay people with energy certificates in place of money. Of course this failed because energy of different types are not of equal wealth... Technocrats wanted to substitute energy value for money, whereas Emergy value is not meant to be used for market, value, but for larger scale evaluation of the economy. Value to the person is market value. Value to the economy is Emergy" (1991, p. 109).

5. See also Abraham's (1991) *A Visual Introduction to Dynamical Systems Theory for Psychology*.

6. Ecological psychology is closely allied with a discipline of ecological physics.

7. Also note that part of the process was random and part was neither pheromone per se or termite per se but the interaction of different geometries in the field (e.g., overlapping gradients). Termite nest building actually represents the very complex functional coupling of the entire ecosystem field at numerous scales and of numerous forms.

8. Note that the extension of one cycle may well be the intention of the next cycle.

9. This small difference makes a big difference, or as Robinson puts it: "Plato never became accurately aware of how much he was straining and distorting the Socratic view by the influence of his own distinct personality ... [for Plato had] a very un-Socratic mind" (cited in Greeley 1990, p. 235).

10. There is a field of evolutionary epistemology started by Karl Popper, Konrad Lorenz, F.A. Hayek, Donald Campbell and others (see Radnitzky and Bartley 1987). They too represent an emerging evolving ecological perspective but with a more analytic bent: "Evolutionary epistemology — which stands in sharp contrast to most traditional approaches — treats knowledge and knowledge-processes as objective evolutionary products, to be compared and contrasted with other such products" (Radnitzky and Bartley 1987, p. 19). Their arguments and concerns, however, are too complicated to pursue here. They are complicated because they seek to bridge the two great problems of metaphysics: a theory of knowledge and a theory of rationality. In a nutshell, the problem is how do you tell good knowledge from bad knowledge or whether there is such a thing as good and bad knowledge — perhaps there are just different perspectives (the radical relativist point of view).

SELECTED READINGS IN CHAOS THEORY IN OTHER FIELDS

Economics/Business

Baumol, W. U., and J. Benhabib (1989). "Chaos: Significance, Mechanism and Economic Applications." *Journal of Economic Perspectives* 3(1):77–105.

Brock, W. A., C. L. and Sayers (1988). "Is the Business Cycle Characterized by Deterministic Chaos?" *Journal of Monetary Economics* 22:71–90.

Candela, G., and A. Gardini (1986). "Estimation of a Nonlinear Discrete-Time Macro Model." *Journal of Economic Dynamics and Control* 10:249–259.

Goldstein, J. (1988). "A Far-From-Equilibrium System's Approach to Resistance to Change." *Organizational Dynamics*, Autumn, pp. 16–26.

Lorenz, H. (1987). "Strange Attractors in a Multisector Business Cycle Model." *Journal of Economic Behavior and Organization* 8:397–411.

Nonaka, I. (1988). "Creating Organizational Order Out of Chaos: Self-Renewal in Japanese Firms." *California Mangement Review*, Spring, pp. 57–73.

Savit, R. (1988). "An Introduction to Chaos in Market Prices." *The Journal of Futures Markets* 8(3):271–289.

Speidell, L. S. (1988). "As a Science, Chaos Can Put Things in Order." *Pensions and Investment Age*, December 12, p. 25.

Waterman, R. H. (1987). "Strategy for a More Volatile World." *Fortune*, December 21, pp. 181–182.

Meteorology and Earth Sciences

Hollingsworth, A. (1986). "Storm Hunting with Fractals." *Nature* 319:11–12.

Lovejoy, S., D. Schertzer, and P. Ladoy (1986). "Fractal Characterization of Inhomogeneous Geophysical Measuring Networks." *Nature* 319:43–44.

Oxall, U., M. Murat, F. Boger, A. Aharony, J. Feder, and K. Jossang (1987). "Viscous Fingering on Percolation Clusters." *Nature* 329:32–37.

Plotnick, R. E. (1986). "A Fractal Model for the Distribution of Stratigraphic Hiatuses." *Journal of Geology* 94:885–890.

Robinson, A. L. (1985). "Fractal Fingers in Viscous Fluids." *Science* 228:1077–1080.

Smalley, R. F., J. L. Chatelain, D. L. Turcotte, and R. Prevot (1987). "A Fractal Approach to the Clustering of Earthquakes: Applications to the Seismicity of the New Hebrides." *Bulletin of the Seismological Society of America* 77(4):1368–1381.

Tsonis, A. A., and J. B. Elsner, (1989). "Chaos, Strange Attractors and Weather." *Bulletin of the American Meteorological Society* 70(1):14–23.

Vallis, G. K. (1987). "Oceanography, El Nino, and Chaos." *Physics Today*, January 1987, pp. 540–541.

Van Damme, H., F. Obrecht, P. Levitz, and P. Gatineau (1986). "Fractal Viscous Fingering in Clay Slurries." *Nature* 320:731–733.

Weisburd, S. (1985). "Fractals, Fractures and Faults." *Science News* 127:279.

Wong, P. (1988). "The Statistical Physics of Sedimentary Rock." *Physics Today*, December 1988, pp. 24–32.

Political Science

Grossmann, S., and G. Mayer-Kress (1989). "Chaos in the International Arms Race." *Nature* 337:701–704.

Peterson, I. (1988). "The Chaos of War." *Science News* 127(1):13.

Saperstein, A. M. (1984). "Chaos — A Model for the Outbreak of War." *Nature* 309:303–304.

Saperstein, A. M. (1988). "SDI, A Model for Chaos." *Bulletin of the Atomic Scientists*, October 1988, pp. 40–43.

Saperstein, A. M., and B. Mayer-Kress (1989). "Chaos Versus Predictability in Formulating National Security Policy." *American Journal of Physics* 57(3):217–223.

Physiology, Medicine and Life Sciences

Anderson, R. M., and R. May (1985). "Vaccination and Herd Immunity to Infectious Diseases." *Nature* 318:323–329.

Babloyantz, A., J. M. Salazar, and C. Nicolis (1985). "Evidence of Chaotic Dynamics of Brain Activity During the Sleep Cycle." *Physics Letters*, Ser. A, 111:152–155.

Basar, E. (Ed.) (1990). *Chaos in Brain Function*. Berlin: Springer-Verlag.

Goldberg, A., D. Rigney, and B. West (1990). "Chaos and Fractals in Human Physiology: Chaos in Bodily Functioning Signals of Health: Periodic Behavior Can Foreshadow Disease." *Scientific American*, February 1990, pp. 43–49.

Lewis, M., and D. Rees (1985). "Fractal Surfaces of Proteins." *Science* 230:1163–1165.

May, F. M. (1986). "The Search for Patterns in the Balance of Nature: Advances and Retreats." *Ecology* 67(5):1115–1126.

May, R. M. (1985). "Ecological Aspects of Disease and Human Populations." *American Zoologist* 25:441–450.

Morse, D. R., J. H. Lawton, M. M. Dodson, and M. H. Williamson (1985). "Fractal Dimension of Vegetation and the Distribution of Arthropod Body Lengths." *Nature* 314:731–733.

Mpitsos, G. J., and S. Soinla (1991). "In Search of a Unified Theory of Biological Organization: What Does the Motor System of a Sea Slug Tell Us About Human Motor Integration?" In: *Lectures in complex systems: Santa Fe Institute Studies in the Sciences of Complexity*, eds. L. Nadel and D. Stein. New York: Addison-Wesley.

Olsen, L. F., and W. M. Schaffer (1990). "Chaos Versus Noisy Periodicity: Alternative Hypotheses for Childhood Epidemics." *Science* 249:499–504.

Pool, R. (1989). "Is It Healthy To Be Chaotic?" *Science* 243:604–607.

Schoner, G., and J. A. S. Kelso (1988). "Dynamic Pattern Generation in Behavioral and Neural Systems." *Science* 239:1513–1520.

Taubes, G. (1989). "The Body Chaotic." *Discover*, May 1989, pp. 63–67.

Psychology

Callahan, J., and J. I. Sashin (1987). "Models of Affect-Response and Anorexia Nervosa." In: *Perspectives in Biological Dynamics and Theoretical Medicine*, pp. 241–258, eds. S. H. Koslow, A. J. Mandell, and M. R. Schlesinger. New York: New York Academy of Sciences.

Gilgen, A., and F. Abraham (Eds.) (1993). *Chaos Theory in Psychology*. New York: Greenwood Publishers.

Hansen, S. J., and W. Timberlake (1983). "Regulation During Challenge: A General Model of Learned Performance Under Schedule Constraint." *Psychological Review* 90:261–282.

Hoyert, M. S. (1992). "Order and Chaos in Fixed-Interval Schedules of Reinforcement." *Journal of the Experimental Analysis of Behavior* 57:339–363.

Kelso, J. A. S., J. D. DelColle, and G. Schoner (1990). "Action-Perception as a Pattern Formation Process." In: *Attention and Performance*, Vol. 13, ed. M. Jeannerod. Hillsdale, NJ: Lawrence Erlbaum Publishers.

Killeen, P. R. (1992). "Mechanics of the Animate." *Journal of the Experimental Analysis of Behavior* 57:429–463.

King, M., and R. A. Abraham (1992). "Netscope: Dynamics From Communication Data." *American Journal of Psychotherapy* 46(1).

King, R., J. D. Barchas, and B. A. Hubermann (1983). Theoretical Psychopathology: An Application of Dynamical Systems Theory to Human Behavior. In: *Synergetics of the Brain*, eds. E. Basar, H. Flohr, H. Haken, and J. Mandell. Heidelberg: Springer-Verlag.

Marr, M. J. (1992). "Behavior Dynamics." *Journal of the Experimental Analysis of Behavior* 57:249–266.

May, J., and M. Groder (1989). "Jungian Thought and Dynamical Systems." *Psychological Perspectives* 20(1):143–156.

Middleton, C, G. Fireman, and R. DiBello (1991). "Consistency in Chaos and Personality." In: Proceedings of the 2nd Annual Meeting of the International Society for Theoretical Psychology.

Redington, D. J., and S. P. Reidbord (1992). "Chaotic Dynamics in Autonomic Nervous System Activity of a Patient During a Psychotherapy Session." *Biological Psychiatry* 31:993–1007.

Sabelli, H. C., L. Carlson-Sabelli, and J. I. Javaid (1990). "The Thermodynamics of Bipolarity: A Bifurcation Model of Bipolar Illness and Bipolar Character and Its Psychotherapeutic Applications." *Psychiatry* 53:346–358.

Schwalbe, M. L. (1991). "The Autogenesis of the Self." *Journal for the Theory of Social Behavior* 21(3):269–295.

Smith, L. B. (1992). "Real Time and Developmental Time: The Geometry of Children's Novel Word Interpretations." Paper presented at the 100th Anniversary Convention of the American Psychological Association, Washington, DC.

Thelen, E. (1992). "Development as a Dynamic System." *Current Directions in Psychological Science* 1:189–193.

Turvey, M. T. (1988). Execution Driven Action Systems and Smart Perceptual Instruments. In: *Dynamic Patterns in Complex Systems*, eds. J. A. S. Kelso, A. J. Mandell, and M. F. Shlesinger. Singapore: World Scientific Publishers.

Vandervert, L. R. (1991). "The Emergence of Brain and Mind Amid Chaos Through Maximum Power Evolution." *World Futures: The Journal of General Evolution* 32:1–21.

CHAPTER 7

Re-Enchantment

> Most of the great religions of the world ... affirm the existence of a
> spiritual being or, at least a spiritual aspect or dimension of reality.
> It may be thought that such religious beliefs ... come directly into
> conflict with the knowledge we have of the material cosmos
> through the physical sciences. But that is not the case. The conflict
> is not with our scientific knowledge of the physical world but with
> the dogmatic materialism of a great many scientists.
>
> *Mortimer Adler (1990, p. 35)*

I would modify the above quotation to say, "a *particular* dogmatic materialistic *interpretation*" instead of materialism per say. As this chapter will explore, it appears possible to have a fully physical (energy-matter) understanding that can nevertheless comprehend the spiritual dimension.

The world under mechanism was a peculiarly sterile place. Awe and mystery, beauty and nobility, connection to something higher — these were all important, but not of this world. As science explained the world more and more, the separation of these things from the world also grew more and more. The deep ecological vision seems to change this. As mechanistic science grew stronger and stronger, its sense that other world hypotheses were absurd also grew stronger and stronger. Humankind became increasingly separated not only from the beauty and nobility of the world but also from the various different parts of itself. Human knowledge systems became more and more fragmented and less and less able to tolerate each other, much less talk to one another. This too seems to change.

This chapter explores the reconciliation between scientific images and spiritual images. Enchantment comes from the wonderment, beauty and delight of reconciliation with each other and with that which is greater than us. Re-enchantment means bringing the wonder of connection back to the real world.

First an outline of the type of world view that ecological science creates.

HOW DOES THE WORLD WORK?: A WORLD VIEW
FOR SCIENCE AND SPIRITUALITY

Classical science painted a picture of a purposeless, passive universe. If one believed this image was fact, then all traditions that described order/purpose/direction were antithetical to science. This particular irreconcilable difference falls away once order building is seen to have a physical basis. Of course, the new physical image of how the world works does not support all spiritual beliefs, just a much more consonant world vision as follows:

A Directed Creative Universe. Until its incommensuration ends, the universe is directed toward creation of increasingly ordered forms. We and all "things" that we see are the net result of this creative drive. A sense of direction, of a process larger than ourselves and of a creative force is restored.

An Opportunistic Universe and a Cooperative One. The delicate balance between forces and flows means that forms will exist in exact proportion to the forces. To the extent that there is force to support it, a form will come into being. In exact opposition to Darwinian thinking, an expanding universe is opportunistic not accidental. Life is no longer an anomaly. Also in contrast to the Darwinian picture, cooperation is an important part of being and becoming. The coming together of existing entities in a new structure is the basis of all new dimensions of being. Competition and cooperation are partners in the process of being. The world is not simply ruthless, and self-interest is dethroned as the sole logic of life.

The One is Many and the Many are One. All forms of being are part of one process; they are differentiated aspects of the field that emerge from, contribute to and then recede back into the ongoing flow. Entity and field are inseparable and co-effecting. The two are like Heidigger's "Being and being," interplaying aspects of one thing. More strongly, entity, other entities and field are all inseparable. The intake and output of each and the context locally and globally — all these are interplaying aspects of one thing. The process exists and evolves only in the interplay of these many forms. Using Buddhist words, it is a co-dependent arising.

This inseparability of all aspects takes ecology to a deeper level. It is not just that living things are curiously interconnected; our interconnection and our existence, each and all, are part of an unfolding process which created us, directs us and to which we contribute. This vision denies the religious and scientific anthropocentrism that has stayed with us despite the Copernican revolution. We are not the center, not the power, not the end-all of

Being. We are members of a community of Being — with rights, privileges, duties, and conditions of membership. We are part of a chain of Being that will not end with us. We have a role, as all elements of the whole do. If we care to continue, the trick to continued existence is clearly in going with the process, not just ourselves.

Constancy and Change. The process I have outlined shows the basic elements of constancy and change so often noted in our world. Each new space-time crisis gives us a way of being that dominates the field by virtue of its new way of accelerating. During its growth and maturity, before its exhaustion and shortfall, we experience relative constancy. Yet, in fact, existence oscillates between local, relative constancy and inexorable change. Absolute rest and permanence do not exist. Adaptation to a homeostatic status quo is not an appropriate model for survival — especially in critical times.

A corollary to constancy and change is that the only real constant is the process. All structure-dependent solutions are doomed to failure. Oddly, if all structural solutions are doomed, one way to serve the pressure to accelerate is to be able to move through forms easily. Forms that change forms (metaforms?) are thus most prone to survive because they can accelerate themselves. Both human consciousness and the process we call "science" are such metaforms. They move us distinctly away from fixation on structure because they can change as a result of critically examining themselves. They are forms that change themselves by learning, not by physical change. Such forms are higher not because they are perfect but because they find their limitations and can move to a new form with relative ease.

Necessity — The Importance of Being Inhomogeneous. When the field context is critical a small fluctuation will seed a transformation and a new form will emerge. Inhomogeneity is a necessity of growth. Our differences, those random uniquenesses, are critically important. The tradition of cherishing the maverick, the odd-ball, the nonconformist, is well founded. Difference is the seed of change and growth.

Chance — Being Inhomogeneous is Not Enough. When the context is critical, a small fluctuation will seed transformation. The fluctuation must fill some critical need but its exact parameters can vary. There will be many suitable fluctuations; *which* one finally becomes amplified is all chance. The situation is a living example of the aphorism: "many may one must."

This understanding speaks to the debate between "Great Man" theories and "Zeitgeist" theories. Is it the times or does a great person force change into being? The reply comes back: yes. Transformation, the creative moment, is a combination of both times and personae. Both the narcissism of personally created change and the impotence of times-generated change are denied.

History: Unpredictable, Idiosyncratic, Lawful. The growth of complexity and the acceleration of the field are inexorable. A cycle of crises is inexorable. But we do not know how any particular crisis will resolve itself. Bifurcations can be conversions, catastrophes, setbacks or terminations for any given self-structure. We cannot predict which of many random fluctuations will seed an event. When seeding does occur it will cause a "frozen accident," both relevant and irrelevant features of the seeding event will shape the path of the system.[1] There is chance and uniqueness, as well as universal rules and necessity. This odd juxtaposition provides a basis for unique, idiosyncratic historical path that is nevertheless part of a lawful, predictable process. Such partial historical particularism speaks to human history's sense of both idiosyncratic uniqueness and logical unfolding.

The Co-Determined Universe. We are members of a creative unfolding based in simplicity but of infinite complexity. Immeasurably small differences will keep evolution forever beyond our control and our knowing. Yet while we cannot be its master, we are not slaves to this process either. We co-create this unfolding. Each living moment arises out of a simultaneous act of effector and effected. Our individual microscale activity, in all its uniqueness is important in a way classical science never imagined.

Demystifying and Reenchanting the World. The new understanding denies dualism, the separation of human- and mind-based dimensions from physical dimensions. We are not a mystery *apart* from the world but part of the mystery *of* the world. So, while we have significantly demystified ourselves, we have also re-enchanted the world and our role in it. Creation is no longer an ancient, surrealistic event but an ongoing mystery unfolding day-to-day in physical reality. And true to religious description, the mystery is in us, of us and more than us all at the same time. Science — our belief in here-and-now facts — and spirituality — our sense of more-to-it-than-this — map to one physically real world.

This sums up the ecological change. How does it fit with spirituality? To explore this I will use the most universal form of spirituality, what is known as the Perennial Philosophy.

ECOLOGY AND THE PERENNIAL PHILOSOPHY

> More than twenty-five centuries have passed since that which has
> been called the Perennial Philosophy was first committed to writ-
> ing; and in the course of those centuries it has found expression,
> now partial, now complete, now in this form now in that, again
> and again. In Vedanta and Hebrew prophecy, in the Tao Te Ching
> and the Platonic dialogues, in the Gospel according to St. John and
> Mahayana theology, in Plotinus and the Areopagite, among the
> Persian Sufis and the Christian mystics of the Middle Ages and the
> Renaissance — the Perennial Philosophy has spoken almost all the
> languages of Asia and Europe and has made use of the terminol-
> ogy and traditions of every one of the higher religions. But under
> all this confusion of tongues and myths, of local histories and
> particularist doctrines, there remains a Highest Common Factor.
>
> *Aldous Huxley, 1954, p. 12*

Ecological science suggests a very strange possibility: traditional spiritual
observations were not superstitious descriptions of a "God" out there but an
accurate description of our very real world and the process from which we
arose, in which we are embedded and which, of necessity, our existence is
designed to serve. Poetical? Perhaps, but also now more physically mean-
ingful than ever before. It is a rather strong possibility that classical science
was too simplistic to fathom the esoteric and the esoterics, being too far
ahead of the world and not systematically grounded to the physical, were
unable to create a reliable conceptual path to their understandings. It took
a lot of scientific progress to build a conceptual structure complex enough
to reach them and still remain connected to the earth. Yet we seem to be
getting there.

The Perennial Philosophy, as the opening quotation notes, is found
across a wide range of spiritual and secular writings, yet, as Huxley says:
"under all this confusion of tongues and myths, of local histories and
particularist doctrines, there remains a Highest Common Factor." I will use
Huxley's (1954) distillation of this basic spiritual essence to show this
essence's similarity to ecological descriptions. Conversely, I'll also use the
distillation to comment on ecological understanding. I use Huxley's words
to describe the Perennial Philosophy and add ecological comments in italics
after each section. Huxley says:

At the core of the Perennial Philosophy we find four fundamental
doctrines:

> 1) The phenomenal world of matter and of individualized consciousness —
> the world of things and animals and men and even gods — is the manifes-
> tation of a Divine Ground within which all partial realities have their being,
> and apart from which they would be nonexistent. (p. 13)

Ecological physics suggests that we are part of a single, unified unfolding
evolutionary process that gives rise to all levels and types of Being. Individual beings arise and then recede in the ever-moving flow. Individual-
ized consciousness are temporary manifestations of the larger whole.

> 2) Human beings are capable not merely of knowing *about* the Divine
> Ground by inference; they can also realize its existence by direct intuition,
> superior to discursive reasoning. This immediate knowledge unites the
> knower with that which is known. (p. 13)

The human mind and no less the human body are the product of a tremendous amount of interwoven, interplaying complexity which connects us
inside and out to all levels of being. We are not separate. We are intrinsically
connected in a way that is much more complicated than just input from the
five senses and mechanical response. Under mechanism, intuition seemed
like a figment of imagination. Under ecology, it seems more like a
reasonable product of a very sensitive and well-connected instrument — a
body/mind that is woven into reality. Rationality has traditionally focused
on the deductive side of the Socratic dialectical loop and that is, at best, half
the equation.

> 3) Man possesses a double nature, a phenomenal ego and an eternal Self,
> which is the inner man, the spirit, the spark of divinity within the soul. It is
> possible for a man, if he so desires, to identify himself with the spirit and
> therefore with the Divine Ground, which is of the same or like Nature with
> the spirit. (p. 13)

Man's double nature makes sense from the ecological perspective. We are
temporary manifestations. It is the whole that is the final Self that is being
evolved. We have a role in that evolution, it is a co-dependent arising. We
have relative autonomy during the space of our existence, and that
autonomy evolved as a function of that larger Self. It evolved as a way to
make the larger Self better — not as a way to escape the whole, as it is often
portrayed. However, our autonomy can be abused, used only for its own
ends, not those of the larger field. And if large enough numbers of us do this
for long enough periods, we will cease to serve the field and we will cease
to exist. The ecological perspective puts a new twist on "identifying with
the Divine Ground"; it is actually an issue of species survival.

> 4) Man's life on earth has only one end and purpose: to identify himself with his eternal Self and so to come to unitive knowledge of the Divine Ground. (p. 13)

I am never sure whether this statement is meant as a fact or a proscription for humankind. The universe is a learning universe. The universe in a certain sense seeks unitive knowledge, as Hegel said "the perfect relations of all its parts" — if such a thing exists. Yet, humankind's position is not privileged in the ecological view. We appear to be able to *not* serve, to use our intelligence stupidly. I hope statement #4 is a fact; I think it should at least be a proscription.

> In regard to man's final end, all the higher religions are in complete agreement. The purpose of human life is the discovery of Truth, the unitive knowledge of the Godhead. (p. 16)

In sum, ecological science appears to have a deep comprehension of and even affinity for the Perennial Philosophy.

PHYSICAL SPIRITUALITY

Ecological science does not validate all spiritual beliefs or all claims made in the name of the different world hypotheses. It simply opens a dialogue between traditionally irreconcilable points of view. One is reminded of the story of the six blind philosophers and the elephant. The structure of their interaction changes when they realize that they *are* all dealing with the same elephant. To my mind, it is nothing short of a miracle that we are beginning to see that it is one elephant and *how* it is one elephant. Who would have believed it? The world is reborn — demystified and re-enchanted — and I expect that 100 years from now it will all seem obvious.

Before closing, let me add two thoughts on how to live in an ecological world. These two thoughts synthesize Perennial Philosophy insights and ecological twists.

Living with the Paradoxes of the Inexorable Co-Dependent Arising. Human beings are in a world that is both inexorable and accidental. We are separate from and yet connected to this world. It is a world of impermanence. We are facing an extended (if not endless) period of becoming. This world creates us at the same time we create it. How does one live in such a world?

The Perennial perspective on action provides some suggestions. In a recursive, complexly interwoven world, whatever one does propagates outward, returns, recycles and comes back in a completely unpredictable form. Like real-life parenting, we can never fully know what we are doing and what will happen. Thus, the Perennial perspective emphasizes doing right as best one can solely because it is right and not for any particular outcome. Outcome is not fully ours to determine. The Perennial perspective leads to what the *Bhagavad Gita* calls High Indifference. One acts from caring concern for the world while knowing that the world is *both* beyond our control yet subject to our actions.

This perspective is exceedingly different from the mechanistic emphasis on outcome with its underlying belief in ability to control outcome. The mechanistic perspective leads to emphasis on winners and the image of winners as the sole "cause" of their successful outcome. This is, of course, accompanied by the tendency to blame losers as being completely responsible for the outcomes they suffer. Mechanism has been very destructive in its simplistic view of how things work.

Giving Up Control. The Perennial Philosophy offers us a yet harder lesson about living in a universe that rushes pell-mell toward change. Trying to hold on to things, to control things is one of the ways we cause our own suffering. The following quotation explains:

> Buddhism avers the possibility of finding lasting peace in the midst of continuous flux... Man is, in fact, obviously prepared to resist just such uncompromising analysis by setting out in single-hearted pursuit of satisfaction, as if it actually represented a *constant*. Yet, in the Buddha's view, it is this very belief in the attainment of lasting happiness, in conventional human terms, that is the true source of suffering. (Ross, 1981, p. 75)

Mechanism did not invent the idea of trying to control things. Control is a deep and fundamental desire attached to the goal of achieving "lasting happiness." It is not something humankind is likely to give up in the near future. Yet, it is a drive we need to relax. The ecological view suggests that change is accelerating (literally). Complexity also accelerates and though we never could control it, our situation seems to be getting worse.[2]

The truly odd thing about giving up the *desire* to control is that it is likely to make us more efficient at improving our condition. This is the deep message of both the Perennial Philosophy and the ecological view. It is not that one does nothing. One simply stops wasting time and energy on trying to force things in a pre-planned, nonnegotiable direction and instead learns to nudge from within, to manage and guide from inside the system — which includes changing oneself as well as one's surroundings. It is very much the kind of notion expressed in Jane Jacobs' "economics of drift." One takes action, the action has a very potent shaping effect, but one also relaxes the drive to control and allows the process to unfold — the process learns, shapes and changes itself through all its component parts, not under the direction of one.

It is going to take some learning for us to believe in this approach, but I think the Perennial Philosophy houses an important lesson for our times. Where individuals might achieve a life time of relative constancy 100 years ago, as things accelerate that possibility becomes more and more remote. Change becomes more and more the norm. Grasping and trying to control becomes more and more dysfunctional. As the Perennial Philosophy teaches, in an evolving world one must anchor oneself in change.

NOTES

1. In Benard cells, the cell-building process is completely repeatable but the particular configuration of cells, their location, relative sizes and directions of roll never occurs the same way twice.
2. This is true because even though our technology grows ever larger, so does its contribution to complexity. Witness the looming specter of ecological disasters portrayed in such recent documentaries as James Burke's "After the Warming." Our more sophisticated technology has both supported poisoning of the planet and allowed us to better understand what we have done to ourselves and our planet. Yet, these things are not easily reversed. I am reminded of the anaerobic bacteria (see Chapter 5) who produced so much oxygen that they poisoned themselves and by doing so served primarily as a stepping stone for the next level, the aerobic bacteria. We can do things, but we are not in control.

Chapter 8

Reconciliation

[There is] a certain Chinese encyclopedia in which it is written that "animals are divided into: a) belonging to the emperor, b) embalmed, c) tame, d) sucking pigs, e) sirens, f) fabulous, g) stray dogs, h) included in the present classification, i) frenzied, j) innumerable, k) drawn with a very fine camel hair brush, l) et cetera, m) having just broken the water pitcher, n) that from a long way off look like flies."

...The wonderment of this taxonomy, the thing we apprehend in one great leap ... as the exotic charm of another system of thought, is a limitation of our own, the stark impossibility of thinking *that*.

Michel Foucault (1973, p. xv)

Having looked at how the ecological vision helps reconcile science and spirituality, let us now look at how it helps reconcile world hypotheses.

I wrote a paper several years ago called "Chaos and Its Implications for Psychology." In that paper I pointed out that one of the amazing things about Chaos was that psychologists from traditionally irreconcilable schools of thought were all embracing it as a way to renew their specialty. I have seen it embraced by Skinnerian Behaviorists, Freudians, Jungians, Gestaltists, Cognitive psychologists, Family Systems therapists, Existential Psychologists, and Transpersonal psychologists. This fact is notable because many of these people would experience Foucault's "stark impossibility of thinking *that*" when faced with the beliefs of the others.

The situation in psychology is not unusual. Some traditions know mystical experiences happen and are an important part of human knowledge of the world. Some traditions tie their understanding to empirical observation and believe that what science has pieced together represents the realistic view of the world. Other traditions see patterns to the vicissitudes of life; they see the world unfolding along some hidden developmental path, like a great organism. Still others see things as being somehow pulled in a direction, attracted toward some destination, some ideal form. These visions of how the world works are Pepper's world hypotheses. They are alive and well, subtly woven into everyday thinking.

What is notable is that these different traditions are generally not on speaking terms. As a result, there are deep schisms between long-standing, well-established knowledge systems. Put more strongly, the result is the *fragmentation* of human knowing. In psychology the fragmentation is obvious and a source of major concern in the field. In human discourses at large the fragmentation is also obvious, but we have become so used to it that people rarely question it. People assume it could be no other way. Seeing differently must of needs mean irreconcilable differences.

This chapter is about why seeing differently might not mean seeing irreconcilably. It is about Chaos and ecologism's very strange ability to support the basic images of all the previous metaphors of how the world works and show how they all fit together. It shows quite concretely how the world is *all* of the above, not *one* of the above.

To lay the groundwork for understanding, I will develop Stephen Pepper's work (1946) to show the nature and history of the different world hypotheses.

PEPPER'S WORLD HYPOTHESES

So far I've talked primarily about two world hypotheses, mechanism and ecologism. However, Pepper discusses six world hypotheses as follows:

Animism uses the metaphor of the human being. — All things animate and inanimate are described as human forms. The sun, stars, trees, rivers, winds and clouds become personal animate creatures that conform to human analogies.

Mysticism uses the metaphor of the mystic experience. — The world and everything in it is understood in terms of revelation, wonderment and our potential contact with the ultimate ground of all things.

Formism uses the metaphor of similarity between two things. The world contains similarity hidden at all levels; real things are approximations to ideal forms.

Mechanism uses the metaphor of the machine. The world and everything in it are described as machines.

Organicism uses the metaphor of a biological organism. The world is described as an evolving organism.

Contextualism uses the metaphor of the unique historical event in a context The world is a poised living moment woven of complex interconnected threads.

I will focus on the four most cognitive of these — contextualism, formism, mechanism, and organicism — as their philosophical traditions are clearer. Pepper describes philosophical traditions behind these core metaphors as follows: (I will explicate each with examples from psychology.)

Formism (similarity). "Formism is often called 'realism' or 'Platonic idealism.' It is associated with Plato, Aristotle, the scholastics, neoscholastics, neorealists, modern Cambridge realists" (Pepper 1946, p. 141). The original source of formism is "the simple common-sense perception of similar things. The world is full of things that seem to be just alike: blades of grass, leaves on a tree... On more careful scrutiny, perhaps we find that blades of grass are not exactly alike... Our discrimination of differences becomes more acute, but so also does our discrimination of the grounds of similarity" (Pepper 1946, p. 151).

Formism taught humankind to classify things. It emphasized that two or more things can have one or more characteristics in common. Often classes can in turn be grouped into higher classes as in biology's familiar series: species, family, genus. etc. "Formistic philosophical systems assume that the phenomena of the world can be understood by assigning them to specific classes of types" (Berry 1984, p. 448).

The original formists also asked *why* things were similar. Their answer was that each member of a class was actually an imperfect material manifestation of an ideal form. The ideal form existed beyond the material world and acted like a magnet, drawing matter toward its ideal. They said that the forms we see in the sensible world are mere shadows of the ideal. This separation between real (material) manifestation and ideal form is a controversial aspect of formist thinking.

Formism is seen in psychology in diagnostic categories and typologies of all kinds. The fact that it is very hard to find a perfect example of any particular category or type shows the formist separation of real phenomena and ideal form. The category exists separate from any particular individual or even any set of individual; it is an ideal which guides both our thinking and the appearance of reality.

Mechanism (the machine). "Mechanism is often called 'naturalism' or 'materialism' and, by some, 'realism.' It is associated with Democritus, Lucretius, Galileo, Descartes, Hobbes, Locke, Berkeley, Hume, Reichenbach" (Pepper 1946, p. 141). "Mechanistic philosophical systems assume that the phenomena of the world can be understood by analyzing them into their working parts, each with a specific location, and by specifying how each part is acted on by other parts, all within a specifiable antecedent-consequent time sequence" (Berry 1984, p. 448).

Mechanism emphasizes quantifiable qualities that can be used to describe an effective relationship of *law* that holds among the parts. Machines are divisible into parts that interact with one another in a cause-and-effect way. Mechanism is where humankind first learned causal analysis, the study of orderly causal relationships between parts and forces.

Various schools of psychological thought have held to the dream of deriving lawful relationships of quantifiable qualities. Early stimulus-response learning theory is probably the best example (e.g., Pavlov, Hull's *Behavior System*, and Skinnerian Behaviorism). However, cognitive psychologists who argue that the human mind is like a computer also fall into a mechanist category.

Organicism (the evolving organism). "Organicism is commonly called 'absolute (or objective) idealism' It is associated with Schelling, Hegel, Green, Bradley, Bosanquet, Royce" (Pepper 1946, p. 141). "Organismic philosophical systems assume that the phenomena of the world exist as parts of some larger unfolding whole that is in the process of developing toward some final end state that is an integrated whole" (Berry 1984, p. 448). The underlying organic process guides a system's development through various qualitative transformations as it moves toward a final form. The final form is believed to have been implicit in the original form. Organicism is where humankind first learned to see a system as a coherent total process with a specific end.

Organicism tends to emphasize the mechanisms and/or stages of development and the end toward which development moves. For example, dialectics (the famous "thesis, antithesis and synthesis") is a form of organicism. This form of organicism emphasizes an organic process hidden beneath a fragmented surface-level experience that proceeds through the mechanism of struggle. At the surface-level, the system struggles with unresolved issues which appear as a thesis and its opposing antithesis. The underlying order is revealed when the thesis and its antithesis dissolve into one, an organic synthesis. The synthesis preserves the opposing truths while showing that the contradictions were in fact not really contradictory at all. The synthesis was thus implicit in the original struggle; polarization was merely part of the process of working through. In dialectics, as in many other forms of organicism, the process moves toward a final absolute and predetermined end. This is a controversial aspect of organismic thinking.

In psychology organicism is seen in Rogerian therapy, Family therapy, and some Jungian therapy. In Rogerian therapy, for example, the organism is described as having a drive towards health that seeks to overcome conditions of worth. These conditions of worth are very much the contradictions and oppositions described in the organic dialectical process. The fully functioning individual is a potential (a final form) implicit in the original child.

Contextualism (the historical event in context). Contextualism is commonly called "pragmatism." It is associated with Pierce, James, Bergson, Dewey, Mead. There may be a trace of it in the Greek, Protagoras (Pepper 1946, p. 141). "Contextualistic philosophical systems assume that the phenomena of the world can be understood by recognizing that all events are unique and must, therefore, be related to the specific context in which they occur, and which are themselves constantly changing" (Berry 1984, p. 448). Contextualism is where humankind first learned to see complexity, uniqueness, and unpredictability — in a way not opposed to order.

The metaphor of contextualism is the historic event in context. However, as Pepper emphasizes, the term "historic event" should not be used to imply *past* event, for the true focus of contextualism is the *living* event. The living moment is intrinsically complex, composed of interconnected activities, with continuously changing patterns. In the living moment the threads of past and future come together in a pivotal moment, and this pivotal moment alone determines the next living moment. It is the job of the contextualist to reveal the many threads woven in the moment. The better one sees the patterns in the fabric, the better one is able to chose a path.

In psychology we see contextualism in Gestalt therapy, Transactional Analysis and Phenomenology. For example, in Gestalt, therapy the living moment, the here-and-now, contains not only the reality of the here-and-now but also the shadows of all of the painful there-and-thens. While the living moment is all there is, these hidden historical shadows cause pain; they produce psychopathology by affecting the living moment from moment to moment. Gestalt exercises move the there-and-thens hidden in the unconscious into view in the here-and-now. Once individuals can see, they can choose.

THE EVOLUTION OF THE FOUR WORLD HYPOTHESES

To get yet a better sense of these traditions, let me give an overview of their historical positions.

Formism, most visible in the writings of Plato and Aristotle (circa 400 B.C.), was the first of the four cognitive world hypotheses. It arose in reaction to the established mythological view, a world governed by temperamental and erratic gods. Greek philosophers such as Plato emphasized the human ability to know in reaction to the sense of impotence that came from the mythological view. Portraying a world filled with ordered forms, the original Greek formism supported the image of a natural cosmos that could be known by human reason. It was one of the earliest types of Western science. Formism in various guises ebbed and flowed in cultural influence until challenged by mechanism beginning around A.D. 1600.

Formism's advance over the previous mythological beliefs made it a triumph of human reason. Aristotle believed that through formistic explanation and ordering, human knowledge would very shortly reach completion. Yet, the course of a philosophy does not seem to run as originally intended. The Greek civilization fragmented over long years of city-state wars and was eventually lost in the rise of the Roman Empire. The Roman Empire in turn was engulfed by barbarians and then transformed by the rise of Christianity.

Around A.D. 400, St. Augustine blended Plato's formist philosophy with Christianity and Scholastic philosophy to the benefit of all. Writing during the collapse of the Roman Empire, Augustine used both Christianity and Platonic formism as an anchor in the descending darkness. In *The City of God* he uses Plato's distinction between the sensible and intelligible worlds as an explanation of the earthly flux that hides the grounding of God's eternal truth. He argued that, despite the chaos all around, humankind was being pulled toward a higher form.

The darkness did descend and through the Middle Ages, the Church grew as a type of firmament. By the 13th century, the church existed as a monolith of surety. It is against this backdrop that Thomas Aquinas brought formism in its Scholastic form to its perfection. Aquinas transformed Christian Scholasticism by blending it with Aristotle's work which had been rediscovered and translated early in the 13th century. In the Thomist view the world exists in a great hierarchy of being, each with its own form and purpose, ending with the Idea of Good (God). Thomism claimed absolute truth based on faith, revelation with support from formistic reason. Ironically, the world view that started as an assertion against supernatural control evolved into a demonstration of supernatural control — God's perfect order.

Mechanism arose then as a reaction to a "perfected" formism. In his *Summa Theologiae*, Aquinas seemed to have worked out everything one could do with formism. Here was a well worked out system that claimed absolute truth and yet had many fundamental gaps. Foremost among these was the complete inability to predict. Formism could explain *after* the fact why something happened and tell you what to call it, but it couldn't tell you what would happen before the fact. It also couldn't tell you what to do to *make* something happen.

From our current perspective it seems strange that people had not reacted against formism's impractical aspects earlier. However, interest in practical concerns was the focus of a budding new context. The rise of guilds in the 13th century reflected a new concern for practical application and accompanying development of techniques. People were beginning to move out of the feudal agrarian world into a world of expanded commerce and non-agrarian technology. People in these times presumed the existence of God. Nevertheless, they were becoming increasingly concerned with earthly issues — even if only as a way to get closer to God, as in the case of the alchemists. Alchemy and the scientific revolution were all part of this great resurgence of earthly concern. It is small wonder that a pragmatic earth-based world hypothesis arose in conjunction with this new focus.

Mechanism began the swing back from a supernatural to a natural universe. It began the re-assertion of human reason's power to know. Since most of us were raised with mechanistic (scientific) assumptions I will not review its history. Suffice it to say that mechanism's ability to predict and design technology has been so compelling that today most westerners know only vestigial formism — categories, classes, typologies, etc. — long since torn from the original theory and philosophy. A modern mechanist generally: 1) doesn't know formism existed; 2) finds it unimaginably primitive; or 3) sees it as essentially a religious not a scientific system. Mechanism's technological power has made it western society's great legitimizer. For mechanists, that which came before seems like religion, not science.

For most Americans mechanism is the last world hypothesis; it is still culturally dominant in the West. However, mechanism's first philosophical successor arose nearly two hundred years ago at the time of the great revolutions (18th century). The story of the French Revolution reveals the omissions of the great mechanistic enterprise.

The material progress that accompanied mechanism spawned a sense of optimism about the ultimate progress of humankind — mechanism seemed to be *the* path to rationality and enlightenment. Enlightenment philosophers such as Voltaire, Diederot and the French Encyclopedists described a "natural law" of progress. At its outset, the French Revolution seemed to be the natural child of this enlightened rationality. Its premises were reason, rational order and harmony of nature. Yet, its actuality included the reign of terror, mob violence, and the eventual rise of a form of absolutism even more complete than the monarchy it overthrew.

The French Revolution is a clear example of where mechanism didn't work. Mechanism could not predict the complex interaction of masses of people in the process of social change, the transformation from one cultural form to another. Its image of prediction and control did not fit chaos, catastrophe and transformation.

Frustration with mechanistic rationality gave rise to the Romantic revolution — a resurgence of human arts which were not dominated by reason. Romanticism gave refuge to those dissatisfied with the mechanistic rationality that could not deal with emotion, social transformation, and cultural change.

While cultural events such as the French Revolution were revealing one set of omissions in mechanism, philosophers such as David Hume were revealing another. As mechanism had grown farther away from the God-given clarity invoked by its founders, it had grown more and more dependent on empiricist or sense-supplied rationales. David Hume's skeptical arguments showed that empirical suppositions actually came from inside the human mind. For example, our belief in cause and effect does not come from sense impressions but from our habit of labeling certain types of association as causal. As far as we can tell, causality exists only in our mind. Science according to Hume, is not based on sense-data but on habits of mind.

Hume's critique lead to Kant's revision of empiricism. Kant accepted Hume's observation that the mind gives order to sense impressions. However, he revised this observation by saying that all knowing is based originally on *a priori* assumptions that stem from an internal direct human knowing. He then restored empiricism by claiming to have found the correct foundational assumptions that give certainty to human knowing. We would never know the things-in-themselves but, according to Kant, with the correct foundation science could still claim to be a machine that cranks out certain knowledge.

It was in the context of Kant's work and German Romanticism that Hegel developed the most famous form of organicism. God is gone, human emotions are beyond mere reason, and empiricism is built in part out of our own minds. Is there any reason, then, to believe that there is order in the universe? Hegel managed to produce an observation and a synthesis that said: "yes, there is order." The observation was his famous dialectical process, thesis-antithesis-synthesis. According to Hegel, world history shows us that as humans think about any concept, they find its limitations and then develop its opposite, the very negation of the original form. The negation in turn is found to have its limitations. The conflict between the two limited forms eventually resolves into a synthesis that transcends the polarity and preserves the truth of the two. For Hegel, the totality of human thought was like an Absolute Mind moving toward its final perfection through the dialectical process. Mechanism couldn't describe such a process because it had no conception of a pull toward something. In mechanism chaos was just chaos with no direction or order underneath.

Hegel's organicism restored the sense of global order moving inexorably toward perfection. But, true to its own vision, its limitations were tied to its strengths. Organicism suggested blind faith in the future; after all, the perfect world was in the process of unfolding. Complacent in this vision, the Romantic tradition failed to react to the growing specter of authoritarianism — a specter that eventually resulted in Hitler, Mussolini, and Franco. Because the Absolute mind is moving toward a final perfection, authors such as Marx claimed that the end, a final complete synthesis of human history, was at hand. The synthesis he claimed was communism and dialectical materialism. This synthesis started with great humanitarian intentions but devolved into dogmatism and totalitarian control. Because the world is unfolding through a process of conflict, it didn't matter how many bodies or how much destruction accrued. Revolutionaries such as Stalin could feel justified in being ruthless — it was part of the evolutionary process. Thus, in assuring us of globally imposed order, organicism invited complacency, dogmatism and unaccountability. It suggested the future was preordained.

Contextualism arose in reaction to organicism's excess of inevitability and globally imposed order. Contextualism retains organicism's sense of historic flow, but it specifically rejects the notion of the pull of some higher order. Contextualists such as Pierce, James, and Mead fix us back in the here-and-now. They look specifically at "how" things happen; "how" a story unfolds and thus why it unfolds in the *specific* way that it does. Human beings are seen as creating their own order in a complex context — the living moment which holds all the threads of past, present and future.

Contextualism is young enough that it is difficult to provide historical examples of its weaknesses. However, its relative lack of internal coherence does give a sense of the most likely problem: dispersiveness. Contextualists have many stories. They truly bring out the richness of the living moment. However, their principles cannot tell how the stories relate or where, if anywhere, they are going. The result is a sense of "anything goes"; prediction or anything that looks like a prescribed direction is particularly absent.

Table 8.1. The Dynamics of World Hypotheses

Hypothesis	Philosopher time	Primary observation	Major weakness
Formism	Plato, Aristotle (400 B.C.)	The pull of form; similarity relates to common attractor.	No description of how parts create the event, hence no prediction.
Mechanism	Descartes, Bacon, Kant (A.D. 1600)	Describes how parts create the event and hence supports prediction. Adds precision and clarity of mathematics.	Mechanism's bottom-up focus cannot see underlying order and does not allow for the pull of a global phenomenon. Could not handle chaos and catastrophe in complex phenomena.
Organicism	Hegel (A.D. 1800)	Describes underlying order indicating global process that operates across chaos and catastrophe.	Loses role of parts in creating this global process hence loses ability to describe why in the here-and-now. Also suggests inexorable final end that opens the door to dogmatic claims.
Contextualism	Heidegger, James (A.D. 1900)	Explains why in the living moment hence restores potency of the parts and restores content to local flows.	Has no sense of global coherence or of precision.

In countering organicism's inexorable order, contextualism seems to have lost all ties to lawfulness and order.

STRENGTHS AND WEAKNESSES

World hypotheses emerge from the dynamics of a particular context. They, in turn, create a new context which spawns an alternative world hypothesis. We have evolved a number of these to date. Table 8.1 summarizes the four cognitive world hypotheses and their major strengths and weaknesses.

Given that new world hypotheses tend to emerge in reaction to the omission of their predecessors, it is not surprising that they might not be on speaking terms. Yet there deeper reasons for not being on speaking terms. Pepper notes that each hypothesis tends to assume both its own completeness and universal scope. In other words, each assumes that it is the final word and that everything in the world works according to the metaphor. Unfortunately, in their traditional forms, none of these ways of looking at the world adequately explains the major focus of any of the others. For example, traditional mechanism doesn't explain the directedness of organismic development and traditional organicism doesn't explain how parts can generate a developmental flow. The common results of assuming one's own view to be complete and seeing no way to another's view is insularity; each view stands alone and may either ignore or throw stones at the others.

We come then to ecologism, a new world hypothesis with the root metaphor of an evolving ecology and specifically an evolving ecology as refined by the set of scientific discoveries reviewed in Part II. In a certain sense the ecological world hypothesis is emerging in reaction to the omissions of *all* of the previous understandings. Yet, the result of this reaction is unusual. Its first unusual characteristic is that it does not see itself as either complete or final. Ecologism sees itself as a *new* stage in the ongoing evolution of human knowledge, but not the final or complete stage. Its second unusual feature is that it sees/includes all of the previous. Thus, ecologism supports and expands the major observations of all of its predecessors. As with spirituality, this does not mean ecologism supports everything that has been said in the name of various world hypotheses, only the major observations. Still the result is unusual. Instead of causing yet a new fragmentation of human knowing, this world hypothesis opens the door to reconciling and hence connecting the existing knowledge traditions. This is a very unusual situation.

Table 8.2 summarizes how ecological science reconciles and extends the existing world hypotheses.

ANIMISM AND MYSTICISM

Perhaps more oddly still, the same reconciliation can be extended to animism and mysticism. So, let me take a moment to review these two hypotheses:

Mysticism. Mysticism understands the world in terms of revelation, wonderment and our potential contact with the ultimate ground of all things. The section on the Perennial Philosophy suggests how the ecologi-

Table 8.2. Reconciling World Hypotheses

Hypothesis/ philosopher	Primary observation	Major weakness	Ecological resolution
Formism Plato, Aristotle (400 B.C.)	The pull of form; similarity relates to common attractor.	No description of how dynamics create form and consequently no ability to predict or explain variations of form or evolution.	Shows how activity of the parts create form and thus expands formist understandings into the realm of variation and evolution of form.
Mechanism Descartes, Bacon, Kant (A.D. 1600)	Describes how parts create the event and hence supports prediction; Adds precision and clarity of mathematics.	Over-focus on independence and reductionism blocks explanation of attraction toward form, direction, spontaneous order-production and top down causality.	Expands mechanism into the realm of non-linear interdependence and thus opens the door to explaining attraction, chaos, bifurcations direction, order-production and top down causality.
Organicism Hegel (A.D. 1800)	Describes underlying order indicating global process that operates across chaos and catastrophe.	Loses the role of the dynamics in sustaining and directing the systems organization hence tendency to assume development follows a fixed path. Fails to integrate historical uniqueness.	Restores an understanding of historical uniqueness, chance, and unpredictability into what is nevertheless an inexorable dialectical developmental flow.
Contextualism Heidegger, James (A.D. 1900)	Explains why in the living moment hence restores potency of the parts and restores content to local flows.	Fails to see the global coherence and underlying order that lies behind the infinitely unique historical events.	Shows how infinitely unique historical events can nevertheless be part of an coherent interwoven global process developing in an overall direction and having rules of competence.

cal vision understands mysticism: we are woven into the whole. It is easy to image the mystical unitive knowing as a form of communing with the community of being that is within us and that connects us to the larger whole. Our bodies and minds are much more sensitively coupled and deeply integrated into a larger process than classical science imagined. We each contain more information than was dreamt of in mechanistic philosophy.

Animism. Animism uses the metaphor of the human being to describe all things animate and inanimate, in human forms. The sun, stars, trees, rivers, winds and clouds become personal animate creatures that conform to human analogies. Animism is the hardest of the world hypotheses for a scientific mind to fathom. Yet the following passage helps provide a reason why it makes sense. Interestingly enough, this passage was written by Jacques Monod as part of a condemnation of animism in its modern form, vitalism.

> Our ancestors, we must presume, perceived the strangeness of their condition only very dimly. They did not have the reasons we have today for feeling themselves strangers in the universe upon which they opened their eyes. What did they see first? Animals, plants; beings whose nature they could at once device as similar to their own. Plants grow, seek sunlight, die... These beings all have an aim, purpose: to live and to go on living... But around them our ancestors saw other objects far more mysterious: rocks, rivers, mountains, the thunderstorm, the stars in the sky. If these objects exist it must also be for a purpose; to nourish it they had also to have a spirit or soul... Thus our forebears were wont to see in nature's forms and events the action of forces either benign or hostile, but never indifferent — never totally alien. [In this way] animism established a covenant between nature and man, a profound alliance outside of which seems to stretch only terrifying solitude. (Monod 1972, pp. 29–30)

Monod argues that the covenant with nature that animism represents is a type of wishful thinking that we must relinquish. We cling to it and this clinging keeps us from looking at the "reality" of evolution. Ecological science allows us to take an opposite tack. Animism's covenant with nature represents an *observation* that we are in a profound alliance with nature. In the ecological perspective this observation is not a wishful thought but a realization that we need to take on. Perhaps animism too can be appreciated for the unrealized accuracy of its observation. The "reality" of evolution is probably much different from what mechanism imagined.

Thus, it might be possible to add another row to Table 8.2:

Hypothesis/ philosopher	Primary observation	Major weakness	Ecological resolution
Mysticism and Animism — predates Western philosophy	Connectedness or relatedness of all things; humanity is part of a larger Being. Direct intuitive knowledge is possible; the things in the world are like us and we are like them.	No explanation of how mystical insights arise and poor ties to empiricism, hence little ability to check the accuracy of mystical insights.	Chaos retains empiricism yet portrays human mind and body as deeply integrated and evolutionarily tuned into the whole system. "Information" can be carried by noise and thus may enter from any part of the body not just the five senses. Mystical experiences may be a form of knowing arising from our deep evolutionary entwinement with the world. It may be our most fundamental form of knowing. We are not alienated, we are connected.

ON SPEAKING TERMS

If you are a traditional mechanist, teleology (pull of form) of any kind is anti-scientific nonsense — but now we know about strange attractors. If you are a traditional mechanist, life is an accident and the universe as a whole is directionless, the only organic unfolding going on is in biology — but now we see the universe as a whole as undergoing a developmental unfolding. If you are a traditional mystic, science is a form of short-sighted dogmatic materialism that has little to offer — but this form of science fathoms spirituality and unitive knowing.

Ecological science provides a basis for an ecology of knowledge built from existing views. A mechanist should no longer laugh at the formist notion of matter being attracted toward a form nor a mystic decry mechanism's inability to fathom humankind's embeddedness in the large mystery. Well-meaning individuals from all quarters can reach each other's perspective. Philosophical dialogue becomes possible where philosophical imperialism has long dominated. This is indeed an unusual state of affairs.

CHAPTER 9

Empowerment

> We make our destinies by our choice of gods.
>
> *Virgil*

Newtonian mechanism resulted in images like: "big effects require big causes"; you are a fixed product of your genes; competition and self-interest are the governing rules of survival; and life is an accident. At various times all of this has been promoted as scientific fact. Contrary to Enlightenment dreams, mechanism ended up producing a very grim god.

One's sense of empowerment in the world comes from one's sense of how the world works and how one fits in it. The amount and type of empowerment we feel defines the amount and type of effort we will exert to improve our own and the world's condition.

Mechanism produced a context for human action marked by extremes: pockets of omnipotence and pockets of impotence. How does the deep ecological vision's very different perspective affect our sense of how we fit in the world and how does that change our sense of empowerment?

THE SHIFTED PERCEPTION OF HOW WE FIT IN THE WORLD

I believe the vision of an evolving ecological world produces the following shifts in perspective:

Emphasizing Becoming Instead of Being (Rejection of Absolutes and Finalities). In the ecological vision, systems do not move to final, constant or repetitive solutions; no system can claim to be "the final system" of anything. This is a major shift from classical-science thinking which expected to reach the end of things. An ecological society knows itself to be just one step in a larger process. Its current state conserves important ways of being but growth will continue, change will occur. Its focus is not on status quo ("this way is best and must be preserved") but on guiding evolution ("what is the best way to go").

Becoming Members Instead of Masters. The notion of systems that are lawful but which can never be precisely predicted puts an end to dreams of human omnipotence. There are definite limits to our ability to know and control. The subtle implication here is that humankind will always remain a member of the world, not its absolute master.

Empowering the Small. The ecological vision shifts our concern from large events that speak for themselves to the myriad of small events that are the heart of any ecology. At a first level this means that individuals can and do make a difference. Sometimes the difference will be pivotal and sometimes not. But regardless of the immediate effect, connectivity suggests that the effects of all acts ripple out and subtly change the world. Thus, the deep implication is that everything we do counts. The religious understanding of "living a right life" becomes a powerful stance, a way in which everyone helps change the world.

Deep Awareness of Subtle Causality (The Responsibilities of Action and Inaction). Classical science promoted the idea that micro-scale interactions did not affect macro-scale systems. In doing so it cut out half the truth of things and found itself unable to understand how order is produced. The history of evolution from chemical networks through civilization provides a graphic sense of subtle causality at work across all scales. The phrase "there are no separate problems anymore" has new meaning. The old blitheness with which we used to discount things goes away. We can never again toss an action out and think we can predict all its effects. Nor can we look at the actions of others and think that they are or can be contained. Everything is grist for the mill and we are all in that mill. Self-interest changes. An old truth becomes more real: injustice anywhere is a threat to justice everywhere. Subtle causality and its direct connection to us makes it harder to hide comfortably in apathy. Taking action is an affair to be done with humility but inaction has its own effect.

Society Centers Its Identity Around Being a Learning System. There is a rubric in business that says the great railroad companies went out of business because they saw themselves in the railroad business, not in the transportation business. These companies died because their identity was centered around a particular manifestation or form rather than the process. Classical thinking encourages identification with form. It thus encourages both resistance to change (clinging to form) and ill-considered change (belief in Utopian final forms). By centering its identity around being a learning system — by looking for ways to grow, improve, and change — an ecological society becomes both more active and more responsible in its search for a more just society.

This last point epitomizes the ecological approach to creating a just society. If one believes that everything evolves, then the solution to the problem of a just society is not a particular structure; it is not even a particular definition of what is "just." Rather "towards a just society" is the name of a quest to which we commit ourselves. It is much like science.

HOW DOES OUR UNDERSTANDING OF ACTION CHANGE?

So: we affect the world both by action and inaction, and we need humility and responsibility to keep us honest. Yet, the ecological understanding also implies a different understanding of what we are doing. Thus, I offer the following additions to the general change in perspective:

Learning to Guide Growth Instead of Trying to Fix Problems. Mechanism, seeing the world as predictable in principle, focuses on solutions to problems. It focuses on actions at single points in time and imagines a change from a wrong state to a right state. Thus operating on the world is like fixing a broken clock. Massive drug enforcement will fix the drug problem; communism (you can substitute any number of other "isms") will solve the problem of human society.

Ecologism, seeing the world as ever-unfolding, focuses on guiding evolution in ways that maximize functional growth. Systems are thought of as evolving through various states which are functional and dysfunctional in a wide range of ways. Evolution is a recursive, learn-by-doing process and is not a problem that is going to be solved in some single-action simplistic way. Ecologism brings home one fundamental message: to apply the simplistic sense of "solving" problems to important complex systems is to fiddle while Rome burns. Complexity grows apace and evolution waits for no system. Simplistic solutions that do not look seriously at the structure of the system offer a short-term distraction at the risk of future disaster.

Emphasizing the Relationship Between Things. In a complexly inter-woven world sequential and either/or logic breaks down. Debates about whether "this" or "that" is the fundamental element seem increasingly absurd — e.g. heredity or environment in psychology; replication or meta-bolism in biology; bottom-up causation or top-down causation in philosophy. And the hardest thing to grasp is that the absurdity comes from the *way* the question is posed — either/or, first, primary, etc. In an inter-woven world questions of either/or, first or primary make no sense. The question is "how do things work?" and this is best addressed by improving our understanding of the relationships between things.

This focusing on understanding relationships is an issue that goes well beyond science. In science two partial truths vying for supremacy look like the heredity/environment debate. In human sectors, two partial truths vying for supremacy are more likely to look like "individual versus society" or "conservatism versus liberalism" debates. Here simplistic dichotomous thinking is much more dangerous. Which should come first, the individual or society? The answer is, of course, Yes-Yes (or No-No), but in human arenas the confusion that results has much more potential for harm. We need to become more subtle in our understandings. Only by understanding how relationships enhance and restrict each other can we optimize syncretism — the good of each and all.

OUT OF ADOLESCENCE?

> COSMIC NONSENSE: is any model of the universe that claims to be final and exhaustive.
>
> *E. M. Robinson (1987)*

The problem with mechanism was that it was both simplistic and arrogant. One is reminded of adolescence. The great sense of power that comes with first real power also tends to make one think one knows everything, can make anything happen, and that shortly the world's problems will be worked out. And then one reaches one's twenties (thirties?). One actually has more power, but it doesn't necessarily seem like it. Usually by forty humility sets in.

The ecological vision does not give us a simplistic vision of the world. It requires that we take the question of how the world works seriously — what are the relationships between things, how do they effect each other, in what ways do they work together or work against each other ... how should we intervene? The answers it suggests are sometimes simple but they are never simplistic.

Empowerment? Yes, in ways that mechanism simply did not allow. We each and all count more. The potential for change and improvement ex-pands. Our current state of being doesn't define the limits of human poten-tial anymore than Cro-Magnon Man defined human potential. Our knowledge of how things work expands even though our sense of control diminishes. Our sense of the importance and sensitivity of action expands with our growing awareness. Survival becomes a much different affair. What can we afford to allow? How must we change? In short, we have more power, more responsibility and a more complex relationship to each other and the world.

How does this type of empowerment change us? For one thing it forces a shift of focus. We stop waiting for the larger-than-life hero to save the world and begin appreciating the everyday "us"es who form the world. Ecologism does not support a single focus of control or a sense of the primacy of big things or special people. It takes all of us to make an ecology and we are all in this together. And this time species survival is more of an issue. We will either stand up en masse and save ourselves or we will probably die.

It is much like growing up. The responsibilities one takes on become broader, more real; the competence required is greater but at the same time the sense of omnipotence grows less. We put away our dreams of being the world's master and begin to appreciate our role as a member of the chain of Being. This is a large part of what the Ecological transformation is about: not a glorious new Utopia, but the possible onset of maturity.

CHAPTER 10

Thoughts on Our Time

> Two dangers threaten the world, order and disorder.
>
> *Paul Valery*

And now to questions about our current moment in history...

It is not possible to look at recent events in Russia, Eastern Europe, and China and not be struck by how well the notions of ecological science fit. The images are there: the inability to restrain change, the limitations of a form which creates conditions that drive the next phase into being; small fluctuations amplified by conditions into a transformation of form; the acceleration of change and the growth of complexity as a cause and requirement of transformation. Nor is the United States immune. Economically, politically, and socially it too shows signs of an impending crisis. And yet, while the model fits, what does it means? What does it suggest is happening and what should we do? This chapter looks at these questions.

PROBLEMS IN THE CURRENT STRUCTURE

In Chapter 1, I noted that the sense of accelerating change and of a complexly interconnected world was more than just a surface phenomenon. The changes occurring now are not just evolution in a metaphoric sense but also part of evolution in a physical sense. Many people already believe that changes are occurring because the level of interconnectedness/complexity and the pace of change in the modern world demand different ways of being, new organizational structures, new types of relating. There are no separate problems anymore — and this requires new ways of doing things. The physics of evolution confirms that the sense of increasing pace of change is not just an impression or an exceptional case; it is and will continue to be the norm. Things will only get faster. The physics of evolution also suggests that in all likelihood, the dramatic changes now occurring represent Western civilization having reached the structural limitations of some dominant form. This section looks at some of the structural limitations that may be driving the current crisis.

The Transactions of Decline

What isn't working? Jacobs (1984) provides some insights from the economic dimension. She notes that certain types of economic actions lead inevitably to economic downfall. Specifically, traditional ways of building empires (explicitly or via sphere of influence) include certain types of economic transactions that both hold the empire together and at the same time provide the seeds of its own eventual downfall. She calls these "the transactions of decline." In order to hold itself together, empires manipulate economic ties to provide the *means* for holding the system together. This includes maintenance of large militaries, economic placation of rebellious factions and artificial economic structuring that centralizes control and fosters dependence on the state. Such relations produce a lot of economic activity, but they do not produce structurally sound, self-generating economic ecologies. The result is the growth of a larger and larger politico-economic entity built on an ever more fragile economic ecology.

Jacobs' analysis provides a clearer picture of how self-generating, organically evolved economic structures are a critical issue in the survival of any economic system. When the fine-grained structure of an economy is manipulated for political purposes the result is a structure that houses the seeds of its own destruction. As she says:

> Successful imperialism wins wealth. Yet, historically, successful empires such as Persia, Rome, Byzantium, Turkey, Spain, Portugal, France, Britain, have not remained rich. Indeed, it seems to be the fate of empires to become too poor to sustain the very costs of empire. The longer an empire holds together, the poorer and more economically backward it tends to become. (p. 182)

Jacobs argues that the very policies and transactions that are necessary to win, hold and exploit an empire are destructive to an imperial power's own economy. Imperial decline is built right into imperial success. The destructive transactions fall into three main groups: prolonged and unremitting military production; prolonged and unremitting subsidies to poor regions; heavy promotion of trade between advanced and backward economies. As Jacobs notes:

> To see why this is so, one need only notice the kinds of economies possessed by military bases... At Camp Lejeune ... North Carolina, loaded trucks rumble throughout ... the receiving hours of the day, bringing in their

freights of peanut butter, business machines, dental drills... A rail line inter-
minably drops off its deposits too. This has been going on day after day,
year after year, decade after decade — all production irretrievably useless
for stimulating or feeding the import-replacing process anywhere, owing to
its very destination. (p. 187)

Note that despite the ideological issues surrounding imperialism, Jacobs'
argument is economic not political. She emphasizes that nations or empires
do not get into these predicaments by choice:

Germany supports French agricultural regions because if it didn't, the
European Economic Community would break down, and France insists on
the subsidies as a condition of its membership because otherwise France
could not contain the anger of its farmers or the ever simmering threat of
separatism in the country's south. Canada frankly calls its systems of national equalization payments to poor provinces the sinews that hold the
country together and combats separatist sentiments in Quebec in the same
fashion that the English combat separatist feelings in Scotland: by remind-
ing pensioners and other recipients of transfer payments ... where their
money is coming from. (p. 213)

It doesn't actually matter how understandable the motives may seem. The
same types of transactions that make the declines of empires inevitable can
also speed stagnation and decay in non-imperial powers that adopt them.
No matter what the motives for them, classic imperial policies and transactions destroy the economic ecology and lead to stagnation and decay.

Writing in 1984, well before the recent events in the former Soviet
Union, Jacobs noted that the governments of both the Soviet Union and
China depend to an extreme degree on transactions of decline to hold their
political units together. Whatever wealth Soviet or Chinese cities created
was promptly devoted to subsidies for other parts of the nation and purposes
of the state.

Her analysis suggests that the Soviet and Chinese communist economies
were/are not significant new episodes in economic history but rather traditional imperialistic economies. Both systems overran old empires on the
brink of dissolution and succeeded in reconsolidating them by force of
arms. The only thing that changed significantly was the greater competence, efficiency and ruthlessness which the communist regimes brought
to the task of holding these sovereignties together.

She also notes that the same transactions of decline can be seen in the
United States — massive foreign aid, massive military investment, large
numbers of people employed in a centralized bureaucracy and equally
massive neglect of such structure-supporting arenas as education, health,

and infrastructure. When you strip away discussions of good and evil, the long-term *survival* implications of such an approach to politics and economics becomes much clearer.

Hierarchy and the Limits of Domination

What else is not working? I've mentioned several times that American businesses are currently struggling with the need for a different way of doing business that can handle the speed and complexity of the modern world. This struggle reflects limitations on another major structural form: current models of hierarchy.

Carneiro's work (1970, see Chapter 5) described the origins of hierarchical society in war and subjugation. Eisler (1988) has similarly suggested that the current form of hierarchy arose out of relations of domination and that most forms of hierarchical relations still reflect a dominator mentality — inside and outside of politics. Hierarchies that employ a dominator mentality are characterized by a flow of information going up and control going down.

The phrase "dominator mentality" carries heavy negative connotations that, as before, can lead to trivializing the situation. And one should not trivialize the power that such hierarchies create. The invention of hierarchical relations — coordination via control from higher levels — opened up vast new realms of human complexity. Greater specialization was possible because larger numbers of people could be coordinated. Greater specialization allowed increasingly detailed refinement of specialty areas. Coordination also created the ability to channel and concentrate resources and energy in ways never before imagined. This allowed projects of much greater size, length and complexity to be undertaken. It also increased efficiency which produced excess wealth that could then be used to support activities not related to immediate survival — science and the arts. The usefulness of such beyond-immediate-survival activities often takes a long time to materialize, but when it does, it creates vast expansions of capacity. And all of this originally became possible as a result of the invention of vertical (i.e., hierarchical) relations.

One must appreciate the power and importance of vertical relations. The catch is that we don't know how much of the current method of vertical relations is critical and how much is frozen historical accident. Further, times change and what is appropriate at one stage of complexity is generally not appropriate at another.

Some of the problems with the current strategy are easy to see. Control is linearized. Information becomes more and more filtered as it is transmitted and retransmitted up the hierarchy. Like a bad game of "telephone," after a certain number of levels the end message no longer resembles the beginning message in any significant way. The top and bottom are effectively disconnected. In addition, linearized control limits the creativity and degrees of freedom of the various components, which further limits efficiency. Using Jacobs' notion, control stifles the very activity — the creative self-organizing activity — that is likely to lead to the greatest strides in development. Since ecological growth unfolds in endlessly surprising ways, trying to over-fit it to a pre-planned direction or to the span of intelligence of a few individuals works only for systems of limited complexity.

And as with the transactions of decline, dominator hierarchies also appear to contain the seeds of their own destruction. Increasing efficiency and structural stability come from increasing levels of reciprocal feedback relations. As Jacobs says:

> In a natural ecology, the more diversity there is, the more flexibility, too because of what ecologists call its greater numbers of "homeostatic feedback loops," meaning that it includes greater numbers of feedback controls for automatic self-correction ... too few homeostatic feedback loops is precisely the failing that renders [systems] disastrously unstable. (1984, p. 224)

The one thing that dominator hierarchies are not designed for is the addition of certain types of feedback loops — particularly bottom-to-top but also side-to-side. This is easy to see in American industry. There is negative feedback from superior levels down but little, if any, going up. An engineering group may submit a schedule to management with 24 months to hit a target market. Management may take 12 months to decide whether to proceed and then require the same dates be met — and all of this is left as management prerogative and the way things have to be. But the net effect is reduction in quality, demoralization and the straining of lower-level resources. The media is full of stories of CEO's who give themselves massive raises in years that their companies have lost massive amounts of money. There is frequent internal empire building that causes tremendous waste to the company.

Side-to-side coupling is also generally poor. To allow top-down control, management hierarchies tend to be organized like inverted trees, with control flowing down the branch. If nodes on two different branches have to work with each other the side-to-side relations are likely to be weak and subject to the contrary whims of the different branches. Thus, despite the fact that many side-to-side relationships are vital to the company at large, they are likely to be fragile and poorly coupled.

Like the railroad companies that failed because they saw themselves in the railroad business rather than the transportation business, dominator (information-up/control-down) hierarchies fail because they focus on being in the control business, not the what-makes-sense-for-the-job business. And let me be very clear: the vast majority of this dysfunctional behavior is not the result of inherent evil but a by-product of the structure. The term "dominator" hierarchy has negative connotations, but what is wrong with them is deeper than their not being nice. Their critical dysfunction comes from their simplistic, poorly coupled structuring, their emphasis on control and their linear implementation of control.

None of this is a surprise to modern industry. As Chapter 8 mentioned, American industry is abuzz with notions of "empowerment" and changing traditional forms of relating. The questions are "how" and "in what way?" The one sure thing is that the final answers to these questions are not in. Industrial America is a real-time example of need searching to amplify a viable new form.

Images of Humankind: Competition and Control

There is one last type of "what isn't working" that relates to common beliefs about how things work and, particularly, about the nature of human beings. There is a long list of images of human nature that have arisen over time (see Table 10.2 given at the end of this chapter). Mechanism gives us what is shown in Table 10.1.

People use their image of what human beings are like in deciding what to do in particular situations. Part of what is wrong in the current time is that mechanism's images are again simplistic. Competition is the classic example. If you believe that the world is Darwinian and competition produces the fittest, then when faced with company-threatening inefficiency, you are likely to make things more competitive internally, with the idea that this will make the company more fit (i.e., externally competitive). But, like other mechanistic thinking, the Darwinian image exaggerates competition's role. It portrays competition as a primary immutable unidirectional cause. People (or companies) who see the world through Darwinian lenses tend to be blind to the dysfunctional aspects of overemphasized competitiveness. For example, environments that over emphasize internal competition ("how well do I do compared to others") are precisely

Table 10.1. Mechanistic Images of Humankind
(after Markeley and Harmon 1982, p. 19)

Source period	Approximate date	Dominant image	Cultures where image is currently active
Industrial Revolution/ Enlighten- ment	A.D. 1500	"Economic man" — individual- istic, materialistic, rationalistic; objective knowledge, utilitari- an/economic values coming into dominance	Most modern industrial nations
Modern social science	A.D. 1900	Human as "beast" — instinctual drives predominant, a "creature of evolution" whose survival depends on competitive adapta- tion and/or suppression of base instincts	Most modern industrial nations
Modern behavioral science	A.D. 1913	Human as "mechanism" — to be understood in ways found successful by nineteenth-century physics	Primarily United States

the ones where company-enhancing cross-group (cooperative) efforts are likely to be stamped out because the incentive structure runs against such cooperation. Environments that over emphasize competition also tend to promote self-oriented status/power-seekers, not producers per se. Since winning out over others is equated with quality, winners are assumed to represent "the best" but the question is "best at what?" Corporate America is filled with individuals who are primarily focused on self-interest, not company or product interest. They are likely to engage in imaging, empire-building, and to increase corporate politics in general — all of which is wasteful to the company as a whole. What is most frightening about this is that the ethic that "competition equals the good" is so strong that many companies not only tolerate but reward this behavior. The bottom line is that over emphasizing competition tends to foster parochial interests. It makes concern about "what's best for the company as a whole" an altruism and a luxury.

Images like "the competitor" (survival of the fittest) are a problem because when faced with a crisis, people are likely to fall back on traditional images to solve their dilemmas. Thus, American business, in its current crisis, speaks of teamwork but tends to fall back into emphasizing competitiveness and rewarding visibility and position in the hierarchy. It speaks of empowerment but finds it hard to relinquish control.

Images like "the competitor" are problematic not because competition isn't important, but because competition's role is exaggerated. As Krugman (1991) notes at the end of his article on the "Myths and Realities of U.S. Competitiveness": "competition is both a subtler and more problematic issue than is generally understood" (p. 814). Mechanism supports simplistic images of control, independence, change, and competition — and simplistic images contribute to current dilemmas.

ECOLOGICAL ALTERNATIVES

> [Now] we approach the difficult question from the practical person — what is to be done? What sorts of actions and programs do the foregoing arguments suggest?
>
> *Markeley, Harmon, et al. (1982, p. 183)*

Ecological science adds to human power, reenchants the world and empowers individuals in ways the old milieu did not. Yet it does not portray a simple world of sweetness and light. The second law is understood as the underlying creative principle, but it is as ruthless as it is creative. The image is of the Dance of Shiva, the creator and destroyer. The field chooses not on what is "good" for human beings, but on a simple tally of what works. And when transformation takes place, it sweeps away relations that existed before. Extinction is a possibility, though perhaps more likely are major economic, social and political regressions, with all the suffering these imply. What does ecologism suggest we do differently?

Economics

First, Jacobs' thoughts on the transactions of decline. What can nations do to handle the inexorable built up of instabilities other than transactions of decline? Jacobs notes one very unusual possibility. Like a dog that realizes he is the object of an approaching hostile advance, nations in which instabilities and stresses have reached a critical point feel like they must do something radically different: prepare to attack, or run — something. The one thing they can't do is just stand around. And if the answer is not to the attack the difficulties by more transactions of decline what else is there?

We are taught that running away from a problem doesn't solve it. However, in real life it occasionally does... The equivalent for a political unit would be to resist the temptation of engaging in transactions of decline by not trying to hold itself together. The radical discontinuity would thus be division of the single sovereignty into a family of smaller sovereignties, not after things had reached a stage of breakdown and disintegration, but long before while things were still going reasonably well. In a national society behaving like this ... division would be a normal, untraumatic accompaniment of economic development itself, and of the increasing complexity of economic and social life. (p. 215)

A nation behaving like this would substitute for the great life force [of] survival, that other great life force, reproduction. In this utopian fantasy, young sovereignties splitting off from the parent nation would be told, in effect, "good luck to you in your independence! Now do try your very best to generate ... a creative city and its region and we'll all be better off. We won't discriminate against you in our trade, and if you should need to raise tariff barriers against our manufactured goods to get a start, we will put up with it without rancor." (p. 215)

These are indeed radical economic thoughts.

Hierarchy and Complexity

Clearly current forms of control can only handle limited complexity. The challenge of our time is the development of other forms of structural relations that, like Carneiro's villages, allow us to expand to a new level of complexity while still retaining social coordination and cohesion. There is little doubt but that these new forms of relations must include greater distribution of control, more feedback loops, and tighter coupling in directions other than top-to-bottom. They will be ecological, not mechanistic.

It is too early to anticipate which particular approach will win out.[1] Ecologism's contribution to the experiment comes in the form of changed images and understandings. For example, ecological understandings help support change simply because they confirm the idea that distributed control is *possible*. Giving up the notion of top-down control will not come easily. Before change can take place, people need reasons to believe that distributed control can work. To this end, self-organization itself is the best example. Whirlpools, entrained cuckoo clocks, and Benard cells have no external constraints or lines of control. The Gaia literature shows how the biosphere forms a self-regulating, i.e., self-controlling entity. Jacobs' city and import-replacement economies are self-organizing. Self-organization is perhaps the most common form of organization.[2] And all of this goes toward confirming that even though we find it hard to imagine, linear information-up/control-down flow may not be the only or even the most efficient form of control. Giving up centralized "dominator" control does not mean there will be no coherence.

Ecologism's other clear message is that, contrary to the usual capitalistic thrust, cooperation is the more likely route to massive increases in efficiency than competition (particularly internal competition). In fact, according to the historical record, the clear evolutionary winners are syncretic organizations, ones that are mutually enhancing. Figuring out ways to facilitate the growth of syncretism is crucial. This is a wide open field because cooperation is often essentially unsupported by the environment. Interestingly enough, however, there are signs that cooperation is being forced into being by the increasing speed and complexity of the modern world. The emergence of open systems cooperatives in the computer industry are an interesting example of the stirrings of complexity-forced cooperation. Consumer pressure for portability, compatibility and variety in application software has begun to force major manufacturers away from proprietary product lines and more and more toward industry standards. The simple fact is that no single company can supply all the computer services the market requires and thus being able to claim "industry standards" is a better survival tool than trying to box consumers into dependence on a proprietary line.

Images of Humankind: The Changing Context for Human Action

The last ecological alternative has to do with images. Ecologism changes our image of the world and how human beings fit in it in very broad ways. In doing so, it produces different understandings about how to live and act in the world; it changes the context of human action. For example, Jacobs' economic ideas and the discussion of syncretism suggest that self-interest is served by taking a larger, longer-term perspective that realizes the world's inherent interconnectivity. This and most other ecological alternatives suggest that the basic ecological rule, "think globally, act locally," is indeed the best way to approach things.

Ecologism says that the self is part of something larger than itself. And, though people come at it from many different perspectives, seeing oneself as part of something bigger changes the way we act. One might argue that parochial self-interest must move toward concern for the whole because

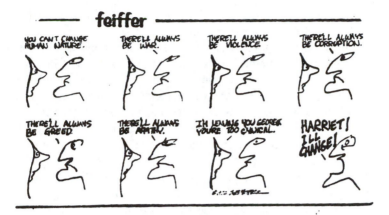

Figure 10.1. "You Can't Change Human Nature," FEIFFER. Jules Feiffer. Reproduced with permission of Universal Press Syndicate. All rights reserved.

global economy and global pollution makes us one world. One might argue that learning cooperation is crucial because evolution requires increasing efficiency and the evolutionary record evidence suggests that the largest increases in efficiency come from cooperation, not competition. Or, one might see the shift in spiritual terms: evolution is a single unified process which gave rise to us and is still taking place here-and-now in ways well-beyond our understanding. Our existence came out of that unfolding process and service to it appears to be what gives life its meaning. Physical, pragmatic, and spiritual; all of these are compatible visions.

Regardless of how you conceive of it, the deep ecological vision's effect on human understanding is quite important. It has the potential to affect two particularly important aspects of human existence: cynicism and morality.

Cynicism, Absurdity and Change

The history of philosophy is marked by epochs: the Age of Reason, the Age of Idealism, etc. It seems likely that the Age we are emerging from should be labeled the Age of Cynicism. God is dead, spirituality a fiction, and self-interest is the way to survive. Mechanism produced an amoral technique-centered age. If people believe that there is nothing in the real world but amoral, parochial self-interest, they do not demand anything more.

Cynicism keeps the world safe for absurdity and the one thing we may not
be able to afford much longer is absurdity.

Fighting cynicism requires reasons to believe that things can be better
and that it is worth fighting the good fight. There is a reason why I went
through those five chapters of physics and biology: the need for a believ-
able path. Ecologism suggests the world looked like it did because we
mistook science's interpretations for fact. But, things change. The view
from ecologism is profoundly different. Ecological science does not
promise omnipotence, control, or utopia, but it does present a profoundly
optimistic vision. The process that drove life, consciousness, and civilization into being is still at work. There is more reason to believe, in Martin
Luther King's words, that though "the arc of the universe is long, it tends
towards justice." With effort, we can learn to go with this flow and see what
else will unfold.

Morality, Choice and Survival

In an accelerating world where the future is made here and now by our
actions large and small, right action becomes a issue of human survival. We
inform our actions as well as possible and fight the good fight the best we
are able — knowing that we cannot know or control, we just dance. In such
a world, differing opinions are the cherished source of future enhance-
ments, and cynicism and closed-mindedness are the two main dangers. In
such a world, morality — *pursuit* of the Good — is a pragmatic real-world
concern.

Morality and choice have a long history of which I believe we are now
entering a new phase. For example, despite their different approaches,
Socrates, Plato and Aristotle all saw the dialectical process[3] as part of a
moral stance which man could choose or not choose. Socrates and Plato
both held that it was man's duty to do the dialectic so that he could find a
way to act responsibly in the world — doing the dialectic defined the life
that's worth living. Aristotle held that choosing to facilitate the world was
Man's duty and not choosing to do so resulted in Man's being left alone
apart from the world. Through the Dark Ages people lost the sense of
choice. Morality became obligation or damnation. The existentialists (for
example, Kierkegaard) rediscovered choice, emphasizing its "or not"
aspect. I can choose to do this, but I don't *have* to choose this.

Ecological thinking also produces a new vision of morality and choice.
Doing the dialectic does seem to be the way humankind learns to act
responsibly in the world. It once more seems to define the life worth living.

However, in the ecological vision the dialectic has more concrete significance. There are no final structures, no final ways of being, no final
absolute knowledge. The dialectic, philosophical questioning, continual
refinement of what we know, how we see and what we do — are precisely
the kinds of things that must be done to keep up with evolution's endless
demand for better ways. It is quite possible that humankind's sense of and
pursuit of the Good, the True, and the Beautiful are very real evolutionarily
inbred survival drives. In the long arc of the universe these things further
survival by uniting us with each other and the world and, at the same time,
increasing our abilities. They may represent our inbred tuning to that very
flow which we must learn to follow.

Thus, ecologism produces a vision of morality and choice embedded in
a very different context. To *not* choose has different implications. We are
no longer threatened with being alone, but with extinction. Choosing
wrongly threatens the species existence more than it did before. The sense
of moral obligation now has deeper meaning. Morality, pursuit of the Good
for its own sake, becomes an issue of the real world, not just metaphysics.

Evolutionary Competence: Learning to Learn

In an evolving ecological world, learning evolutionary competence is a
critical task (Banathy 1987). And towards this end, perhaps the most fundamental of all lessons is that learning is continual. In an evolving ecological world, "all structure-dependent solutions are doomed to failure"
(Swenson 1989c). Whatever we have now is perhaps the best we can do for
the moment but it is also something to be grown beyond. This attitude must
become foundational in all spheres: science, government, education, human
relations, morality, spirituality, etc. Without this attitude, the structures our
forebears built to increase their being, become cages that suffocate new
growth.

The second most important lesson of ecologism is that evolution is real
and we *must* learn its rules in order to realistically pursue evolutionary
competence, i.e., competence at continuing. The physics of evolution extends our physical understanding about when, why and how systems arise,
change or decay. Thus, it provides a more critical basis for discussion of
evolutionary competence. For example, we now know that: (i) physical law
predicts ongoing qualitative change of relationships between elements; (ii)
this restructuring is seeded at particular evolutionary moments by unpredictable, microscopic events; (iii) there is a finite number of such microscopic events that are capable of seeding a restructuring; (iv) small

differences in these events may lead to drastically different macroscopic outcomes (futures); (v) the process is irreversible (Swenson 1989d, p.20). The theory suggests that the future *is* unpredictable; change making is not privileged — anyone can do it.

The theory also suggests that (in Olaf Stapledon's words): "mankind is irrelevant to the purposes of the universe." The future may be more ordered from the field's point of view but catastrophic from a human point of view. Using Swenson's (1989d) words, access to the seeding of future states is not privileged, but "not privileged" should be heavily underscored. All of this must be taken seriously and used to inform our behavior because both actions and inactions shape the future.

IMAGES OF HUMANKIND

The arc of the universe is long, but it tends toward justice.

Martin Luther King, Jr.

The one obvious thing I haven't mentioned is that the Ecological Transformation itself appears to be a product of the evolutionary process. Evolution shapes the context which shapes individuals and events. In turn, individuals and events change the context and shape evolution. Not only does "everything affect everything" but the timing and unfolding of things is significantly more ordered than previously imagined. We get the Ecological Transformation at this juncture in history in part because generations of "standing on others' shoulders" has allowed us to reach a level of complexity that can deal with greater complexity in the world. We also get it because the modern world's level of complexity — its pace of change, level of economic interconnectedness and skyrocketing increase in knowledge — forces a crisis. The old ways simply cannot deal with the pace and complexity of modern society. The conditions are ripe for change because the failure of the old and necessity of something new is forced into our vision on a daily basis.

Adam Smith talked of the "invisible hand" operating behind economic vicissitudes — the invisible hand seems now to have a farther range. Where it once seemed strange that Newton and Leibnitz both invented the calculus at the same time, it now seems utterly reasonable. Where it once seemed amazing that a physical picture of evolution and ecology was coming about exactly at the time it seemed most needed; it now seems utterly reasonable. This book is my product, yet it and I are a product of these times and evolution's invisible hand. It all seems so utterly reasonable.

By way of closing let me use the words of a group of scholars who are apparently shaped by this same hand, for they invented the same thoughts I have and I had no knowledge of them until near the completion of this book. The book I shall cite, *Changing Images of Man* (Markeley and Harmon 1982) was produced as a collaborative effort of the Stanford Research Institute and was reviewed and shaped by such notables as Joseph Campbell, Margaret Mead, Carl Rogers, B. F. Skinner, and Ervin Laszlo. It is a serious effort to evaluate our current dilemmas and possible future course. It has this to say about our dilemma:

> 1) An interrelating set of fundamental dilemmas, growing apparently ever more pressing, seem to demand for the ultimate resolution a drastically changed image of man-on-earth.

They note that humankind is threatened by the ecological consequences of continued material growth but fears the economic effects of a sudden stoppage. People recognize the global instability caused by economic nationalism and a growing gap between rich and poor nations, yet seem unable to turn the trend around. We face a cultural crisis of meaning. The legitimacy of business and government systems that pursue economic ends that counteract human needs comes ever more into question. We no longer have any sense of who is at the helm, how the ship is steered, nor toward what shores we either are or should be aiming for.

> 2) There are increasingly evident signs of the imminent emergence of a "new image of man." It is very much a challenger to the dominant scientific world view as that has evolved over the past few centuries... Yet, it is not new since traces of it can be found, going back for thousands of years, in the core experiences underlying the world's many religious doctrines.

They note that the new image reactivates cultural myths whose meaning had become forgotten and seems to be substantiated by advances in science (even though science had previous played a role in discrediting the same images.)

In their view the central emphasis in the new image is on the role of creative work in the life of the individual. Thus they note:

> In "true Freemasonry" there is one lodge, the universe — and one brother-hood, everything that exists. Each person has the "privilege of labor," of joining with the "Great Architect" in building more noble structures and thus serving in the divine plan.

In their view the new image of humankind has the potential to reactivate traditional American images such as the work ethic, free-enterprise and a

democratic society while at the same time embracing long-standing images
from other parts of the globe. But they also give caution:

> The degree to which the characteristics described ... are realized may well
> determine the degree to which highly undesirable future outcomes
> (economic collapse, a garrison-police state) can be avoided. The emerging
> image of humankind has increasingly widespread acceptance and long his-
> torical roots. It can be opposed and suppressed, but probably at great social
> cost. The necessary condition for a stable society in the medium-term future
> ... is that the behavior patterns and institutions of the society shall have
> transformed themselves to be compatible with the new image. (p. 186)

I will close with these scholars' list of the images of humankind over
history — and the thought that we are entering a very new phase.

Table 10.2. Dominant Images of Humankind Over History (after
Markeley and Harmon 1982, p. 18)

Source period	Dominant image	Cultures in which image is at present active	Significance for post-industrial era
Middle Paleolithic 250,000–40,000 B.C.	The hunter, focus of the male-dominated culture field of the "Great Hunt"	Few cultures in its pure form; most in its militaristic equivalent	Jeopardizes cross-cultural peace; may be necessary for police operations, however
Upper Paleolithic 30,000–15,000 B.C.	A sense of spiritual affinity between beasts and man, of which totemism is an expression	Various American In-dian cultures with tradi-tions intact	Has relevance for a renewed sense of partner-ship with other life forms on the planet
Neolithic after 9000 B.C.	The planter, the child of the Goddess; woman the giver of life	Hindu and certain other cultures	Has possible relevance for balancing mail-em-phasis of Western culture
Sumerian 3500 B.C.	The human civilized through submission to seasonal variations and ruling elites	Most cultures	Has relevance as historical analogy; shows "political func-tion" of new images

Semite 2350 B.C.	The human as a mere creature fashioned of clay to serve the gods, or some god, as a slave; but superior to and having dominion over nature. Notion of the "chosen people"	Orthodox Jewish, Christian, Islamic faiths	Stands in its present form as an obstacle to emergence of new ecological understandings
Zoroastrian 1200 B.C.	The human having free will, having to choose between good and evil, mythology of individual salvation	All Western cultures, in secular form	Presents a basic polarity needing to be dialectically transcended/synthesized
Age of Polis 500 B.C.	Greece: Aeschylus and image of human as *tragic hero* Greece: Mystery religions, the person becomes so attached to the material things of this world that he/she has lost touch with his/her own true nature which is not of these things, but spirit — our self is the very being and model of that spirit of which each is but a particle	Most Western cultures to some degree. All cultures, but never very visible	Could provide a guiding image for personal/societal transformation in time of crisis. Could contribute to deemphasizing material overconsumption and ecological understanding
Age of Polis 500 B.C. cont'd	Greece: science and objective knowledge as aesthetic rather than utilitarian activity; naturalistic emphasis in science, art, and philosophy	None in which dominant	Has relevance to counterbalancing the "technological ethic"

cont'd

Early Christian (and Muslim) A.D. 100	Two contrary images: 1) following the Semite and Zoroastrian traditions, God's servant — obey or be dammed; 2) that of the Gnostics similar to the image of the Greek mystery religions, the person "saved" by self-knowledge	1) Traditional Judeo/Christian/Muslim cultures; 2) Most cultures as an underground view	1) A dominant image that needs to be incorporated into a larger synthesis; 2) Could contribute to a new "self-realization ethic" for our culture if incorporated into a larger synthesis
Industrial Revolution/ Enlightenment A.D. 1500	"Economic man" — individualistic, materialistic, rationalistic; objective knowledge, utilitarian/economic values coming into dominance	Most modern industrial nations	Likely inappropriate for transition to post-industrial era
Modern social science A.D. 1900	Human as "beast" — instinctual drives predominant, a "creature of evolution" whose survival depends on competitive adaptation and/or suppression of base instincts	Most modern industrial nations	An image needing to be incorporated into a larger synthesis
Modern behavioral science A.D. 1913	Human as "mechanism" — to be understood in ways found successful by nineteenth-century physics	Primarily United States	Promoted as providing the most appropriate basis for man's next era, perhaps now itself needing to be incorporated into larger synthesis
Modern transdisciplinary science A.D. 1945	Human as "goal-directed, adaptive learning system"	Image has not yet reached "takeoff point"	Provides a possible conceptual basis for integrating most other images of many in an evolutionary frame of reference
Various times and places from ca. 1500 B.C. to present	Human as "spirit" — the "philosophia perennis" view of man and the universe as essentially consciousness in manifest form	Most cultures, in various degrees of purity	Could contribute to needed synthesis of "opposing" images as it sees apparent opposites as differing aspects of the same underlying reality

NOTES

1. Management literature is filled with theories for new forms of relating (see for example, Peters 1989, *Thriving on Chaos*). It is interesting that distributed control and tighter coupling are common themes.

2. Even in computers, neural nets (networks of interconnected independent nodes each running their own rules) provide an uncanny model for the potential of non-centralized interactive control. Each node runs its own rule using input from other nodes, and in turn, sending its own results out to affect others as well. The surprising result is vastly increased computational speed and some rather unexpected computational results, like the ability to mimic patterns without having an algorithm for the pattern.

   There are also some interesting game-theoretic analyses that suggest ways of interactive social control and cohesion. For example, Taylor (1976) used an iterated version of the Prisoner's Dilemma to show that cooperation eventually evolves if there is a high probability of recurrent interaction. Taylor used his argument to attack the State's "public good" justification of coercion (i.e., "if the State doesn't enforce cooperation, public goods like defense and clean air won't be provided and everyone will be worse off.") Apparently, coercion is not needed if people are organized into face-to-face communities where there is a high degree of recurrent balanced interaction. People learn it's in their long term interest to cooperate (supplied by Cariani 1991).

3. Which we now see as self-evolution.

Retrospective

This book sought to answer three basic questions: 1) what is the evolving ecological vision; 2) how did it come about; and 3) how will it affect us. With the previous chapters as reference, I can now answer these questions quite parsimoniously:

What is it? The evolving ecological vision is a metaphoric vision of how the world works, supported by a physical vision of how the world works. Both appear to be emerging out of the same pressures. Metaphorically and physically we begin to see the world as a tightly interdependent system evolving through interactive dynamics. Not only does this restless world ecology hide order in what looks like chaos, it *produces* order through chaos.

How did it come about? The scientific shift has been building for a long time. It came about as a result of a set of new tools and small insights showing just how non-Newtonian most of the world is. It started with finding structure hidden in nonlinear interactive systems. It moved through understanding how systems self-organize and it is unified by the vision of how higher and higher levels of ordered complexity are driven into being via energy flow. The bottom line is that the new science reorganizes our vision around broader-case systems rather than the limited systems that have so long been the center of our scientific universe.

How will it affect us? The evolving ecological viewpoint produces a very powerful vision of the world. Its images of how complexity works produce a new form of pragmatism which includes concepts such as big changes through small effects, co-creation, and the importance of cooperation, endless learning, and endless change. The deep ecological view offers hope of bridging the breaks between traditionally antagonistic knowledge systems. It re-enchants the world by making the mystery of creation an ongoing reality and producing a vision of the physical world that is consonant with many spiritual traditions. In fact, it implies a spirituality all by itself. How did we get here, what we are doing, where we are going — all the questions that lie behind what each of us does on a daily basis are put in a very different context. All of this changes our everyday sense of how the world works. And most impressively, the physical, the pragmatic and the spiritual are no longer so disjoint.

Appendices

Appendix A

Basic Concepts of Modern Nonlinear Dynamics (Chaos)

This appendix provides a brief overview of some of the concepts of modern nonlinear dynamics (Chaos). See Abraham and Shaw (1982–88), Thompson and Stewart (1987), and Schuster (1984) for more thorough introductions to the field.

THE GEOMETRY OF BEHAVIOR

Analytic methods focus on finding "solutions" to equations. In essence they use the assumption that if you have a vector describing the instantaneous change the system takes at one moment, you can solve an equation that will describe what the system will do any time in the future (and presumably did do any time in the past). With the equation and a starting point (initial conditions), you can predict what the system will do any time in the future.

But, unfortunately, you can only solve the equation from instantaneous change vectors for a few systems that behave in very simple ways. Also, for many systems you can't find precise initial conditions and for others the initial conditions are completely unknown (e.g., the weather, the economy, human beings). If calculus is your primary tool and you find that it only works on a limited set of simple systems, how else does one make a precise description of how a system works?

The answer that has come to fruition in Chaos is that you try to obtain a graphic "overview of how the whole system evolves and how this is influenced by the starting conditions" (Thompson and Stewart 1987, p. xi).

Poincaré was the first person to study the global properties of solutions to equations using the qualitative techniques of geometry and topology. As Abraham and Shaw (1982, p. 12) note: "the key to the geometric theory of dynamical systems created by Poincaré, is the phase portrait of a dynamical systems." These portraits are called phase space diagrams.

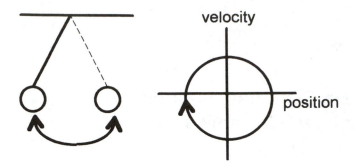

Figure A1. Phase space map of a frictionless pendulum (after Crutchfield et al. 1986).

Phase Space

Phase space is one of the fundamental concepts of dynamics and was around long before Poincaré and Chaos. In dynamics one creates a model of the system under study that allows one to represent the motion of the system as the motion of a point in a space of appropriate variables. The model's "independent variables" are the minimum set of variables that must be known if one wishes to be able predict the motion of the system in the next infinitesimally small step in time. Phase space is defined as the space created by using these independent variables as axes. The number of dimensions in the space is equal to the number of independent variables. Phase space is a powerful concept because with a model and a set of appropriate variables, dynamics can represent a real-world system as the geometry of behavior of a single moving point.

A pendulum provides a simple example of phase space. If you graphed the behavior of a pendulum in phase space, one axis would be the velocity and the other axis would be the position of the bob in the horizontal direction. A plot of the pendulum in phase space would show all the velocity/position pairs that the system generates. Figure A1 shows the phase space map for an imaginary frictionless pendulum.

Phase space diagrams allow you to map all the possible states the system can go through. If one has an actual system, one can map phase space points and connect them in order of occurrence to show how the system evolves (i.e., the trajectory it follows). Figure A2 shows a hypothetical phase diagram of voltage and current in an electronic black box.

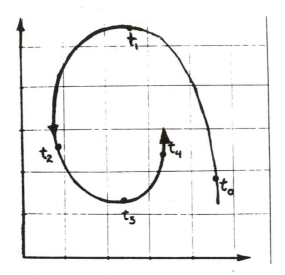

Figure A2. Phase diagram of voltage vs. Current (Abraham and Shaw 1982, p. 16).

If one had a large number of observations one could chart where all points go. Such a map is called a vector field and the trajectories it reveals show the system's phase portrait as shown in Figure A3.

Basins and Separatrixes

One of the advantages of using phase space is that one can see how the system will behave over the entire region of phase space. As Figure A4 shows, a system may not flow uniformly in a particular spiral or direction. It may have one or more critical points or junctures which separate distinct regions of flow. Such boundaries between different flow regions are called separatrixes.

Initial conditions (i.e., points) from one side of a separatrix will be drawn toward one type of flow and those on the other side will be drawn toward another. The two sides of a separatrix are distinct basins of attraction; points in the two regions are attracted different ways.

Charting basins of attraction defines the form of behavior that the system will have under different conditions. As Figure A5 shows, basins of attraction may be complexly intertwined.

Sally J. Goerner

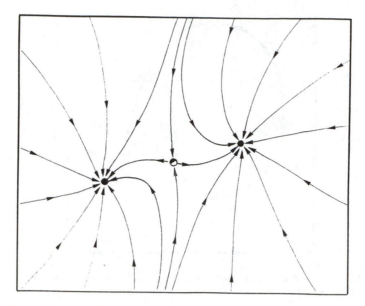

Figure A3. Vector field of a dynamical system (Abraham and Shaw 1982, p. 30).

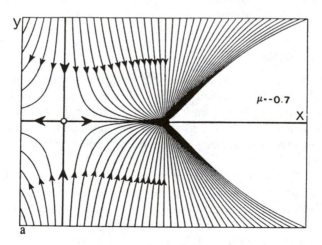

Figure A4. Separatrixes and complex flow (Thompson and Stewart 1987, p. 123, Copyright ©). Reprinted by permission of John Wiley & Sons, Ltd.

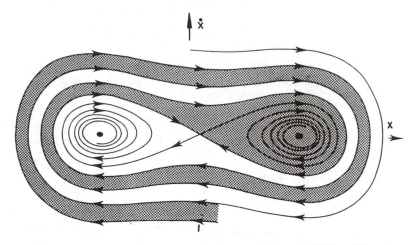

Figure A5. Basins of attraction (Thompson and Stewart 1986, p. 50).

It is notable that the boundary between basins of attraction is not always as clean and distinct as the one shown above. In fact, these boundaries are often fuzzy. Here fuzzy is a technical term used to describe a complex type of boundary in which immeasurably close points are drawn toward different attractors. Fuzzy boundaries are an important concept in Chaos. For example, at the quantum level chaotic and regular regions are inseparably interwoven in the fabric of phase space. Because of finite precision and measurement error, chaotic and regular points cannot be separated.

Charting basins of attraction highlights the system's potential for distinctly different behavior depending on conditions; such diagrams counter the impression that one equation (model) means one type of behavior. Quite the contrary, multiple competing attractors are more likely the case.

DISSIPATIVE VERSUS CONSERVATIVE DYNAMICS

As Figure A6 shows, nonlinear systems are divided into two main groups, dissipative and conservative systems.

The common understanding of the distinction between dissipative and conservative is that in conservative systems energy is conserved and in dissipative systems energy is dissipated into the surrounds. Technically the distinction between dissipative and conservative systems has to do with the model of the system in phase space. Dissipative systems are one whose

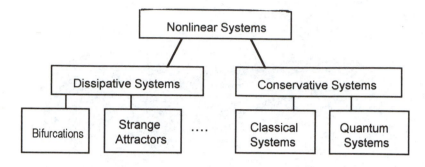

Figure A6. Nonlinear systems (after Schuster, 1984, p. 3).

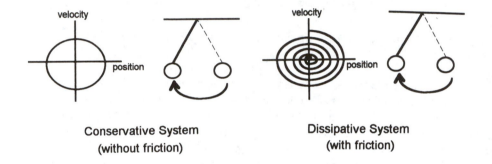

Figure A7. Pendulums in phase space (after Crutchfield et al. 1986, p. 49).

phase space maps shrink in volume. Conservative systems are ones whose map in phase space do not shrink in volume. As Thompson and Stewart (1987, p. 1) put it: "Dissipative systems ... have the property that an evolving ensemble of states occupies a region of phase space whose volume decreases with time."

Figure A7 shows the phase-space maps for pendulums with and without friction. The pendulum with friction is a dissipative system it dissipates energy to friction and its points in phase space contract into a smaller and smaller region, in this case, the origin. The pendulum without friction is a conservative system. It doesn't lose energy and its points in phase space don't contract into a smaller and smaller region.

Note that the definition of conservative versus dissipative systems is based on characteristics of the *model* of the system and not on characteristics of the system per se. This is important to remember. In the final analysis all systems are "conservative" because energy is neither created nor destroyed; it's always conserved. The real difference between "dissipative" and "conservative" systems is in the models people use to show how the energy flows. If a system's energy flow is very difficult to follow at a single scale of measure (the "macro"-scale) people use models that leave out energy lost to the microscale, for example, heat created by friction. This energy isn't gone, we just aren't including it in the model. Dissipative models chart how energy moves from macroscale to microscale. Dissipative systems are conservative systems which we model with dissipative models. [Note: This point may seem obscure now but it is part of a larger issue of categorizing the world by models which are actually artifacts of our own abilities rather than facts of the world. It is the insidious problem of mistaking one's model for the system, or in Korzybski's words, confusing "maps for terrain." It is relevant because it is part of the problem with classical physics' metaphysics.]

It is important to know about dissipative versus conservative system models because some phenomena are found only in conservative systems and some only in dissipative systems. Much of what is commonly associated with the science of Chaos actually applies only to dissipative-system dynamics. I will review these findings first and conclude with a section on conservative-system chaos.

NONLINEAR DYNAMICS IN DISSIPATIVE SYSTEMS

> A dissipative dynamical system is one in which the volume of phase space shrinks as time evolves, with the result that the system ends up in a special region of phase space, with a lower number of dimensions, and this region is called an attractor.
>
> *Baranger (1990, p. 86)*

The quotation above summarizes the distinctive features of dissipative- versus conservative-system chaos. Getting smaller means the system's final behavior can be described by an equation of much smaller degree than that of the actual system. It is this getting smaller and simpler that results in the phenomenon of attractors and universality both of which are described below.

Attractors

In general a dissipative system may have some initial transient behavior and then settle into a stable type of behavior. The pattern of behavior that a system moves toward over time is called an attractor.

Although phase space was used long before Chaos. However, before Chaos only a few simple types of attractors were known. In the case of the pendulum with friction, the long-term behavior of the system tends toward the final, fixed resting point. This point is said to "attract the system"; it is called a fixed-point attractor. Other systems, like the driven pendulum (for example, a clock), do not come to rest in the long term but instead cycle periodically through a series of states. A phase space diagram of such systems have a corresponding periodic orbit that attracts the system; such periodic phase space orbits are called limit cycle attractors.

Strange Attractors

In two-dimensional systems (i.e., models with two phase space variables), only fixed-point or limit cycle attractors are possible. However, in three dimensions or higher (Shaw 1980) it is possible to have a completely different type of attractor, a strange attractor. Figure A8 shows the strange attractor of a weather modeling system graphed in three-dimensional phase space and also in standard time series output (upper left). Note just how erratic the time series data looks yet how orderly the strange attractor seems.

Strange attractors have a number of interesting features. The output never repeats but no point falls outside a limiting shape; the output is bounded by a complex topological shape. The limiting form (strange attractor) acts like an asymptote: the longer the model runs the more completely the limiting form is approximated. Nevertheless, the output never reaches or completes the form.

Strange attractors show how a complex system may have endlessly unique behavior that is nevertheless clearly ordered. The long-term behavior of the system is non-repeating yet attracted to a clear form. And, notably, endless uniqueness can be lawful; it can be described by simple equations.

Sensitive Dependence and Lawful Unpredictability

Strange attractors provide a very important understanding being lawful and being predictable are not equivalent. For many systems, prediction of local

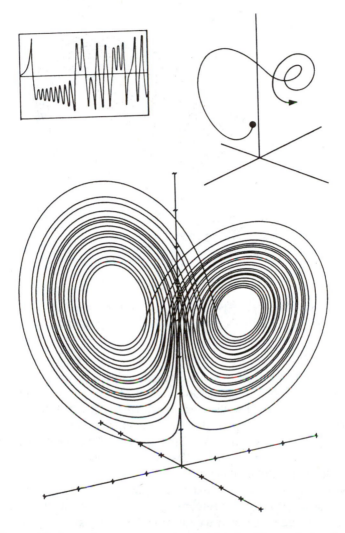

Figure A8. Lorenz's strange attractor (reprinted with permission from James P. Crutchfield).

behavior will be impossible even with the precise equations of motion. Let me explain how this comes about.

Refer back to the Lorenz attractor in Figure A8. Remember, the Lorenz attractor is a graph of precise equations of motion. Note that, in certain

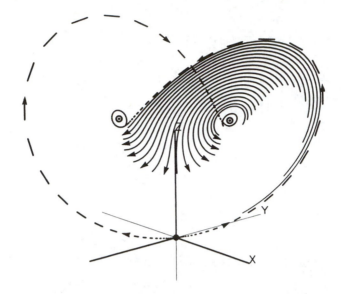

Figure A9. Diverging orbits (Thompson and Stewart 1986, p. 22, Copyright ©). Reprinted by permission of John Wiley & Sons, Ltd.

places, the orbit lines come so close together that they almost appear to touch. Mathematically, it can be shown that in strange attractors orbits can come arbitrarily close together yet never cross. The distance between separate orbits can be smaller than any measurement error, yet two immeasurably close orbits will not stay immeasurably close; they will diverge. Figure A9 shows an enlargement depicting how once very close orbits diverge along very different paths.

"Sensitive dependence on initial conditions" is the technical phrase for equations with orbits that come arbitrarily close together. Classically, scientists presume that if you start an equation from very similar points (i.e., initial conditions), it will produce very similar outputs. However, if a system has sensitive dependence, two indistinguishably close initial points can lead to two widely different endpoints. For example, imagine you start the equation running with an initial position from one of the regions or arbitrarily close orbits. Because even computers use finite precision, you cannot select a particular orbit. You will arbitrarily end up on one of many immeasurably close orbits. As Stewart (1989) notes, the one you get will even depend on how your particular computer handles truncation and round

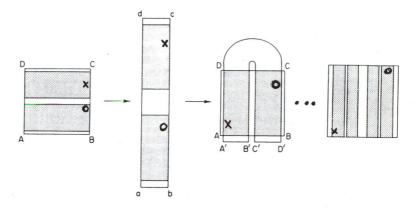

Figure A10. The baker's transformation (after Thompson and Stewart 1987, p. 246, Copyright ©). Reprinted by permission of John Wiley & Sons, Ltd.

off. Furthermore, if you run the program a little while, the path you did obtain will go one way while its once immeasurably close neighbors will end up somewhere else. All of this happens before you ever leave the computer model, much less enter the real world.

Sensitive dependence is nicknamed "The Butterfly Effect": even with the exact equation of motion, finite precision and measurement error will be enough to foil any attempts at prediction. You can describe the global form but you cannot predict the actual path. This is lawful unpredictability.

Efficient Mixing: The Baker's Transformation

Strange attractors suggest that dynamical systems can produce endlessly unpredictable outcomes from a simple rule of operation (equation). Mathematician Stephen Smale (1967, 1980) provides a simple model of how this can happen. The model, called the baker's transformation shows graphically how: 1) unpredictability can arise from a simple operation; and 2) how small differences in starting position can lead to dramatically different end points (i.e., sensitive dependence).

The baker's transformation works like this. Imagine a square of metal with two marks very close together. Now stretch the square upward into a tall bar. Now fold the bar in half. Now stretch the folded bar upward again and fold the new bar in half again. Figure A10 shows this process. The baker's transformation is a kind of efficient mixer much like an automated

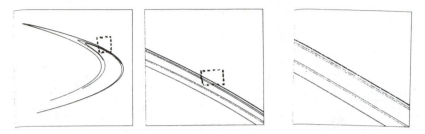

Figure A11. Detail with magnification (after Helleman 1984, p. 462).

taffy puller. As a result of the iterated transformations (stretching, squeezing and folding), the two points that started so close together end up in very different places. Also, because the folding causes a sharp break with the previous location, a chart of any point's location does not follow a smooth (linear) path.

The stretching, squeezing and folding in the baker's transformation actually refers to topological transformations applied to a shape in phase space. If you look at the dark bars in the baker's transformation, you see that neat little nonoverlapping layers build up. As the iteration continues, the layers get finer and finer, never overlapping. Points in the original form move to divergent locations over time, yet they stay within the same space.

The stretching, squeezing and folding transformations that produce the features of the attractor in phase space presumably correspond to some physical operation in the system. For example, in the case of the pendulum with friction, the spiral attractor contracting in phase space to a point results from a squeezing transformation. This squeezing (contraction) corresponds to the system's shrinking energy, the dissipation that reflects energy lost to friction.

The breadmaker's transformation, suggest that regions of chaos may actually represent well-mixed regions of phase space. Chaos is not so much random as it is well mixed.

Fractals

When you stretch a piece of dough and fold it, you get two layers. When you stretch and fold it again, you get four layers, and so on. In principle, a strange attractor, like well-kneaded dough, contains an infinite succession of layers within layers. As Figure A11 shows, if you magnify the attractor you see finer and finer levels of detail.

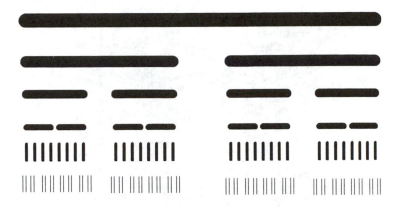

Figure A12. Cantor dust.

Georg Cantor, a nineteenth-century mathematician, described similar infinitely layered structures as abstractions built out of a simple operation being repeated over and over (iterated). For example, divide a line in thirds and remove the middle third. Then take each of the remaining line segments, divide them in thirds and remove those middle thirds, and so on. The result is the Cantor "dust" structure shown in Figure A12.

In the 1920s Birkhoff realized that such forms they might arise naturally in dynamical systems, but it was not until Benoit Mandelbrot's work in the 1960s that such geometries were explored in detail and applied to real-world things. Mandelbrot coined the term fractal for them because their infinitely bent structure was fractured and because such structures have a spatial dimension that is a fraction rather than an integer (e.g., not one-dimensional nor two-dimensional, but 2.3-dimensional). Mandelbrot (1983), Barnsley (1989) and others have shown that the form of most natural objects coastlines, lightning bolts, fern leaves is fractal. Fractals of the Cantor dust type also fit noise on electrical lines and cotton prices. Here again much of what was thought to be random or irregular is in fact highly ordered and describable. If the world is a giant machine, it may be a breadmaking machine.

Figure A13 shows an iterative geometry version of a landscape. Note that the picture is not a photograph but the output of an iterative equation. Fractals have some unusual characteristics. Primary among them are the phenomena of scaling and self-similarity. Self-similarity refers to the fact that the same form repeats itself (at least approximately) at all levels, which results in a form built of a form built of a form, etc.

Figure A13. Fractal landscape (Plate 9.8.11, Michael Barnsley, Arnaud Jacquin, Francois Malassenet, Laurie Reuter, and Alan Sloan, from *Fractals Everywhere* by Michael Barnsley; Copyright © 1988 by Academic Press, Inc.).

Because the microcosm mirrors the macrocosm at each level, the degree of complexity remains constant over different scales as seen in Figure A14.

Scaling means that the self-similar form is proportional at each level. Thus, if you magnify a fine area of the structure, you get increased information in proportion to the new scale.

Scaling has some important implications for measurement. For scaled phenomena, measurement is relative to the scale used; it varies with the size (scale) of the ruler used. You can grasp this intuitively when you remember

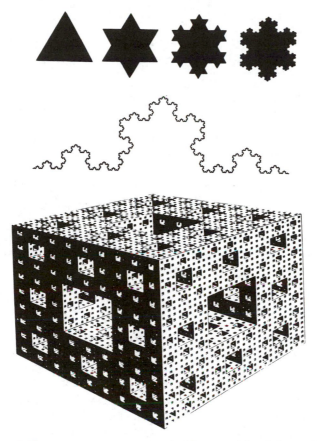

Figure A14. Koch snowflake and Serpinski sponge (after Schuster 1984, p. 49).

that what appears to blend into a curve is actually made up of a huge number of complex bumps. For example, if you measured the coastline of France using a ruler on a standard size globe you would get a different result than if you measured it on a two-foot square map of France. The result would be even more different if you gathered topographic maps showing detailed contours of the entire coastline and even more so if you took a ruler and walked the coastline yourself. Each result would be significantly longer because each would include levels of detail that could not be measured at higher levels.

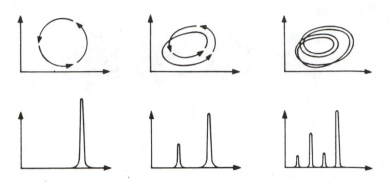

Figure A15. Qualitative changes of attractor (after Cvitanovic 1989, p. 6).

The existence of a fractal microstructure, a kind of infinite self-similar layering is a characteristic of strange attractors and the phenomena they describe (Abraham and Shaw 1984).

Bifurcations: Qualitative Change

Normally one models a system with the equation's parameters fixed at particular value (i.e., $r = 3.2r(x-1)$). However, in dynamical systems if you vary the parameter, you might find that the system followed one attractor at one setting and another attractor at another setting. Many of those attractors will be similar, if not identical, but at certain points a qualitatively different attractor may come into being. This qualitative change in behavior is called a bifurcation. Figure A15 shows some qualitative changes of attractor.

Figure A15 shows three qualitative changes in patterns that a fluid makes during its transition from calm to turbulence. The upper charts show the attractors themselves and the lower chart shows the attractor's frequency. If there is one repeating cycle the frequency chart shows one spike; if the attractor loops around twice before repeating, its frequency chart has two spikes; and if it loops four times, it has four spikes.

These three attractors point out a particular twist to phase space maps. While we say that phase space maps are handy because they allow us to see the entire range of a model's behavior at once, in fact, phase space maps only show the model's behavior for a particular parameter value. Each attractor in Figure A15 holds for a certain temperature; the fluid system passes through the three as the temperature increases.

Robert May's bifurcation diagram allows you to see the model's entire range of behavior over all parameter values. A bifurcation diagram of the fluid system would show the temperature ranges where each attractor holds and where the bifurcations between them take place. Without a bifurcation diagram you don't see where slightly different parameter values result in qualitatively different behavior in fact, you might not realize that the model had many different forms of behavior.

May (1974) developed the bifurcation diagram using the logistic equation, a well-known equation used in the study of population dynamics. The logistic equation, $x = rx(1 - x)$, is very simple, reminiscent of high school algebra. In this equation, x represents an animal population value and r is a parameter representing fertility rate.

For a long time, scientists knew that if you ran the logistic equation long enough it either converged to a stable equilibrium point or it didn't. Because scientists were primarily interested in stable equilibriums, no one ever investigated the "non-converging" situations. May was the first to systematically explore this equation's entire range of behavior. His work showed how the equation evolves through wide variety of different behaviors and that there is a specific pattern, an order, to the way the system evolves as the parameter r changes. Depending on small differences in the parameter, the system can evolve into any of a number of different stable behaviors, steady state equilibrium being only one.

His bifurcation diagram shown below, collapses all this variety into a single map. To obtain the bifurcation diagram above, you take the general equation:

$$x = rx(1 - x).$$

Then you compute the long-term behavior for each specific value of parameter r. For example, you would run each of the following equations for many iterations:

$$x = 2.9x(1 - x) \quad \text{and} \quad x = 3.0x(1 - x).$$

Do this for all values of r and map the results using fertility parameter r values for the horizontal axis and attractor frequency (how many cycles before it repeats) on the vertical axis. The bifurcation diagrams collapses the attractor's more complete flow information into a set of points on the vertical axis.

Figure A16 shows a bifurcation diagram. Where the graph is a single line, the equation's output stabilized at a single equilibrium point. Where it breaks into a parabola, the final pattern was an alternation between two

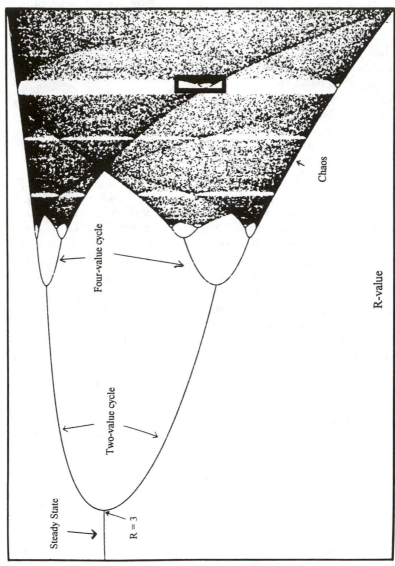

Figure A16. A bifurcation diagram (after figure from James P. Crutchfield).

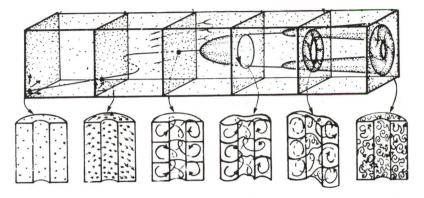

Figure A17. The bifurcation diagram and attractors (Abraham and Shaw 1988, p. 46).

values. Where the parabola splits into two smaller parabolas, the final pattern alternated among four values. Note that in the early part of the map, bifurcations follow a geometric progression: they go from 1 to 2 to 4 to 8. Where the graph is dark the equation is exhibiting chaos; the final population values hop around, never repeating.

This bifurcation diagram points out another set of classical assumptions. Traditionally, scientists assume that a small change in parameter value won't change the systems behavior significantly. Now we see that small differences in parameters as well as initial conditions can make a big difference. Sometimes a small change in a parameter will cause the system to enter an entirely different type of behavior.

Figure A17 shows another view of a bifurcation diagram with the corresponding attractors given in cross-section and the motion the attractors describe shown below. This diagram highlights the fact that a system can have multiple attractors. One major area of study in complex dynamics is when and how a system shifts between competing attractors; this includes bifurcations and transitions to chaos.

Universality

The bifurcations in May's bifurcation diagram for animal population values occurred on a geometric ratio: 1, 2, 4, 8, 16. If you look closely at the frequency diagrams of the fluid going to turbulence you will see this same

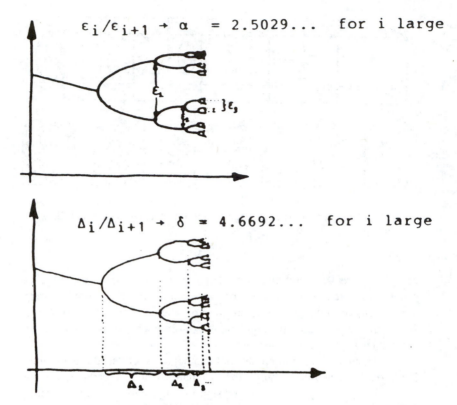

Figure A18. The alpha and delta universal constants (Cvitanovic 1989, p. 10).

ratio repeated: 1, 2, 4, ... The amplitudes of the fluid's frequency spikes also seem to show a certain proportionality.

Feigenbaum's Universality Theory proves that none of this is coincidental. The period-doubling into chaos is a standard pattern exhibited by large numbers of seemingly very diverse models. More remarkably this pattern's geometric convergence follows two universal constants $\alpha = 4.669$ and $\delta = 2.5029$, where δ is the ratio of the distance between two successive bifurcations on the horizontal axis and α is the ratio of the vertical distances of successive bifurcations. Figure A18 shows how these two ratios work.

Universality has two important implications. First, many quantitative aspects of the system can be predicted. Chaos works on geometries (called qualitative mathematics) but it can predict behavior quantitatively. For example, Universality predicts the spacing and amplitude of the fluid's frequency spikes and the final values of the animal populations.

The second and more important aspect of Universality Theory is its implication that complexity can be dealt with simply. Universality Theory shows that large classes of equations (models) behave the same way, qualitatively and quantitatively. For example, 4.669 holds for both the logistic equation and the sine function. All the possible equations in the world only generate a few basic types of behavior and it turns out that only a few properties of the system determine what type of behavior a system will exhibit. Two quotations give some sense of what this implies:

> The wonderful thing about this universality is that is does not matter much how close our equations are to the ones chosen by nature; as long as the model is in the same universality class ... as the real system, both will undergo a period-doubling sequence. That means that we can get the right physics out of very crude models. (Cvitanovic 1989, p. 11)

> Rolling streams, swinging pendulums, electronic oscillators many physical systems go through transition on the way to chaos... Equations for fluids, even pendulums, were far more challenging than the simple one-dimensional logistic map. But Feigenbaum's discovery implied that those equations were beside the point... When order emerges, it seems to have suddenly forgotten the original equation. (Gleick 1987, p. 174)

Thus, Universality suggests there are certain universal patterns of motion. "Dissipation bleeds complex systems of many conflicting motions, eventually bringing the behavior of many dimensions to one" (Gleick 1987, p. 209).

It is quite possible for infinite-dimensional systems as fluid turbulence was long considered can be effectively modeled with very simple equations. The specifics of the equation are not so important; you only need to be in the same class.

Universality dramatically simplifies complexity in three ways; by giving us: 1) the ability to describe classes of systems; 2) the understanding that high-dimension systems can be effectively modeled by simple equations; and 3) the understanding that the behavior described for a class of systems holds regardless of the physical nature of the system. It also suggests something very startling: many systems with exceedingly different "physics" at work will behave identically. Universality represents patterns of behavior that are inherent in the interaction of elements regardless of the mechanism involved.

Qualitative mathematics makes the notion of common forms of behavior rigorous. It makes a science of similarity, that is, having the same shape or pattern (remember similar triangles in high school geometry). Topology, for example, explores the range of perturbations which a system can undergo and still remain the same in essence, referred to as topological conjugacy. Modern geometric approaches use topological conjugacy to classify systems that will behave in geometrically similar ways. This ability to identify general classes of systems means that you can prove theorems for a class that then apply to all systems in that class.

The Big Picture

I have described attractors as pictures of the system's global behavior for a fixed value of a control parameter (e.g., $x = 3.14156x(1 - x)$). I have described the bifurcation diagram as a picture of the systems global behavior for all values of the parameter. Now, what happens if there is some dynamic that guides the control parameter? For example, in the logistic equation for population values, control parameter r represents fertility rates. In real-life systems, the fertility rate is itself a function of other variables perhaps food supply, crowding, and/or weather conditions. Can one know anything about the system's global behavior for all possible dynamics of the control parameter? The answer turns out to be "yes" and the work that is done on this topic is work on the Big Picture.

Work in the Big Picture looks at how different bifurcation diagrams would emerge from different control pattern dynamics. This work is important because it highlights the fact that "control parameters" themselves are part of a dynamic, part of a bigger picture. In the classical view, someone controls the control parameters. For example, when applied to amplifier feedback systems, r represents the music's volume. Here, the control parameter (volume) changes only when the experimenter turns the knob. In real life, "control parameters" often represent effects that a higher-level system has on the system we are studying. For example, the fertility rate is a single number that summarizes the net effect of a number of environmental factors. These environmental factors also form a system in which the animal system is embedded. The animal system probably even affects this environmental system. Thus, one system's control parameter is another system's output, and these two systems are likely interactive. The nice thing about work in the Big Picture is that it makes all of this interconnected tangle much simpler, more orderly, and accessible. Figure A19 shows a map

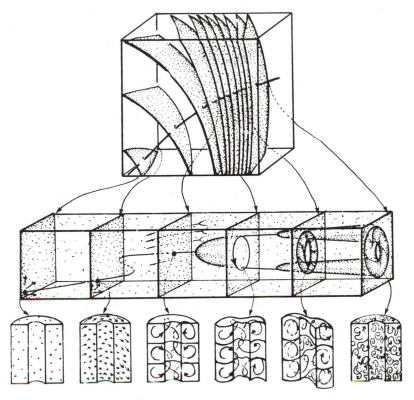

Figure A19. The dynamical superspace (Abraham and Shaw 1988, p. 46).

of the dynamical superspace, the qualitative change map for all possible dynamics of the control parameter.

In Figure A19 the curved sheets represent planes of structural instability, known as the bad set. Whenever a system crosses one of these sheets, it will change form. Thus, the Big Picture shows the global terrain of transformation.

Abraham and Shaw (1988) have created a pictorial atlas of the possible ways in which a system with one control parameter can go through its morphogenesis. For example, there are a finite number of paths into chaos and these have been catalogued in an Encyclopedia of Bifurcations. The Encyclopedia shows three major transformation types: subtle, catastrophic and explosive. Each of these major paths has subtypes, including such poetically named types as the Periodic Blue Sky catastrophe and the Noisy

Cascade. All of this means that there is a lot we can say about the possible things that can happen to a system depending on which way it goes.

NONLINEAR DYNAMICS IN CONSERVATIVE SYSTEMS

As Baranger (1991) notes: "The two things that are striking about dissipative chaos are strange attractors and universality. The two things that are striking about conservative system chaos is the KAM theorem and the homoclinic tangle."

The KAM Theorem

For the applied mathematician of the nineteenth century the paramount problem was the problem of the solar system. Since the time of Kepler, very good approximations of the motion of solar system had been worked out as a two-body problem; that is, because the sun is far heavier than any planet, one can get a very good approximation of the solar system by just looking at how each planet revolves around the sun (two bodies) without considering more complex interactions. The three-body problem represented the next simplest extension. Between 1850 and 1950 virtually every great mathematician attempted to find a viable approach to the three-body problem.

The KAM theorem finally determined why the three-body problem could not be resolved at least with the approaches being used. Until the KAM theorem mathematicians had been using an approach called "perturbation theory." Like calculus, perturbation theory attempted to simplify parts of the problem by breaking them down into small pieces and attempting to approximate them with lines or simple curves. The KAM theorem showed that such approximation cannot work because phase space for the three-body problem contains a fractal.

The fractal keeps the three-body problem from being approximated by simpler curves because when you try to break a fractal into smaller pieces it doesn't become simpler, it's equally complex at all levels. Hence, a straight line can't approximate a smaller piece any better than a larger one.

The KAM theorem shows that the boundary between the system's regular region and the chaotic region is fractal. This means that not only is there no nice, smooth boundary between regularity and chaos, but there is some chaos everywhere. If you take a very small region of phase space, no matter how small, no matter where in phase space, inside this volume there will always be some chaos. Chaos is dense everywhere. The boundary fills all space; that's part of its fractal nature.

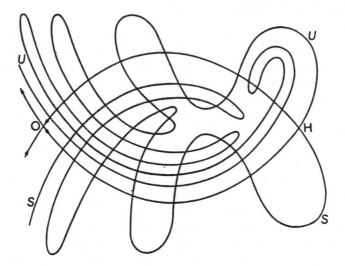

Figure A20. Homoclinic tangle (Abraham and Shaw 1986, p. 86).

Looking at the solar system from the perspective of two bodies made it seem endlessly stable and precisely regular. The three-body approach suggests that the solar system has the capacity for chaos. This suggestion has been born out. For instance, it has now been shown that the orbit of Pluto is chaotic. Pluto revolves around the sun and never quite returns to where it was before, it changes its speed of rotation, and it changes its inclination over the ecliptic.

Homoclinic Tangles

Conservative systems have chaos (with sensitive dependence and fractal structure) just as dissipative systems do. However, chaotic conservative systems do not have strange attractors. The primary diagram of chaos in conservative systems is the homoclinic tangle. Poincaré discovered and tried to draw the homoclinic tangle but gave up, saying it was simply too complex. The KAM theorem established the homoclinic tangle as a fractal. Figure A20 shows a homoclinic tangle as a cross-section of the three-dimensional case.

CHAOS AND INFORMATION FLOW

The final characteristic of chaos I will discuss joins together a number of the previous points. Shaw's (1980) theory of chaos and information flow suggests how chaos' peculiar characteristics help interconnect the world.

Energy in systems has traditionally been divided into two levels: the macro-scales (macroscopic level) and the micro-scales (the microscopic heat-bath level). Classically, science expects to be able to gain complete knowledge of interactions at the macro-scales while having complete ignorance of the micro-scales. These two levels are held to be essentially separate, the effects of each upon the other being negligible.

Shaw believes that this implicit separation breaks down in a system at or near the chaotic level where strange attractors appear. At these points minute amounts of change can produce massively different behavior. Thus, at these points even the minute activity of the micro-scales can have a measurable effect at the macro-scales.

Shaw translates this connection between micro- and macroscales into information theoretic terms in order to develop a theory of how information flows in and out of systems. To summarize this work briefly, Shaw sees the systems described by classical mechanics as "informationally dead"; after the first complete cycle, all further positions are repeated. The system is completely predictable; it tells us nothing new. Strange attractors, however, show a system that is orderly yet continually new (unpredictable). There is more information in the system than that specified in the initial conditions alone; the system is said to be "generating information." It appears that at or near chaos, the heat bath can channel information via strange attractors. Strange attractors seem to act as channels for information flowing between microscale activity and macro-scale activity.

Shaw shows that some attractors lose information, some generate information and some are informationally static. The net result is a world in which information flows back and forth between different systems.

While Shaw's work is still controversial, it does fit with a growing view of the world as an information-processing system (e.g., Rucker (1987) and Kuhn (1988)). Most importantly for us, his theory further demonstrates the interconnectivity hidden in apparently separate phenomena. The Butterfly Effect means that large- and small-scale events far from being disconnected may provide a channel of connection between widely separate macro-scale phenomena.

Appendix B

Entropy

Thermodynamics is a codification of what has been experienced (in a quantitative, objective fashion) by a broad spectrum of scientific investigators. The very same juxtaposition of phenomena observed in the 19th Century by engineers working with steam engines is seen to occur without fail in diverse modern areas of study such as mechanics, electronics, chemistry, physics, biochemistry and ecology.

Ulanowicz (1986, p. 9)

This appendix provides a more detailed discussion of entropy and the second law. It is largely about why entropy is useful for fields as diverse as biology, physics and information theory.

WHAT IS ENTROPY?

The concepts of energy and entropy were developed together during the mid-19th century and have been tightly intertwined ever since. The concept of energy was developed to represent the constant "thing" that could be moved among different forms (chemical, electrical, etc.) to do work. The concept of entropy was developed to represent the "thing" that was always lost when energy exchanges took place. In those early days, what was lost was a certain percentage of the potential to do work. It was as if the energy, while remaining constant, was degraded as a result of each exchange. A little bit of it ran through our fingers like sand, and once lost, it could not be retrieved.

Western culture has been using the concept of energy for so long now that energy feels like a "thing." Unfortunately, we have no such common feel for entropy. This is understandable given the facts of entropy: energy is a thing that is conserved and allows us to do work; entropy is a thing that is created when we lose work potential. Entropy is hard to intuit. Worse, what is hard to intuit at the energy-exchange level becomes quite mystifying when applied to things like information.

The early researchers were working on steam engines. In its early incarnation, entropy was a measure of work potential lost because energy went irretrievably into micro-scale motion (heat dissipation). In this early work, entropy was measured by a ratio of temperatures at one point in time versus a later point in time. However, entropy has come a long way from steam engines. Entropy measures are now made for a wide range of systems, including information-theoretic models and quantum-mechanical models ... and in neither of these cases is entropy defined as the work potential lost because of molecular motion. So, what is lost? What is entropy? To answer this we need to explore how the concept of entropy got from steam engines to information theory.

Boltzmann established the core modern definition of entropy in the process of working on the problem of thermal equilibrium. Where the original definition of entropy was in terms of steam engine parameters:

$$dS = dQ/T,$$

where S = entropy, Q = heat energy, and T = temperature. Boltzmann's model was completely generic; it was developed in terms of states of a system. The states of a system are defined by the variables used in the model. So, Boltzmann's definition of entropy was a phase-space definition (see Appendix A), i.e., the variables of the model define the axes of the space. He developed this generic approach to entropy in the process of trying to explain the thermal version of entropy in terms of molecular motion. This was at a time when the existence of molecules was not well accepted and he was trying to explain how entropy could be a product of molecular collisions. What he showed was that a generic state-space definition covered the thermal definition.

What was his generic definition? Boltzmann was looking at molecular motion in terms of particle position and velocity, the states of his system were position/velocity states. Yet, he was also looking at large numbers of molecules, so he actually had a large number of such microsystems interacting with each other. These of course were impossible to follow individually, but they could be dealt with as a whole probabilistically.

In this generic definition, entropy turns out to be the volume of the model in phase space. It is a single measure, a snapshot of the volume in multi-molecular phase space at a particular moment.

This might have been the story of entropy except a quirk about the volume in multi-molecular phase space when the dimensions are changing.

Such a phase space is a conglomerate of many smaller spaces. If phase space #1 contains variable x_1 and phase space #2 contains variable x_2 then when we put the variables x_1 and x_2 together to make a single phase space, the volume of resultant phase space is the product of the volumes of the two smaller phase spaces. Thus, if the generic definition of entropy were left as just the volume of phase space, when we put two systems together the entropy of the joint volume would be the product of the entropies of the individual systems. This is not pleasing to our intuition. It seems more natural to have the entropy of the joint system be the sum of the entropies of the two systems. Therefore, by convention, we change the definition. We take entropy as the logarithm of the volume in phase space. With this definition, when we join together two systems we do not multiply but add the entropies. Thus, by convention the generic definition of entropy is:

$$S = \log V.$$

This is a fine definition, one which appeals to our intuition. But it needs to be refined for those cases in which different volumes of the phase space have different probabilities of being occupied by the system, in other words, if the probability distribution function of the system over the whole volume is not uniform. In this case, one must replace the volume by a weighted average of all possible positions. Summing over all possible positions is essentially an integration operation and the result of an integration is a volume. What the "weighted average" gets you is the volume in phase space of a best (i.e., most probable) estimate of where the system is. This is done as follows: one breaks up the phase space into small volumes v_i and assigns to each a probability p_i that the system is in that volume. The sum of the small volumes must equal the whole volume and the sum of the probabilities must add up to unity. Thus:

$$\Sigma v_i = V \qquad \text{and} \qquad \Sigma p_i = 1.$$

The formula for the entropy of the system is then:

$$S = \Sigma p_i \log(v_i/p_i).$$

Note that you get the original formula $S = \log V$ when the probability is uniformly distributed. For instance, assume that the volume V has been split up into N equal volumes v_i and p_i is equal to $1/N$. Then the weighted sum S is $N(1/N) \log(V/N)N$ which is $S = \log V$.

Boltzmann couldn't know where any particular real molecule was (i.e., its position/velocity), but he had Maxwell's estimate of the probability of the different position/velocity pairs for all possible position/velocity pairs at equilibrium. Therefore, he used this distribution to compute a most probable volume in phase space using the formula shown above. His real contribution is that this definition of entropy, which maps well to the original, is so generic that it can be applied to all types of systems. And in the generic definition entropy amounts to a snapshot volume in phase space.

So, Boltzmann gave us a generic definition of entropy. It is the one general and consistent definition of entropy across all systems the log of the volume in phase space or the weighted sum. It is generic and thus has nothing per se to do with energy, temperature or any other particular variable. The second law (increasing entropy) holds for all these different abstract systems. Thus, entropy has nothing to do with any variable per se but rather what happens to phase-space snapshots as the system evolves.

What happens to the phase-space snapshot as the system evolves and what do such changes mean? The key to understanding this has to do with the fact that the entropy measure is based on probabilities and on models, not on actualities of where the system is. The generic entropy measure gives the volume of a best estimate of the system. What changes as the system evolves is the volume of our best estimate of the volume.

What could possibly make our best estimate get bigger and bigger and why should that be a fundamental law of the universe? I believe the best answer to this is "complexity," and one of the reasons why generic entropy is so hard to understand is that you really need a good grasp of Chaos to fathom why it should happen at all. Harken back to Chaos, the Breadmaker's Universe, stretching and folding in phase space ... and most of all to fractals. Imagine that each time something interacts with something else there's a stretch and a fold, a new layer, a new nook and cranny of phase space. Our models can't follow all that detailed complexity. Indeed, thanks to fractals and certain Russian mathematicians we can now prove that it is impossible to follow. No matter how far down you go, a fractal map has the same complexity. So, the universe grows in complexity with each motion. And we cannot follow it all. Instead we draw a little outline around how it is mostly distributed. Then, like a ball of tangled string, each wrap around the ball increases the complexity a little, increases the volume of our outline a little and adds a little more to what we don't know. That is entropy. It happens regardless of the nature of the system. At each interaction the world gets a little more complex and we know a little less about it.

Let's take a brief visit to conservative systems theory to see how this works. By definition, conservative systems conserve their volume in phase space. However, even though the volume in phase space remains the same in principle, in practice it becomes very, very complicated (like the ball of string) to the point where it can't be followed anymore. So it is replaced with a kind of envelope which takes in the whole complex thing and which is bigger than the original volume because it also includes all the little nooks and crannies of complexity. That increase is the increase in entropy.

The generic concept of entropy brings home the realization of models, modeling abilities and modeling choices. Chaos helps us understand what entropy is in terms of increasing complexity. It also where what we lose is going; it is being woven into finer and finer levels of complexity.[1]

But, what does all this mean in terms of concrete things like steam engines. Early workers, like Clausius and Carnot, were concerned with efficiency of engines. They lost something. From their perspective, potential to do mechanical work was lost in a very physical sense. The proof that you can't construct perpetual motion machines is a proof that you can't get all the energy back. How do we reconcile this very concrete aspect of something lost and the grand abstraction that is entropy?

This is a very nasty conceptual problem. It is nasty for two reasons. For one thing, from the generic perspective what is lost is unique to each particular type of system. In steam engines what is lost is the ability to do mechanical work; in information theoretic models what is lost is the ability to extract information. Entropy is a universal phenomenon that is supported by a whole variety of unique things getting lost. Secondly, when whatever is lost gets lost, it is really lost (i.e., the perpetual motion machine). How can such a plethora of unique things getting lost all have a common physically real basis?[2]

The claim is that all these unique things getting lost is a function of the increasing complexity of the system and our inability to follow all that complexity. So, let me comment on quandary #2 the physical sense of losing something. When whatever is lost gets lost, it is really lost (i.e., the perpetual motion machine) but only to that scale of measure. Understanding why entropy increase is physical is tied to the scale dependency of measurement.

Thank God for fractals, or this would never make sense. In the steam-engine days people only knew how to measure temperature, pressure and volume. We can measure much smaller scales now, so the micro-scale heat energy those researchers lost is not missing to scientists working at the atomic level. It is causing a lot of work at the atomic scale. What was lost at the macro-scale is alive and well at the micro-scale. This is conceptually true for all systems. Thus, any phase space model treats its variables as a macro-scale. Producing entropy means that interactions at this macro-scale level result in increased complexity that can only be studied and operated on at a finer scale of measure. The reason potential is lost to the macro-scale level because macro-scale action (for example, Carnot cycles) cannot retrieve it and it takes work to retrieve it from the micro-scale by other means. Morowitz summarizes it as follows:

> Our current concepts of thermodynamics are rooted in the industrial revolution and the attempts to determine how much mechanical work is available from heat engines. Entropy provides a measure of the work that is unavailable because of our lack of knowledge of the detailed state of the system. The whole structure acquires consistency only because it requires work to obtain information. If this were not true, a Maxwellian demon could indeed continuously violate the second law of thermodynamics. The second law and the entropy measure tell us as much about the observer as about the system. (1968, p. 130)

NOTES

1. So the most general and consistent way to define entropy is in terms of the (log) of the volume of phase space computed by weighted averages. In applying this definition people develop a host of substitute definitions for their particular system. For example, in chemistry there will be a variety of chemicals, with different chemical potentials, concentrations, boundary conditions, etc. All of these factors make a particular phase space and a particular probability distribution within that space.

    Unfortunately, unique phase spaces and unique entropies create an open door for conceptual misappropriation. Substitute definitions require a set of assumptions used to define the weighting function (probability distribution). Of course, the substitute definition does not hold outside of these assumptions but people are often not aware of this. It is also common for people to try to reduce all entropies to their particular definition of it. Both information theory and dissipative-structure theory have used this approach. This just further clouds the issue. Entropy is more than just heat dissipation or chemical mixing. Only from the perspective of the generic understanding do we stand any chance of comprehending its full import.

2. Entropy's connection to modeling can be seen in the traditional approach to energy. The energy relationships that people have traditionally drawn out are based on dividing energy into two categories. There is one category that "cannot" be analyzed (called heat) and there is another category that can be analyzed (called other things like mechanical energy, chemical energy, electrical energy etc.). The energy that can be analyzed is analyzed and that which can't be analyzed becomes an aspect of entropy and is assumed to be evenly distributed over phase space.

References

Abraham, F. D. (1989). "A Dynamical Model of the Attributional Process in Cognitive Motivational Theory." In: *Basic Principles of Dynamical Systems in Psychobiology*, eds. F. Abraham, R. Abraham, and C. Shaw. Santa Cruz, CA: Aerial Press.

Abraham, F. D., and C. Shaw (1990). *A Visual Introduction to Dynamical Systems Theory for Psychology*. Santa Cruz, CA: Aerial Press.

Abraham, R. (1985). *On Morphodynamics*. Santa Cruz, CA: Aerial Press.

Abraham, R., and C. Shaw (1982). *Dynamics of the Geometry of Behavior, Part One: Periodic Behavior*. Santa Cruz, CA: Aerial Press.

Abraham, R., and C. Shaw (1984). *Dynamics of the Geometry of Behavior, Part Two: Stable and Chaotic Behavior*. Santa Cruz, CA: Aerial Press.

Abraham, R., and C. Shaw (1986). *Dynamics of the Geometry of Behavior, Part Three: Global Behavior*. Santa Cruz, CA: Aerial Press.

Abraham, R., and C. Shaw (1987). "Dynamics: A Visual Introduction." In: *Self-Organizing Systems*, pp. 543–597, ed. F. Yates.

Abraham, R., and C. Shaw (1988). *Dynamics of the Geometry of Behavior, Part Four: Bifurcation Behavior*. Santa Cruz, CA: Aerial Press.

Amato, I. (1992). "Putting Gentle Reins on Unruly Systems." *Science* 256:1283.

Arthur, W. B. (1990). "Positive Feedback in the Economy. *Scientific American*, February 1990, pp. 92–99.

Artigiani, R. (1991). Unpublished presentation at the 35th Annual Meeting of the International Society of the System Sciences, Ostersund, Sweden.

Banathy, B. (1987). "The Characterization and Acquisition of Evolutionary Competence." *World Futures*, April 1987.

Baranger, M. (1990). "Chaos: A Primer." In: *Proceedings from the Summer School of Computational Atomic and Nuclear Physics,* eds. C. Bottcher, M. R. Strayer, and J. B. McGrory. Held at the University of the South, Sewanee, TN. Singapore: World Scientific Publishing Co.

Baranger, M. (1991). Personal communication.

Barnsley, M. (1989). *Fractals Everywhere*. San Diego, CA: Academic Press.

Barry, M. (1991). "Electronic Communication via CSGnet, July 7, 1991." G. Cziko, Coordinator. Internet address: g-cziko@uiuc.edu.

Bartlett, J. (1980). *Bartlett's Familiar Quotations*. Boston, MA: Little, Brown and Company.

Bateson, G. (1976). *Steps to an Ecology of Mind*. New York: Bantam Books.

Bateson, G. (1979). *Mind and Nature: A Necessary Unity*. New York: Bantam Books.

Barrow, J. D., and F. J. Tipler (1988). *The Anthropic Cosmological Principle*. Oxford: Oxford University Press.

Bartley, W. W. (1987). The Philosophy of Biology Versus the Philosophy of Physics. In: *Evolutionary Epistemology, Rationality and the Sociology of Knowledge*. eds. G. Radnitzky and W. W. Bartley III, pp. 7–40. La Salle, IL: Open Court.

Berger, P., and T. Luckmann (1967). *The Social Construction of Reality*. Garden City, NY: Doubleday and Co.

Berry, F. M. (1984). "An Introduction to Stephen C. Pepper's Philosophical System via World Hypotheses: A Study in Evidence." *Bulletin of the Psychonomic Society* 22(5):446–448.

Bohm, D. (1970). "Further Remarks on Order." In: *Towards a Theoretical Biology*, ed. C. H. Waddington. Chicago: Aldine Publishing.

Bohm, D. (1980). *Wholeness and the Implicate Order*. New York: Routledge and Kegan Paul, Inc.

Bohm, D. (1985). *Unfolding Meaning*. New York: Routledge and Kegan Paul, Inc.

Boltzmann, L. (1886). "The Second Law of Thermodynamics." Populare Schriften, Essay 3. Reprinted in *Ludwig Boltzmann, Theoretical Physics and Philosophical Problems*, ed. B. McGuiness. Boston: D. Reidel Publishing Co.

Briggs, J., and F. D. Peat (1989). *Turbulent Mirror*. New York: Harper and Row.

Brooks, D., and E. Wiley (1988). *Evolution as Entropy*. Chicago: The University of Chicago Press.

Burke, J. (1978). *Connections*. Boston, MA: Little, Brown and Co.

Byers, H. R. (1974). *General Meteorology*. New York: McGraw Hill.

Cairns-Smith, A. G. (1982). *Genetic Takeover and the Mineral Origins of Life*. New York: Cambridge University Press.

Campbell, J. (1956). *Hero With a Thousand Faces*. New York: World Publishing Co.

Cariani, P. (1991). Electronic communication distributed on CSGNet. April 12.

Carneiro, R. (1967). "On the Relationship Between Size of Population and Complexity of Social Structure." *Southwestern Journal of Anthropology* 23:234–243.

Carneiro, R. (1970). "A Theory of the Origin of the State." *Science* 169:733–738.

Carneiro, R. (1987). "The Evolution of Complexity in Human Societies and Its Mathematical Expression." *International Journal of Comparative Sociology* 28:111–128.

Chaisson, E. (1987). *The Life Era*. New York: Atlantic Monthly Press.

Chaitin, G. (1987). *Algorithmic Information Theory*. Cambridge: Cambridge University Press.

Chua, L. O., and T. Lin (1990). "Chaos and Fractals from Third-Order Digital Filters." *International Journal of Circuit Theory and Applications* 18:241–255.

Crutchfield, J. P., F. Doyne, N. H. Packard, and R. S. Shaw (1986). "Chaos." *Scientific American*, December, pp. 46–57.

Csanyi, V. (1989). *Evolutionary Systems and Society: A General Theory of Life, Mind and Culture*. Durham, NC: Duke University Press.

Cvitanovic, P. (1989). *Introduction to Universality in Chaos*. Bristol, England: Adam Hilger.

DeGroot, S.R., and R. Mazur (1969). *Non-Equilibrium Thermodynamics*. Amsterdam: North Holland.

Delattre, P. (1986). "An Approach to the Notion of Finality According to the Concepts of Qualitative Dynamics." In: *Dynamical Systems a Renewal of Mechanism*, pp. 273–290, ed. S. Diner, D. Fargue, and G. Lochak. Philadelphia: World Scientific Publishing.

Deneubourg, J. L., J. M. Pasteels, and J. C. Verhaeghe (1983). "Probabilistic Behavior in Ants: A Strategy of Errors." *Journal of Theoretical Biology* 105:259–271.

Devaney, R.L. (1986). *An Introduction to Chaotic Dynamical Systems*. Menlo Park, CA: Benjamin/Cummings.

Dewdney, A. K. (1987). "Probing the Strange Attraction of Chaos. *Scientific American* 257(1):108–111.

Diner, S. (1986). "Epilogue: A Renewal of Mechanism, Toward an Instrumental Realism." In: *Dynamical Systems a Renewal of Mechanism*, pp. 273–290, eds. S. Diner, D. Fargue, and G. Lochak. Philadelphia: World Scientific Publishing.

Dreyfuss, H., and J. Rubin (1989). "The Invention of the Modern Self." Audiotape Lectures. University of California at Berkeley, Department of Philosophy.

Dyson, F. (1985). *Origins of Life*. Cambridge: Cambridge University Press.

Eigen, M. (1981). "The Origin of Genetic Information." *Scientific American* 244(4):88–118.

Eigen, M., and P. Schuster (1979). *The Hypercycle: A Principle of Natural Self-Organization*. Berlin: Springer-Verlag.

Ekeland, I. (1984). *Le Calcul, L'Imprevu*. Paris: Editions du Seuil.

Eisler, R. (1988). *The Chalice and the Blade*. New York: Viking Press.

Feigenbaum, M. J. (1978). "Quantitative Universality for a Class of Nonlinear Transformations." *Journal of Statistical Physics* 19:25–33.

Feigenbaum, M. J. (1980). "Universal Behavior in Nonlinear Systems." *Los Alamos Science* 1:4–27.

Foucault, M. (1973). *The Order of Things*. New York: Random House.

Ford, J. (1986). "Chaos: Solving the Unsolvable, Predicting the Unpredictable." In: *Chaotic Dynamics and Fractals*, pp. 123–140, eds. M. F. Barnsley and S. G. Demko. New York: Academic Press.

Ford, J. (1989). "What is Chaos, That We Should Be Mindful of It?" In: *The New Physics*, eds. S. Capelin and P. Davies. Cambridge: Cambridge University Press.

Freeman, W. J. (1991). "The Physiology of Perception." *Scientific American*, February, pp. 78–85.

Gazzaniga, M. S. (1985). *The Social Brain. New York: Basic Books.*

Gilbert, G., and M. Mulkay (1984). *Opening Pandora's Box*. Cambridge: Cambridge University Press.

Gilgen, A., and F. Abraham (Eds.) (1994). *Chaos Theory in Psychology*. New York: Greenwood Publishers.

Glass, L., and M. C. Mackey (1988). *From Clocks to Chaos: The Rhythms of Life*. Princeton, New Jersey: Princeton University Press.

Gleick, J. (1987). *Chaos, Making a New Science*. New York: Viking.

Goerner, S. (1990). "Chaos and the Evolving Ecology World Hypothesis: Implications for Just Systems." In: *Proceedings of the International Society of the Systems Sciences*, 34th Annual Meeting, Portland, 1990.

Goldstein, J. (1990). "Freud's Theories in Light of Far-From-Equilibrium Research." *Social Research* 52(1):9–45.

Goleman, D. (1972). "The Buddha on Meditation and States of Consciousness, Part I: The Teachings." *Journal of Transpersonal Psychology* 4:151–214.

Greeley, L. (1990). *Philosophical Spacing (PS): Key to the Nonlinear Complex Dynamics of the Attentional System of the Cognitive Learning Process in the Philosophical Dialectic Method*. Doctoral Dissertation. School of Education, Harvard University, Cambridge.

Greeley, L. (1991). "The Implications of Chaos Theory for the Metaphysics of Psychology." Paper presented at the first annual meeting of the Society of Chaos Theory in Psychology, San Francisco.

Gurel, O. (1979). "Preface." In: *Bifurcation Theory and Applications in Scientific Disciplines*, pp. 1–27, eds. O. Gurel and O. E. Rossler. New York: New York Academy of Sciences.

Gutzwiller, M. (1983). "Mild Chaos." In: *Chaotic Behavior in Quantum Systems*, pp. 149–165, ed. G. Casati. New York: Plenum Press.

Haldane, J. (1954). "On Being the Right Size." In: *A Treasury of Science*, eds. H. Shapely, S. Rapport, and H. Wright. New York: Harper and Brothers.

Hayes, S., L. Hayes, and H. Reese (1988). "Finding the Philosophical Core: A Review of Stephen C. Pepper's World Hypotheses." *Journal of the Experimental Analysis of Behavior* 50:97–111.

Hegel, G. F. (1962). *The Philosophy of History*. Trans. W. R. Boyce-Gibson. New York: Harper and Row.

Helleman R. H. (1984). "Self-Generated Chaotic Behavior in Nonlinear Mechanics." In: *Universality in Chaos*. ed. P. Cvitanovic. Bristol, England: Adam Hilger

Hofstadter, D. (1985). *Metamagical Themas: Questing for the Essence of Mind and Matter*. New York: Bantam Books.

Holland, H. (1978). *The Chemistry of the Atmosphere and Oceans*. New York: John Wiley & Sons.

Hubel, D., and T. Wiesel (1962). "Receptive Fields, Binocular Interaction, and Functional Architecture in the Cat's Visual Cortex." *Journal of Physiology* 160:106–154.

Hunt, E. R. (1991). "Stabilizing High-Period Orbits in a Chaotic System: The Diode Resonator." *Physical Review Letters* 67(15):1953–1954.

Huxley, A. (1954). "Introduction." In: *Bhagavad-Gita [The Song of God]*, pp. 9–23, trans. S. Prabhavananda and C. Isherwood. New York: New American Library.

Jacobs, J. (1969). *The Economy of Cities*. New York: Random House.

Jacobs, J. (1984). *Cities and the Wealth of Nations*. New York: Random House.

Jantsch, E. (1980). *The Self-Organizing Universe*. New York: Pergamon Press.

Jaynes, J. (1976). *The Origins of Consciousness and the Breakdown of the Bicameral Mind*. Boston: Houghton Mifflin.

Johnson, R. C. (1988). "Neural Model: One Equation Does It All." *Electronic Engineering Times*, March 28, 53–54.

Jung, C. (1956). *Collected Works*, Vol. 5: *Symbols and Transformation*. Trans. R. C. Hull. New York: Pantheon. (Original work published in 1912).

Kidder, T. (1982). *Soul of a New Machine*. New York: Simon and Schuster.

Kimura, M. (1983). *The Neural Theory of Molecular Evolution*. New York: Cambridge University Press.

King, M., and R. A. Abraham (1989). "Communicative Chess." Paper presented to the American Society for Cybernetics Annual Convention, Norfolk, VA.

King, M., and R. A. Abraham (1992). "Netscope: Dynamics from Communication Data." *American Journal of Psychotherapy* 46(1).

King, R., J. D. Barchas, and B. A. Hubermann (1983). "Theoretical Psychopathology: An Application of Dynamical Systems Theory to Human Behavior." In: *Synergetics of the Brain*, eds. E. Basar, H. Flohr, H. Haken, and J. Mandell. Heidelberg: Springer-Verlag.

King, R., J. D. Barchas, and B. A. Hubermann (1984). "Chaotic Behavior in Dopamine Neurodynamics." *Proceedings of the National Academy of Sciences of the United States of America* (Neurobiology) 81:1244–1247.

Koerner, J. (1989). *Nontriviality of Nonlinear Dynamics in Psychology of Learning*. Doctoral Dissertation. University of Minnesota, Minneapolis.

Koestler, A. (1972). *The Roots of Coincidence*. New York: Vintage Books.

Krippner, S. (1987). *Learning Guide for Eastern Psychologies*. San Francisco: Saybrook Institute.

Krugman, P.A. (1991). "Myths and Realities of U.S. Competitiveness." *Science* 254:811–814.

Kugler, P., and R. Shaw (1990). "Symmetry and Symmetry-Breaking in Thermodynamic and Epistemic Engines: A Coupling of the First and Second Laws." In: *Synergetics of Cognition*, ed. H. Haken. Heidelberg, Germany: Springer-Verlag.

Kugler, P., R. Shaw, K. Vincente, and J. Kinsella-Shaw (1990). "Inquiry into Intentional Systems: Issues in Ecological Physics." *Psychological Research* 52:98–121.

Kuhn, H. (1988). "Origin of Life and Physics: Diversified Microstructure Inducement to Form Information Carrying and Knowledge Accumulating Systems." *IBM Journal of Research and Development* 32(1):37–46.

Kuhn, T. (1972). *The Structure of Scientific Revolutions*. New York: Houghton Mifflin.

Lampl, M., J. D. Velduis, and M. L. Johnson (1992). "Saltation and Stasis: A Model of Human Growth." *Science* 258:801–803.

Langs, R. (1989). "Psychotherapy and Psychoanalysis Defined by Mathematical Models." *Psychiatric Times*, March 1989.

Laszlo, E. (1987). *Evolution: The Grand Synthesis*. Boston: Shambhala.

Lintilhac, P. (1974). "Differentiation, Organogenesis, and the Tectonics of Cell Wall Orientation." *American Journal of Botany* 61(2):135–140.

Lotka, A. J. (1922). "Contribution to the Energetics of Evolution." *Proceedings of the National Academy of Science* 8:147.

Lovelock, J. (1979). *Gaia: A New Look at Life on Earth*. Oxford: Oxford University Press.

Mandelbrot, B. B. (1977). *Fractals: Form, Chance and Dimension*. San Francisco: W.H. Freeman and Co.

Mandelbrot, B. B. (1982). *The Fractal Geometry of Nature*. New York: W.H. Freeman and Co.

Mandelbrot, B. B. (1987). "Towards a Second Stage of Indeterminism in Science." *Interdisciplinary Science Reviews* 12(2):117–127.

Mandelbrot, B. (1990). "Fractals and Visual Perception." Presentation at the Annual Meeting of the Sigma Xi Science Foundation, Research Triangle Park, NC.

Margulis, L. (1970). *Origin of Eucaryotic Cells*. New Haven: Yale University Press.

Margulis, L. (1981). *Symbiosis in Cell Evolution*. San Francisco: Freeman and Co.

Margulis, L. (1982). *Early Life*. Boston: Science Books International.

Margulis, L. (1990). "Gaia and Microcosmos." Paper presented at the 8th International Congress of Cybernetics and Systems, Hunter College, New York.

Markeley, O., and W. Harmon (1982). *Changing Images of Man*. New York: Pergamon Press.

Marr, M. J. (1992). "Behavior Dynamics." *Journal of the Experimental Analysis of Behavior* 57:249–266.

Maturana, H.R., and F. J. Varela (1980). *Autopoiesis and Cognition: The Realization of the Living*. Boston Studies in the Philosophy of Science, Vol. 42.

Maturana, H., and F. Varela (1987). *The Tree of Knowledge*. Boston: Shambhala.

May, J., and M. Groder (1989). "Jungian Thought and Dynamical Systems." *Psychological Perspectives* 20(1):143–156.

May, R. (1969). *Love and Will*. New York: W.W.Norton and Co.

May, R. M. (1976). "Simple Mathematical Models with Very Complicated Dynamics." *Nature* 261:459–467.

May, R. M. (1974). "Biological Populations With Non-Overlapping Generations: Stable Points, Stable Cycles, and Chaos." *Science* 186:645–647.

May, R. M. (1987a). "Chaos and the Dynamics of Biological Populations." In: *Dynamical Chaos*, pp. 27–43, eds. M. V. Berry, I. C. Percival, and N. O. Weiss. Princeton: Princeton University Press.

May, R. M. (1987b). "Nonlinearities and Complex Behavior in Simple Ecological and Epidemiological Models." In: *Perspectives in Biological Dynamics and Theoretical Medicine*, pp. 1–15, eds. S. H. Koslow, A. J. Mandell, and M. R. Schlesinger. New York: New York Academy of Sciences.

Mayer-Kress, G., and S. P. Layne (1987). "Dimensionality of the Human Electroencephalogram." In: *Perspectives in Biological Dynamics and Theoretical Medicine*, pp. 62–86, eds. S. H. Koslow, A. J. Mandell, and M. R. Schlesinger. New York: New York Academy of Sciences.

Meinhardt, H. (1979). "The Random Character of Bifurcation and the Reproducible Processes of Embryonic Development." In: *Bifurcation Theory and Application in Scientific Disciplines*, pp. 188–203, eds. O. Gurel and O. E. Rossler. New York: New York Academy of Sciences.

Miller, S. L. (1953). *Science* 117:528.

Minsky, M. (1985). *The Society of Mind*. New York: Simon and Schuster.

Mizutani, H., and E. Wada (1982). "Material Cycles and Organic Evolution." *Origins of Life* 12:369–376.

Monod, J. (1972). *Chance and Necessity*. New York: Random House.

Moon, R. C. (19??). *Chaotic Vibrations*. New York: John Wiley & Sons.

Morowitz, H. J. (1968). *Energy Flow in Biology: Biological Organization as a Problem in Thermal Physics*. New York: Academic Press.

Nicholis, G., and I. Prigogine (1989). *Exploring Complexity*. New York: W.H.Freeman & Company.

Nicolis, J., and S. Tsuda (1985). "Chaotic Dynamics of Information Processing: The 'Magic Number Seven Plus-Minus Two' Revisited." *Ichiro Bulletin of Mathematical Biology* 47(3):343–365.

Odum, E. P. (1969). "The Strategy of Ecosystem Development." *Science* 16:262–270.

Odum, E. P. (1983). *Systems Ecology: An Introduction*. New York: John Wiley.

Odum, H. T. (1988). "Self-Organization, Transformity, and Information." *Science* 242:1132.

Odum, H. T. (1991). *Energy and Policy*. New York: John Wiley.

Olsen, L. F., and W. M. Schaffer (1990). "Chaos Versus Noisy Periodicity: Alternative Hypotheses for Childhood Epidemics." *Science* 249:499–504.

Onsager, L. (1931). "Reciprocal Relations in Irreversible Processes." *Physical Review* 37:405.

Oparin, A. I. (1957). *The Origin of Life on The Earth*, 3rd ed., trans. Ann Synge. Edinburgh: Oliver and Boyd.

Pagels, H. (1988). *Dreams of Reason*. New York: Simon and Schuster.

Palmer, L. S. (1957). *Man's Journey Through Time*. London: Hutchinson.

Pantzar, M. (1991). *Economics and Replicative Evolution*. New York: Gordon and Breach.

Pattee, H. (1991). "Measurement-Control Heterarchical Networks in Living Systems." *International Journal of Systems Science*.

Pattee, H. H. (1982). "Cell Psychology: An Evolutionary Approach to the Symbol-Matter Problem." *Cognition and Brain Theory* 5(4):325–341.

Peitgen, H., and P. Richter (1986). *The Beauty of Fractals*. Berlin: Springer-Verlag.

Pepper, S. (1946). *World Hypotheses: Prolegomena to Systematic Philosophy and a Complete Survey of Metaphysics*. Berkeley: University of California Press.

Peters, E. (1991). *Chaos and Order in the Capitol Market*. New York: John Wiley & Sons.

Peters, T. (1989). *Thriving on chaos*. New York: Simon & Schuster.

Pettersson, M. (1978). "Acceleration in Evolution, Before Human Times." *Journal of Social and Biological Structures* 1:201–206.

Peyla, W. L. (1992). "Dynamics in the Fine Structure of Schedule-Controlled Behavior." *Journal of the Experimental Analysis of Behavior* 57:267–287.

Popper, K. (1965). *Conjectures and Refutations*. New York: Bantam Books.

Popper, K. (1968). *The Logic of Scientific Discovery*. New York: Harper & Row.

Pribram, K. (1976). *Consciousness and the Brain*. New York: Plenum Press.

Pribram, K. (1991). Keynote Address at the First Annual Conference of Chaos in Psychology, San Francisco.

Price, D. J. (1956). *Discovery* 17:240.

Prigogine, I. (1972). "Thermodynamics of Evolution. *Physics Today,* December 1972.

Prigogine, I. (1978). "Time, Structure and Fluctuation." *Science* 201:777.

Prigogine, I. (1980). *From Being to Becoming*. New York: W.H.Freeman and Company.

Prigogine, I., and G. Nicolis (1971). "Biological Order, Structures and In-stabilities." *Quarterly Review of Biophysics* 4:107–148.

Prigogine, I., and E. Stengers (1984). *Order Out of Chaos*. New York: Bantam Books.

Radnitzky, G., and W. W. Bartley III (1987). *Evolutionary Epistemology, Rationality and the Sociology of Knowledge*. La Salle, IL: Open Court.

Robson, E. M. (1987). *Freedom, Cannibalism, Creative Love, and the Values of Cosmic Nonsense*. Parker Ford, PA: Primary Press.

Rogowitz, B. E., and R. F. Voss (1990). "Shape Perception and Low-Dimension Fractal Boundary Contours." In: *Proceedings of the Conference on Human Vision: Methods, Models, and Applications, SPIE/SPSE Symposium on Electronic Imaging*, Vol. 1249, eds. B. E. Rogowitz and J. Allebach. Santa Clara, CA (or contact: Rogowitz and Voss, IBM T.J. Watson Research Center, Yorktown Heights, New York, 10598).

Rosen, R. (1970). *Dynamical System Theory in Biology*. New York: John Wiley & Sons, Inc.

Rosen, R. (1985). *Theoretical Biology and Complexity*. Orlando, FL: Academic Press.

Rosen, R. (1991). *Life Itself*. New York: Columbia University Press.

Ross, N. W. (1980). *Buddhism: A Way of Life and Thought*. New York: Vintage Books.

Rossi, E. (1989). "Archetypes as Strange Attractors." *Psychological Perspectives* 20(1):143–156.

Roth, G., and H. Schwegler (Eds.) (1981). *Self-Organizing Systems: An Inter-disciplinary Approach*. Frankfurt: Campus Verlag.

Rucker, R. (1987). *Mind Tools*. Boston: Houghton Mifflin.

Sacks, O. (1990). *Awakenings*. New York: Harper Collins Publishers.

Schrödinger, E. (1944). *What is life? The Physical Aspect of the Living Cell*. Cambridge: Cambridge University Press.

Schuster, H. (1984). *Deterministic Chaos*. Weinheim, FRG: Physik-Verlag.

Schwalbe, M. L. (1991). "The Autogenesis of the Self." *Journal for the Theory of Social Behavior* 21(3):269–295.

Schwarz, E. (1991). "From Thermodynamics to Consciousness: A Model for Evolution." In: *Proceedings of the International Society of the Systems Sciences, 35th Annual Meeting*, Vol. I, pp. 235–241, Ostersund, Sweden.

Shaw, R. (1980). "Strange Attractors, Chaotic Behavior, and Information Flow." *Zeitschrift Fur Naturforsch* 36A:80–112.

Shaw, R. (1984). "The Dripping Faucet as a Model Chaotic System." Santa Cruz, CA: Aerial Press.

Sheldrake, R. (1981). *A New Science of Life*. Boston: Houghton Mifflin Company.

Skarda, C. A., and W. J. Freeman (1987). "How Brains Make Chaos in Order to Make Sense of the World." *Behavioral and Brain Sciences* 10:172.

Skinner, H. A. (1989). "Butterfly Wings Flapping: Do We Need More 'Chaos' in Understanding Addictions." *British Journal of Addiction* 84:353–356.

Smale, S. (1967). "Differentiable Dynamical Systems." *Bulletin of the American Mathematical Society* 747–814.

Smale, S. (1980). *The Mathematics of Time: Essays on Dynamical Systems, Economic Processes, and Related Topics*. New York: Springer-Verlag.

Smith, H. (1985). *The Cell and The Womb*. Ithaca, NY: Art Matrix.

Smith, H. (1986). *Mandelbrot Sets and Julia Sets*. Ithaca, NY: Art Matrix.

Smith, H. (1988). Personal Communication.

Smith, L. B. (1992). "Real Time and Developmental Time: The Geometry of Children's Novel Word Interpretations." Paper presented at the 100th Anniversary Convention of the American Psychological Association, Washington, DC.

Spencer, H. (1862). *First Principles*. London: Williams and Norgate.

Stewart, I. (1989). *Does God Play Dice: The Mathematics of Chaos*. New York: Basil Blackwell.

Suppe, F. (1972). "Afterword." In: *The Structure of Scientific Theories*, pp. 617–731, ed. F. Suppe, Chicago: University of Illinois Press.

Swenson, R. (1988). "Emergence and the Principle of Maximum Entropy Production: Multi-Level Systems Theory, Evolution and Nonequilibrium Thermodynamics." In: *Proceedings of the 32rd Annual Meeting of the International Society for the Systems Sciences* (St. Louis, May), pp. 32–43.

Swenson, R. (1989a). "Emergent Attractors and the Law of Maximum Entropy Production: Foundations to a Theory of General Evolution." *Systems Research* 6(3):187–197.

Swenson, R. (1989b). "Emergent Evolution and the Global Attractor: The Evolutionary Epistemology of Entropy Production." *Proceedings of the 33rd Annual Meeting of the International Society for the Systems Sciences* 3:46–53.

Swenson, R. (1989c). "The Earth as an Incommensurate Field at the Geo-Cosmic Interface: Fundamentals to a Theory of Emergent Evolution." In: *Geo-Cosmic Relations: The Earth and Its Macro-Environment*, pp. 299–306, eds. G. J. M. Tomassen, W. de Graff, A. A. Knoop, and R. Hengeveld. Wageningen, The Netherlands: PUDOC Science Publishers.

Swenson, R. (1989d). "Engineering Initial Conditions in a Self-Producing Environment." In: *Proceedings of IEEE and SSIT Conference* (October 20–21). California State University, Los Angeles.

Swenson, R. (1990). "Gauss-in-a-Box: Nailing Down the First Principles of Action." *PAW Review* 4(1).

Swenson, R. (1991). "Order, Evolution, and Natural Law: Fundamental Relations in Complex Systems Theory." In: *Handbook of Systems and Cybernetics*, ed. C. Negoita. New York: Marcel Dekker, Inc.

Swenson, R. (1991). "Autocatakinetics, Yes — Autopoiesis, No: Steps Towards a Unified Theory of Evolutionary Ordering." *International Journal of General Systems*.

Tarrant, J. (1988). *The Design of Enlightenment in Koan Zen*. Doctoral Dissertation. San Francisco: Saybrook Institute.

Taylor, M. (1976). *Anarchy and Cooperation*. New York: John Wiley & Sons.

Thom, R. (1975). *Structural Stability and Morphogenesis*. Reading, MA: W.A. Benjamin, Inc.

Thompson, J., and H. Stewart (1986). *Nonlinear Dynamics and Chaos*. New York: John Wiley and Sons.

Tipton, J., and F. Barrow (1988). *The Anthropic Cosmological Principle*. Oxford: Oxford University Press.

Turing, A. M. (1952). "The Chemical Basis of Morphogenesis." *Philosophical Transactions of the Royal Society of London* 237:37–72.

Turvey, M. T. (1988). "Execution Driven Action Systems and Smart Perceptual Instruments." In: *Dynamic Patterns in Complex Systems*, eds. J. A. S. Kelso, A. J. Mandell, and M. F. Shlesinger. Singapore: World Scientific Publishers.

Turvey, M. (1990). "Perceiving Shape by Wielding." *Perception and Psychology* 48:477.

Turvey, M. (1991). "Perceiving Aperature Size by Striking." *Journal of Experimental Psychology*, vol. 17.

Turvey, M. T., and C. Carello (1981). "Cognition: The View From Ecological Realism." *Cognition* 10(1081):313–321.

Ulanowicz, R. (1986). *Growth and Development: Ecosystems Phenomenology*. Berlin: Springer-Verlag.

Varela, F. J., H. R. Maturana, and R. B. Uribe (1974). "Autopoiesis: The Organization of Living Systems, Its Characterization and a Model." *Biosystems* 5(4):187–196.

Von Bertalanffy, L. (1968). *General Systems Theory*. New York: George Braziller.

Weber, B., and D. Depew (1985). *Evolution at a Crossroads: The New Biology and The New Philosophy of Science.* Cambridge: The MIT Press.

Wheeler, J. A. (1988). "World as System Self-Synthesized by Quantum Networking." *IBM Journal of Research and Development* 32(1):4–15.

Wicken, J. (1987). *Evolution, Thermodynamics, and Information: Extending the Darwinian Program.* Oxford: Oxford University Press.

Wilber, K. (1982). "Introduction." In: *The Holographic Paradigm and Other Paradoxes*, ed. K. Wilber. Boulder, CO: Shambhala.

Wilber, K. (1983). *Up From Eden.* Boulder, CO: Shambhala.

Willson, S. J. (1986). "A Use of Cellular Automata to Obtain Families of Fractals." In: *Chaotic Dynamics and Fractals*, pp. 123–140, ed. M. F. Barnsley and S. G. Demko. New York: Academic Press.

Wolmuth, P. (1991). "Contractual Allocation of Resources Reconsidered: Value, Markets and the Myths of Human Autonomy." In: *Proceedings of the International Society of the Systems Sciences, 35th Annual Meeting*, Ostersund, Sweden.

Wright, R. (1988). "Did the Universe Just Happen?" *The Atlantic Monthly*, April, pp. 29–44.

Zeeman, C. (1977). *Catastrophe Theory: Selected Papers.* Reading, MA: Addison-Wesley Publishing Company.

Zeeman, C. (1986). "The Dynamics of Darwinian Evolution." In: *Dynamical Systems a Renewal of Mechanism*, pp. 273–290, eds. S. Diner, D. Fargue, and G. Lochak. Philadelphia: World Scientific Publishing.

Zeleny, M. (1981). "What is Autopoiesis?" In: *Autopoiesis: A Theory of Living Organization,* ed. M. Zeleny. New York: North Holland.

Zerin, E. (1989). "Epistemology and Psychotherapy." *Transactional Analysis Journal* 19(2):80–85.

Index